SANTA FE
ALBUQUERQUE
ACCESS®

P9-CTA-569

Orientation

Northern New Mexico is a region of the American continent that bypasses the mind and speaks directly to the unconscious, a place with a primitive attraction that many find irresistible. "Land of Enchantment" is the state motto, and it is more than a license-plate slogan. Thousands of writers, artists, scientists, and celebrities, as well as countless unwary travelers, have been seduced by the land. Visitors to **Santa Fe**, in particular, have been known to begin house-hunting after their first hour in the city; others have moved here after seeing it in their dreams. Weary of Europe, writer D.H. Lawrence came here seeking new inspiration from "the aboriginal Indians

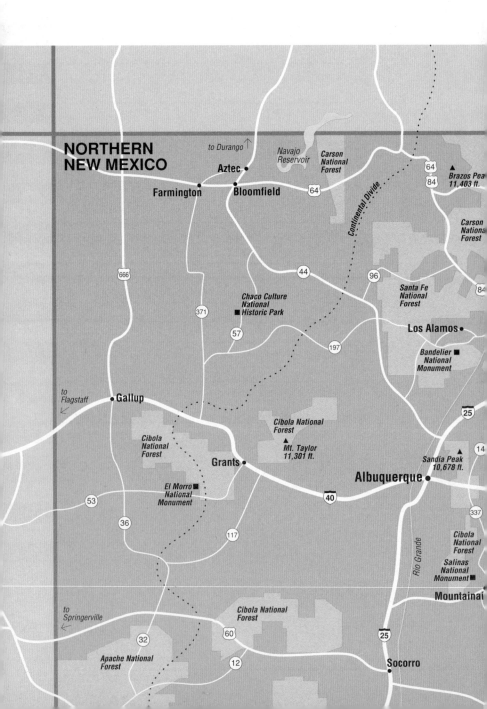

NORTHERN NEW MEXICO

to Durango

Navajo Reservoir

Carson National Forest

Aztec

Farmington   Bloomfield   64

64

84   Brazos Peak 11,403 ft.

Carson National Forest

666

44

96

Santa Fe National Forest

84

Chaco Culture National Historic Park

371

57

197

Los Alamos

Bandelier National Monument

to Flagstaff   Gallup

25

Cibola National Forest

Cibola National Forest

Mt. Taylor 11,301 ft.

Sandia Peak 10,678 ft.

14

53

Grants

Albuquerque

El Morro National Monument

40

337

36

117

Cibola National Forest

Rio Grande

Salinas National Monument

Mountainair

to Springerville

Cibola National Forest

25

32

60

12

Apache National Forest

Socorro

and from the aboriginal air and land." Painter Georgia O'Keeffe, after visiting for one summer, was not at peace until she had made the region her home. Physicist J. Robert Oppenheimer, exposed to the area in his boyhood, chose it as the perfect place to construct an atomic bomb. And many film stars have turned their backs on the Hollywood nightmare to come live in the Santa Fe dreamscape, among them the late actress Greer Garson, who settled in Santa Fe decades before it was chic, and actor Dennis Hopper, who made **Taos** his home in the 1960s. Continuing this trend, actors Carol Burnett, Brian Denehy, Gene Hackman, and Shirley Maclaine have their principal homes in Santa Fe.

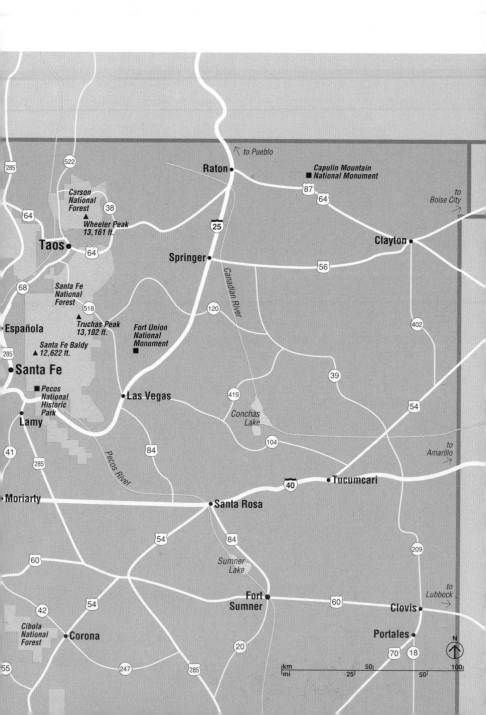

Today Northern New Mexico is a land of first-class hotels decorated with Indian and Hispanic motifs and crafts, well-publicized restaurants featuring Southwestern food (as well as most every other cuisine in the world), down-home restaurants that offer blazing hot chile-based local food, art galleries displaying work ranging from regional artists to painters of international renown, plus excellent skiing, hiking, and fishing. But more than anything else, Northern New Mexico is a land of stark and powerful images. The first sight of a single twisted piñon tree clinging to life in the crevice of a barren rock speaks directly to the loneliness of the human condition. As the tree becomes more familiar, it may come to symbolize the three very different cultures that coexist here. The piñon survives in the high desert against all odds, like the Indians of the 19 nearby pueblos, whose spirit has withstood centuries of material deprivation and hostile invasions. Its tenacious roots suggest the deep faith of the Hispanic population, whose ancestors carved villages and cities in a region where there was little commercial reason for either. And the needle-sharp green branches symbolize the prosperity brought in recent decades by Anglo expatriates. This triad is visible in a thousand variations: in the bleached bones painted by O'Keeffe, in the black pottery of **San Ildefonso Pueblo**, in the folk art of Hispanic *santeros* (carvers and painters of religious icons).

At once as austere as a moonscape and as brightly colored as a Mexican garden, this high-desert region is a striking blend of nature's grandeur and human humility. Mountain peaks as high as 13,000 feet rise into pristine blue skies, snowcapped in winter, studded with wildflowers in spring, alive with rushing streams in summer; in autumn whole mountainsides, especially above Santa Fe, turn a bright gold courtesy of enormous spreads of aspen trees. In the valleys, a spring or summer downpour can suddenly transform dry gullies (arroyos) into rushing rivers hazardous to anything in their path. The first settlers, ancient Indians called Anasazi, made their homes high in cliff dwellings that can still be visited at such historic sites as **Bandelier National Monument.** Their descendants, the Pueblo Indians, built flat-

Taos Pueblo

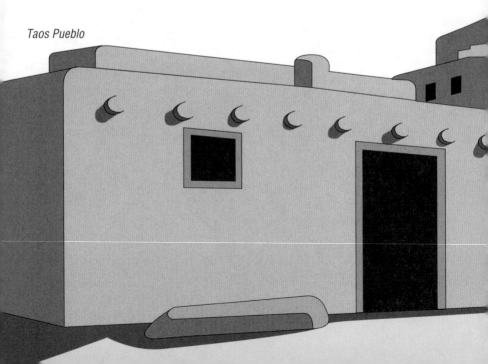

roofed villages of adobe (dried mud) that have remained inhabited for centuries. Spanish conquistadores and settlers who arrived in 1540 followed suit, and flat adobe construction, real or imitation, remains the norm today—as mandated by zoning statutes—in Santa Fe, Taos, and the older sections of **Albuquerque.** Few structures are more than two stories high, and the colors run the full spectrum from beige to brown. Only in downtown Albuquerque, a modern metropolis of almost 650,000 people, have glass-and-steel skyscrapers been hurled into the face of the natural order.

Settled by the Indians more than one thousand years ago, the region was claimed by Spanish explorers in the 16th century and became part of New Spain, later called Mexico. Numerous mission churches are reminders of Catholic missionaries who came to convert the Indians. US troops conquered the area during the Mexican-American War in 1846, and for a half-century it was the New Mexico Territory, a land of desperadoes such as Billy the Kid and unscrupulous lawyer-landgrabber politicians like the Santa Fe Ring. Not until 1912 was the territory divided in half and given statehood as New Mexico and Arizona—the last two of the contiguous 48 states.

The most recent invaders of the region are the hordes of Anglos, many of them wealthy, who have built million-dollar homes in the hills, mostly near Santa Fe. In almost 25 years the majority population of Santa Fe has gone from 65 percent Hispanic to 51 percent Anglo. The presence of wealthy newcomers has induced the establishment of acclaimed upscale restaurants and high-priced boutiques. These changes have caused consternation among many locals, who long for the sleepier days of yore.

Santa Fe, the spiritual and artistic heart of the region, is the oldest state capital in the US. Here, in a city of only 62,000 residents, you can choose from among more than 4,500 rooms in large and small hotels and motels as well as in charming bed-and-breakfasts. Wandering through the narrow streets that once were burro paths or Indian trails reveals 200 restaurants offering a wide selection of tastes that ranges from the haute cuisine

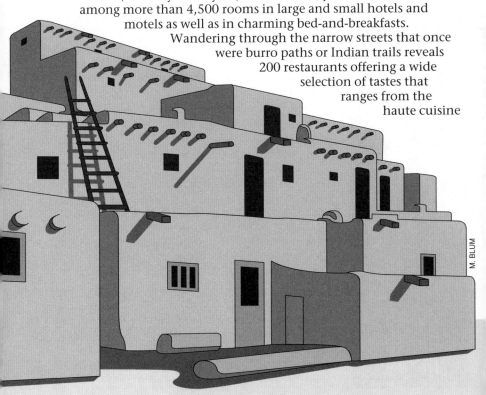

M. BLUM

of **Santacafe** and **Coyote Cafe** to the grilled meat of **Roque's Carnitas;** more than 200 art galleries featuring everything from traditional Western paintings to contemporary abstractions; and over 50 Indian jewelry shops laden with silver and turquoise bracelets and belts, with pottery, baskets, kachina dolls, and every other variety of Indian craft. Six museums display the best of the best in every art and craft, and in July and August the world-famous open-air **Santa Fe Opera** fills the night with music, as do both the world-class Santa Fe Chamber Music Festival and the equally distinguished **Desert Chorale.**

Santa Fe is also a convenient jumping-off point for day trips. The red-and-yellow striated hills near **Abiquiu**—which O'Keeffe made famous—are not to be missed, and the **Santuario de Chimayó,** an old village church where miraculous healings have allegedly occurred, is also fascinating. The many Indian pueblos in the area offer a glimpse and perhaps insight into another way of life.

For those who prefer similar attractions in a more compact package, Taos sits 70 miles to the north up a scenic drive through the canyon of the **Rio Grande.** Several dozen galleries offer a wide range of art, and a handful of restaurants, notably **Lambert's,** reach the level of Santa Fe's best. Two fine museums— the **Millicent Rogers Museum** and the **Harwood Foundation**—specialize in the works of the early Taos art colony. And the skiing at **Taos Ski Valley** is indisputably the most challenging and spectacular in the state. More than 500 years old, **Taos Pueblo,** which sits just on the outskirts of town, is the oldest continuously inhabited apartment dwelling in the country. Five stories high in some places and all adobe, it is, along with **Acoma Pueblo,** among the most intriguing sights in the US West.

Nearly 300 years old, Albuquerque has its own historic attractions—from the buildings of **Old Town** to huge numbers of ancient Indian petroglyphs in the lava mesas to the west—although they have been overshadowed by the urban and commercial sprawl that now surrounds them. The city is better known, however, as the hot-air ballooning capital of the world; as the home of the **University of New Mexico;** and as a center for high-tech industries.

If possible, make the northerly 60-mile drive from Albuquerque to Santa Fe in the late afternoon, when the setting sun lends an extra grace to the rolling hills dotted like leopard skins with piñon and juniper bushes, when the red earth blushes, when the mountains turn a mysterious purple, when the fairies of enchantment come out to play.

How To Read This Guide

SANTA FE/TAOS/ALBUQUERQUE ACCESS® is arranged by neighborhood so you can see at a glance where you are and what is around you. The numbers next to the entries in the following chapters correspond to the numbers on the maps. The text is color-coded according to the kind of place described:

Restaurants/Clubs: Red   **Hotels:** Blue

Shops/ 🍵 Outdoors: Green   **Sights/Culture:** Black

♿ **Wheelchair accessible**

Wheelchair Accessibility

An establishment (except a restaurant) is considered wheelchair accessible when a person in a wheelchair can easily enter a building (i.e., no steps, a ramp, a wide-enough door) without assistance. Restaurants are deemed wheelchair accessible *only* if the above applies *and* if the rest rooms are on the same floor as the dining area and their entrances and stalls are wide enough to accommodate a wheelchair.

Rating the Restaurants and Hotels

The restaurant ratings take into account the quality, service, atmosphere, and uniqueness of the restaurant. An expensive restaurant doesn't necessarily ensure an enjoyable evening; however, a small, relatively unknown spot may have good food, professional service, and a lovely atmosphere. Therefore, on a purely subjective basis, stars are used to judge the overall dining value (see the star ratings at right). Keep in mind that chefs and owners often change, which sometimes drastically affects the quality of a restaurant. The ratings in this guidebook are based on information available at press time.

The price ratings, as categorized at right, apply to restaurants and hotels. These figures reflect the general price range of establishments in the area.

The restaurant price ratings are based on the average cost of an entrée for one person, excluding tax and tip. Hotel price ratings reflect the base price of a standard room for two people for one night during the peak season.

Restaurants

   ★ Good

   ★★ Very Good

   ★★★ Excellent

   ★★★★ An Extraordinary Experience

   $ The Price Is Right (less than $10)

   $$ Reasonable ($10-$15)

   $$$ Expensive ($15-$20)

   $$$$ Big Bucks ($20 and up)

Hotels

   $ The Price Is Right (less than $100)

   $$ Reasonable ($100-$175)

   $$$ Expensive ($175-$250)

   $$$$ Big Bucks ($250 and up)

Map Key

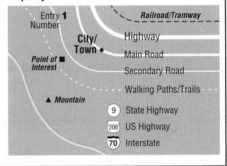

Area code 505 unless otherwise noted.

Getting to Northern New Mexico

Airports

Albuquerque International Sunport (ABQ)

If you're flying on a commercial airline to Northern New Mexico, Albuquerque will be your first destination. **ABQ** recently underwent a $10.5-million expansion to add four gates and moving sidewalks. Decorated with Southwestern furniture and art, the airport has about 19,000 passengers passing through it daily. **ABQ** is located on the south side of the city off **I-25** and serves eight commercial airlines, a regional carrier (**Mesa Airlines**), and a commuter line (**Ross Aviation**). **Mesa Airlines** provides air-

shuttle service between Albuquerque and Santa Fe up to seven times daily. In winter **Mesa** also offers service from Albuquerque to some New Mexico ski resorts, including **Angel Fire** and **Red River.**

Airport Services

Airport Emergencies.................................842.4004

Customs and Immigration........................766.2621

Ground Transportation..............................842.4366

Information 842.4366

Lost and Found 842.4379

Paging..842.4379

Police 842.4379, 842.4366

Airlines

American Airlines 842.4229, 842.4360,

....800/433.7300

America West Airlines 247.0737, 800/247.5692

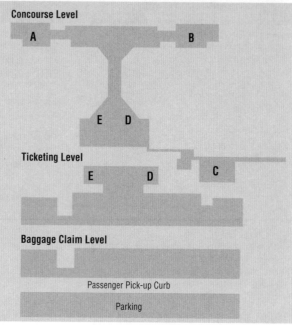

ALBUQUERQUE INTERNATIONAL SUNPORT (ABQ)

Concourse Level

A   B

E   D

Ticketing Level

E   D   C

Baggage Claim Level

Passenger Pick-up Curb

Parking

Gate Locations for Major Airlines

A Southwest
  USAir Express

B American
  America West
  Continental
  Delta
  Northwest
  United
  USAir

C TWA

D Ross Aviation

E Mesa Airlines

Continental Airlines 842.8220, 800/525.0280
Delta Airlines 243.2794, 800/221.1212
Mesa Airlines 842.4414, 800/637.2247
Ross Aviation 242.2811
Southwest Airlines 245.1717, 800/435.9792
TWA 842.4010, 800/221.2000
United Airlines.....................................800/241.6522
USAir 842.4903, 800/428.4322

Getting to and from Albuquerque International Sunport

By Car
ABQ is about three miles from downtown Albuquerque. To get there, head north on I-25. To reach Santa Fe, continue north on I-25 for about 60 miles. For Taos, follow directions to Santa Fe, then continue north on **US 285** approximately 15 miles to **Española** and then head east about 40 miles on **NM 68** into Taos. To get to the airport, simply reverse the above directions.

Rental Cars
Car-rental companies at **ABQ** include:

Alamo...............................842.4057, 800/327.9633
Avis 842.4080, 800/331.1212
Budget 768.5900, 800/828.3438
Dollar 842.4224, 800/369.4226
Farr Better Car Rental 884.2554, 800/247.9556
Hertz 842.4235, 800/654.3131
National............................842.4222, 800/227.7368
Thrifty 842.8755, 800/367.2277

By Bus
Greyhound/Trailways (243.4435, 800/231.2222) and **Texas, New Mexico & Oklahoma Coaches** (**TNMO**; 243.4435 in Albuquerque, 471.0008 in Santa Fe, 758.1144 in Taos) provide regular service to Santa Fe (a 1.5-hour trip) and Taos (2.5 hours). **Shuttlejack** (243.3244 in Albuquerque, 982.4311 in Santa Fe, 800/452.2655) also offers daily service from **Albuquerque International Sunport** to Santa Fe and Taos.

By Limousine
American Limousine (891.5466), **Lucky's Limousine Service** (836.4035), or **VIP Limousine Service** (883.4888) provide service.

By Taxi
There is a taxi zone on the airport's lower level where **Albuquerque Cab** (883.4888) and **Yellow Cab** (247.8888) cars are available.

Private Albuquerque Airports

For those wealthy enough to own their own planes, various private airports in Albuquerque service single- and double-engine airplanes as well as small private jet airliners. Three such airports are: **Coronado Airport** (10000 Pan-American Fwy NE, 821.7777), **Double Eagle Airport** (7401 Paseo del Vulcan, 842.7007), and **Cutter Flying Service** (2502 Clark Carr Loop SE, 842.4184).

Santa Fe Municipal Airport

This small airport (473.7243), which is located approximately 15 miles south of downtown at the end of Airport Road, is used by private planes and shuttle lines.

Taos Airport

Approximately 12 miles west of Taos, off **US 64**, this airport (758.4995) services only private planes.

Train Station (Long-distance)

Amtrak's (842.9650 in Albuquerque, 988.4511 in Santa Fe, 800/872.7245) *Southwest Chief,* which runs between Chicago and Los Angeles, stops in Albuquerque daily. The train arrives at **First Street** and **Silver Avenue** and continues northeast to the town of **Lamy**, where the **Lamy Shuttle Service** (982.8829) is available by reservation to take travelers 19 miles farther north to Santa Fe. There is no railway service to Taos.

Getting Around Northern New Mexico

Bicycles

Santa Fe has numerous bike routes. The **Santa Fe Convention and Visitors Bureau** (201 W Marcy St, at Grant Ave, 984.6760, 800/777.2489) offers a bicycle map full of information about riding in and out of town; you can also get the map by calling 988.RIDE. Rentals are available from **First Powder/Last Chance General Store** (Hyde Park, 982.0495), **Palace Bike Rentals** (409 E Palace Ave, at Delgado St, 984.2151), **Santa Fe Schwinn** (1611 St. Michael's Dr, between Llano St and Cerrillos Rd, 983.4473), and **Tees and Skis** (107 Washington Ave, between E Palace Ave and Nusbaum St, 983.5637).

In Taos, rentals and information are available at **Gear Up Bicycle Shop** (129 Paseo del Pueblo Sur, between Kit Carson Rd and Kit Carson State Park, 751.0365).

Albuquerque also has a large network of bicycle paths. For a free map, call the **Office of Cultural Recreational Services** (768.3550). Rentals are available from **Rio Mountain Sport** (1210 Rio Grande Blvd NW, between Floral and Indian School Rds NW, 766.9970) and **REI (Recreational Equipment Inc.;** 1905 Mountain Rd NW, between 18th and 20th Sts NW, 247.1191).

Buses

Santa Fe Trails (984.6730) is the city's public bus system. Covering most of Santa Fe, the buses run on natural gas. Park at the **De Vargas Center Mall** (N Guadalupe St, at Paseo de Peralta) and ride to the congested downtown plaza area in less than five minutes.

Taos has no bus system.

In Albuquerque, the **Sun Tran** (843.9200) buses cover the entire city but only during daylight hours. There is regular service from 6AM to 7PM Monday through Friday and from 6AM to 6PM on Saturday and Sunday. Buses run less frequently to the more remote parts of town and on weekends. The bus stops are well marked with the company's sunburst logo.

Driving

Navigating a vehicle through New Mexico can be an adventure. Year after year the state ranks among the worst three in automobile deaths per capita. It is also always near the top in alcohol-related auto accidents. Many New Mexicans have an ornery streak: They hate to stop at red lights, and they refuse to use directional signals. Drive defensively, and expect the drivers around you to do the unexpected at any time. Pedestrians have the right-of-way by law, and in Santa Fe and Taos people take full advantage of it. Drivers in Taos, perhaps because of the narrow streets, tend to drive slowly and with courtesy, and they follow the rules. If possible, avoid I-25 or **I-40** in Albuquerque during the rush hours—traffic is dense and speeders offensive (the maximum speed limit on both roads is 75 miles per hour).

Parking

In June through August, parking is a serious problem in downtown Santa Fe and Taos. There are municipal parking lots at 216 W San Francisco Street (at Sandoval St) and 102 E Water Street (between Shelby St and Don Gaspar Ave) in Santa Fe and on Padre Martinez Lane (between Ranchitos Rd and Don Fernando St) in Taos, but the crush of visitors tends to fill them up by around 10AM.

Parking in Albuquerque is abundant, except for the Old Town and **University of New Mexico** areas, which can be horrendous. There are municipal lots on Mountain Road NW (at San Felipe St NW) and on Central Avenue (between San Felipe and Romero Sts NW). Parking meters are in effect in some places in all three cities (these spots get taken quickly), except after 6PM and on Sunday and holidays.

Taxis

There are no cabs cruising the streets of Santa Fe, Taos, and Albuquerque. The following companies offer pick-up service:

Santa Fe:

Capital City Cab 438.0000

Taos:

Faust's Transportation 758.3410

Albuquerque:

Albuquerque Cab....................................883.4888

Checker Cab 243.7777

Yellow Cab 247.8888

Tours

Walking and vehicular tours in Santa Fe, rafting tours on the Rio Grande (departures from Santa Fe or Taos), and bus tours to such outlying areas as the Indian pueblos are offered by several companies. Contact the **Santa Fe Convention and Visitors Bureau** (984.6760, 800/777.2489), the **Santa Fe County Chamber of Commerce** (510 N Guadalupe St, behind the De Vargas Mall annex, 988.3279), or the lobby desks of most hotels for information about specific operators and schedules. The **Taos Chamber of Commerce** (1139 Paseo del Pueblo Sur, between Paseo del Cañon and Salazar St, 758.3873, 800/732.8267) has details about white-water rafting trips.

Riding and walking tours are available in Albuquerque through **Rio Grande Super Tours** (242.1325), **Gray Line of Albuquerque** (242.3880, 800/256.8991), and **Okupin Tours** (867.3817). Ballooning is a popular pastime as well, and the city is home to a number of companies that will take you up, up, and away. Try **Hot Alternatives Etcetera Inc.** (269.1174, 800/322.2262), **Braden's Balloons Aloft** (281.2714, 800/367.6625), or **Hot Air Extraord-in-air** (266.9744). All will pick you up at your hotel or other convenient locations.

Walking and Hiking

Downtown Santa Fe is best seen on foot. The maze of narrow old streets is as pleasurable to stroll as it is frustrating to maneuver in a car. This is also true of Santa Fe's **Canyon Road,** Albuquerque's Old Town district, and the entire town of Taos.

For more ambitious walks, in addition to the many miles of trails in national forest areas near all three cities, both Santa Fe and Albuquerque offer excellent hiking opportunities within minutes of downtown. In Santa Fe, the favorite is the **Atalaya Trail,** which starts at the **St. John's College** parking lot (the entrance to the college is at the intersection of Camino Cabra and Camino de Cruz Blanca) and climbs gradually to the summit of the 9,000-foot **Atalaya Peak** overlooking the city. The Sierra Club publishes a good guide to the many hiking trails in the Santa Fe area. Available at local book stores, the book rates the trails according to difficulty. In Albuquerque, a paved walking, jogging, and biking trail accessible from the **Rio Grande Nature Center** (entrance on Candeleria Rd NW, west of Rio Grande Blvd NW) runs the full length of the city through the cottonwood forest on the banks of the Rio Grande. There are also numerous trails on **Sandia Crest,** a 10,000-foot mountain just north of the city.

In the **Sangre de Cristo Mountains** is the **Pecos Wilderness** (a broad expanse located in the **Carson** and **Santa Fe National Forests**). Its most popular trailhead is the **East Portal** near the parking lot of the **Santa Fe Ski Basin,** 17 miles east of town on **Hyde Park/Ski Basin Road.** From here, the 20-mile **Windsor Trail** leads to the **South Portal** at the upper end of the **Pecos River Canyon** and provides access to the other trails through the wilderness. There are two other trailheads for the Pecos Wilderness—at **Santa Barbara Campground** near **Rodarte** (south of Taos) and at **El Porvenir** (west of **Las Vegas**).

The **Carson National Forest Service** (1139 Paseo del Pueblo Sur, between Paseo del Cañon and Salazar St, 758.6200) provides information on hiking in the forests.

FYI

Accommodations

Make hotel reservations ahead of time in all three cities. Santa Fe and Taos are jammed with tourists in summer and skiers in winter. Summer weekends in those two cities are the busiest; show up without a reservation on a Saturday, and your chances of finding a room are not good, despite the fact that booming Santa Fe now has more than 4,500 hotel rooms. Santa Fe's **Indian Market,** the third weekend in August, draws buyers and browsers from all over the country, and some downtown hotels get booked for that event up to a year in advance. Even the cheapest motels fill up early, and without a reservation you might have to stay in Albuquerque, 60 miles to the south, or Española, 24 miles to the north.

Albuquerque has 8,500 hotel rooms, but many are often booked by conventions. This city is most crowded during the New Mexico State Fair in September and during the Albuquerque International Balloon Fiesta in October.

Bed-and-breakfasts proliferate throughout Santa Fe, Taos, and Albuquerque. For information, call one of the following:

Albuquerque Bed & Breakfast Association...............
 PO Box 7262, Albuquerque, NM 87504, no phone
Bed & Breakfast Inns of Taos 758.4747,
 ....800/876.7857
Bed & Breakfast of New Mexico.................982.3332
New Mexico Central Reservations 766.9770,
 ....800/466.7829
Santa Fe Central Reservations 983.8200,
 ....800/776.7669
Santa Fe Reservation and
 Lodging Service....................................989.3799
Taos Central Reservations........................776.2233,
 ....800/776.1111

Altitude

Albuquerque is perched a mile above sea level, and Santa Fe and Taos are even higher at 7,000 feet. Some people are unaffected by the height; others find that they tire easily at first. It's good to follow a relaxed schedule the first day or two to give the body time to adjust, and to drink lots of water. Those with heart problems should check with their doctors first to see if travel at these altitudes is advisable.

Climate

Average Temperatures (°F)			
	Month	High	Low
Santa Fe	January	40	18
	April	59	35
	July	91	56
	October	62	38
Taos	January	40	10
	April	53	21
	July	87	50
	October	67	32
Albuquerque	January	46	24
	April	69	42
	July	91	64
	October	71	44

Northern New Mexico has four distinct seasons, and winter is definitely one of them. However, the sun shines more than 300 days a year, and rainfall is usually limited to scattered afternoon thunderstorms, mostly in spring (when the wind kicks up) and summer; normally there are not more than a handful of rainy days each year. Albuquerque gets a few light snowfalls in winter, while Santa Fe and Taos have been known to experience six or eight substantial storms. The low humidity throughout the area makes hot summer days much more bearable than at lower altitudes.

Drinking
New Mexico's legal drinking age is 21. Bars close at 2AM Monday through Saturday and at midnight on Sunday.

Hours
Throughout this guide, opening and closing times for shops, attractions, coffeehouses, and other establishments are listed by day(s) only if normal operating hours apply (opening between 8 and 11AM and closing between 4 and 7PM). In all other cases, specific hours are given (for example, 6AM-2PM, daily 24 hours, noon-5PM).

Money
Most banks in Albuquerque, **The Bank of Santa Fe** (241 Washington Ave, at Paseo de Peralta, 984.0500) in downtown Santa Fe, and the currency exchange counter at the **Albuquerque International Sunport** (no phone) will exchange Mexican and Western European currencies. **Sunwest Bank of Albuquerque** (303 Roma Ave NW, at Third St NW, Albuquerque, 765.2205) and **United New Mexico Bank** (200 Lomas Blvd NW, between Second and Third Sts NW, 765.5000) will change all foreign monies. Banks are generally open Monday through Friday from 9AM to 3PM; drive-ups usually remain open later. Traveler's checks are accepted virtually everywhere.

Museum Passes
New Mexico's four state-run museums are the **Palace of the Governors,** the **Museum of Fine Arts,** the **Museum of International Folk Art,** and the **Museum of Indian Arts and Culture.** At press time, a one-day pass to all four cost $5; a four-day ticket, $8. Seniors are admitted free on Wednesday.

Personal Safety
Santa Fe, Taos, and Albuquerque are safe, but it's a good idea to avoid alleys and unattended parking lots in Santa Fe and Taos and not to wander around alone after dark in Albuquerque's **Downtown** or **East Central** areas.

Publications
Santa Fe's daily newspaper since 1849, the *New Mexican,* publishes a small calendar of events every day, and a more inclusive weeklong list appears every Friday in the arts section, *Pasatiempo.* The free, weekly *Santa Fe Reporter,* which has won a slew of national awards, publishes a complete calendar of art openings, and theater, music, and other events on

Wednesday. The weekly *Taos News* does the same for Taos each Thursday. The daily *Albuquerque Journal,* the state's largest newspaper, and the *Albuquerque Tribune,* the afternoon daily, both publish weekend arts sections with a calendar of events on Thursday.

Radio Stations
AM:

KSWV (Spanish)	810
KVSF (news/talk)	1260
FM:	
KSFR (classical)	90.7
KNYN (country and western)	95
KHFM (classical)	96.3
KIOT (eclectic)	102.3 in Santa Fe, 102.5 in Albuquerque
KOLT (country)	106
KBOM (oldies)	106.7
KBOM (rock)	107

Restaurants
Reservations are strongly suggested at the upscale restaurants in all three cities. Most inexpensive dining spots do not take reservations, and you may have to wait for a table, especially on Friday and Saturday nights. Casual dress is acceptable almost everywhere.

When a server in a New Mexican restaurant asks "red or green?" he or she wants to know if you want red chile or green chile on your food. Green is usually more popular; red can be harder for some people to digest. Either can be hotter than the other on any given day. If you want half and half, say "Christmas." If your lips, tongue, and throat feel like they're burning, drinking water is *not* the way to dowse the fire. Instead, eat something sweet. Many New Mexican dishes come with sopaipillas, a local delicacy that is served instead of bread; put some honey on it and take a bite to reduce the chile heat.

Shopping
The best gift and souvenir shopping in Santa Fe is in the **Plaza,** Canyon Road, and **Guadalupe Street** districts, as well as at **Jackalope Pottery** (2820 Cerrillos Rd, between Camino Carlos Rey and Clark Rd, 471.8539) and **Trader Jack's Flea Market** (Hwy 84-285, eight miles north of Santa Fe). On the west end of town is **Villa Linda Mall** (Cerrillos and Rodeo Rds), the city's major shopping mall; and **Santa Fe Factory Stores** (at Cerrillos Rd and I-25), a large factory outlet mall with upscale stores. **De Vargas Center Mall** (N Guadalupe St, at Paseo de Peralta) is another popular shopping spot.

The historic district of Taos—the **Plaza, Kit Carson Road,** and **Bent Street**—and the **Taos Pueblo** have the best gift and souvenir shopping. **Paseo del Pueblo Sur** (from Kit Carson Road to Ranchos de

Taos) offers everything from supermarkets to discount department stores.

In Albuquerque, Old Town and the **Nob Hill** areas offer the best gift and souvenir shopping; major shopping malls are the **Coronado Center** (6600 Menaul Blvd NE, at Louisiana Blvd NE) and nearby **Winrock Center** (Louisiana Blvd NE, just north of I-40).

Smoking

No-smoking sections exist in most restaurants in Northern New Mexico. In Albuquerque, a city ordinance prohibits smoking in such public areas as the airport and shopping malls. It's okay to smoke in malls in Santa Fe. Smoking is banned in some of Taos's public buildings.

Street Plans

Visitors can easily get lost in Santa Fe's narrow, winding thoroughfares. Not only are the streets a maze, but addresses are often not consecutive or just don't make sense. Either follow a map or ask a friendly local for directions. Taos's small size makes navigating easy—there really is only one main street. Albuquerque is laid out on a grid pattern and all addresses are designated by quadrant (NE, NW, SE, SW), with the **Atchison, Topeka, and Santa Fe** railroad tracks and **Central Avenue** downtown as the dividing points.

Taxes

The three cities have a sales tax—known technically as a gross receipts tax—that varies from 5.5 percent in Albuquerque, to 6.25 percent in Santa Fe, to 6.3 percent in Taos County, to 6.8 percent in the city of Taos. This tax is levied on all goods and services, and applies not only to hotel and restaurant bills, but to all purchases, including food bought at supermarkets. Medicine and doctor and dental bills are not exempt from the tax. Hotels also tack on a lodgers' tax—4 percent in Santa Fe, 3.5 percent in the city of Taos, 3 percent in Taos County, and 5 percent in Albuquerque—to room charges. And car-rental agencies add a hefty tax of over 11 percent.

Telephone

The area code for the state of New Mexico is 505.

Tickets

Tickets for rock concerts and other national events can be purchased through **Ticketron** outlets at most record stores. For local cultural events, buy tickets at most of the larger hotels and at Santa Fe's **Galisteo News** (202 Galisteo St, between W Alameda and W Water Sts, 984.1316). Tickets to the **Santa Fe Opera** can be purchased by mail or phone (PO Box 2408, Santa Fe, NM 87504, 986.5900, 986.5955).

Tipping

In restaurants the standard tip is 15 to 20 percent of the bill. Some eateries add a service charge of 15 to 18 percent for parties of five or more. Taxi drivers normally get 10 to 15 percent depending on the quality of the service, and tips for maids and porters are discretionary.

Visitors' Information Offices

The **Santa Fe Convention and Visitors Bureau** (201 W Marcy St, at Grant Ave, 984.6760, 800/777.2489) is open Monday through Friday. The **Taos Chamber of Commerce** (1139 Paseo del Pueblo Sur, between Paseo del Cañon and Salazar St, 758.3873, 800/732.8267) is open daily. The **Albuquerque Convention and Visitors Bureau** (20 First Plaza NW, at Tijeras Ave NW and Second St NW, Suite 601, 842.9918, 800/733.9918) is open Monday through Friday.

The **State of New Mexico Welcome Center** (open daily; 491 Old Santa Fe Trail, at Paseo del Peralta, 827.7400), the **Santa Fe County Chamber of Commerce Information Center** (open Monday through Friday; 510 N Guadalupe St, behind the De Vargas Center Mall annex, 988.3279), and the **Albuquerque Convention and Visitors Bureau**'s walk-in center (open daily; 303 Romero St, between Old Town Plaza and Mountain Rd NW, no phone) also supply information on New Mexico.

Phone Book

Emergencies

Ambulance/Fire/Police 911

AAA Emergency Road Service

    Santa Fe and Taos 800/726.4222

    Albuquerque 291.6600

Dental Society Referrals, Albuquerque 242.0345

Handicapped Transportation Services,

    Albuquerque 764.1550

Hospitals

    Santa Fe: St. Vincent Hospital 983.3361

    Taos: Holy Cross Hospital 758.8883

    Albuquerque:

    Presbyterian Hospital 841.1234

    University of New Mexico Hospital 843.2411

24-Hour Pharmacies

    Santa Fe: Walgreen Drug Store 982.4643

    Albuquerque: Walgreen Drug Store 881.5210

Poison Control 800/432.6866

Police (nonemergency)

    Santa Fe 827.9126

    Taos 758.4656

    Albuquerque 768.1986

Rape Crisis Center

    Santa Fe 473.7818

    Taos 758.2910

    Albuquerque 266.7711

Visitors' Information

Amtrak 800/872.7245

Greyhound/Trailways 243.4435, 800/231.2222

Passport Information		Time and Temperature	
Santa Fe	988.6351	Santa Fe	473.2211
Albuquerque	848.3895	Albuquerque	247.1611
Sante Fe Trails	984.6730	24-hour Albuquerque Events Line	243.3696,
Shuttle Jack	243.3244		800/284.2282
Sun Tran	843.9200	Weather and Road Conditions	800/432.4269

Main Events

New Mexicans love fiestas of every description, and from the beginning of May through Christmas there is rarely a slow day on the special-events calendar. Whether the occasion is a solemn religious procession by candlelight or a wild citywide street party, a world-renowned classical music festival or a spectacular hot-air balloon competition, New Mexicans observe it with boundless enthusiasm. Here are some of the most popular celebrations in **Santa Fe, Taos,** and **Albuquerque:**

January
Three Kings Day All Indian pueblos observe 6 January, the traditional end of the Christmas season. The governor and other tribal officers of each pueblo take office on this day, and it is marked by sacred animal dances. Although dance times are not prescheduled, they usually get going in the late morning. These events are free, but most pueblos charge for parking. Contact the individual pueblos for more information.

February
Celebrity Ski Classic Scheduled for three days in the second week of February during the otherwise uneventful off-season, film and television stars come to Santa Fe to raise funds for charity by competing against local skiers in this highly publicized ski race. Call 983.5615 for more information.

Mardi Gras in the Mountains A weeklong party in the tradition of New Orleans, complete with masquerade balls, Mardi Gras parades, music, and costumes takes place at the **Red River Ski Area.** Ski races and snow sculptures are also featured. Call 800/348.6444 for more information.

March
Rio Grande Arts and Crafts Festival During the second weekend in March, the **New Mexico State Fairgrounds** in Albuquerque is the venue for one of the year's best arts-and-crafts shows, attracting many of New Mexico's best artisans. Call 292.7457 for more information.

April
Pilgrimage to Chimayó On Good Friday thousands of Catholics from all over New Mexico make a pilgrimage on foot to **Santuario de Chimayó,** a small sanctuary in the hills between Santa Fe and Taos where it is believed that miracles occur. Pilgrims, walking on their knees and making the journey in wheelchairs—some carrying large wooden crosses—line US 285 north of Santa Fe for more than 30 miles. Call 753.2831 for more information.

Gathering of Nations Powwow The largest American Indian powwow in the US is held in Albuquerque. Elaborate costumes and competition dancing for big cash prizes highlight the traditional ceremony, which climaxes in **American Indian Week,** the third week of the month. Admission is charged. Call 836.2810 for more information.

Albuquerque Founder's Day This commemoration, usually held concurrently with the **Gathering of Nations Powwow,** focuses on Albuquerque's Spanish Colonial heritage. **Old Town Plaza** is the site of cultural and historical celebrations, food vendors, and live entertainment. The festivities are free. Call 842.9918 for more information.

Taos Talking Picture Festival A multicultural celebration of new independent films, Native American film and video, Latino film, and cutting-edge technology in special effects, animation, and multimedia productions takes place in Taos the third week of the month. Call 751.0673 for more information.

May
Cinco de Mayo Celebration This huge celebration on the Sunday preceding 5 May at Albuquerque's **Civic Plaza** marks the anniversary of Mexico's defeat of the French in Puebla in 1862. The city's residents join this free, colorful extravaganza of Mexican food and dancing in the streets to live music. The festivities last from late morning through the evening. Call 525.8313 for more information.

Taos Spring Arts Festival The whole community of Taos collaborates to produce this exhibition of the arts that marks the beginning of the tourist season. Spanning the last two weeks of May, events include an arts-and-crafts show, artists' receptions at most galleries, literary readings, and musical performances. Most events are free. Call 732.8267 for more information.

June
Spring Festival at El Rancho de las Golondrinas In early June volunteers dress in Spanish Colonial garb and demonstrate traditional crafts, skills, and chores at this large Spanish hacienda near Santa Fe. Admission is charged. Call 471.2261 for more information.

Pedal the Peaks Bicycle Tour During the third week of June, seven days of bicycle races attract cyclists from around the world to a varied, challenging series of courses on mountainous roads around Santa Fe, Taos, Albuquerque, **Las Vegas,** and **Los Alamos.** Call 800/795.0898 for more information.

Opening Night at the Santa Fe Opera The start of the six-week opera season (usually late June or early July) is marked by an elegant tailgate party, where opera-goers—men in black tie and women in exclusive designer gowns—enjoy dinners individually catered by Santa Fe's leading restaurants. Everything is set up outdoors on folding tables in the opera parking lot. Opening night tickets for the opera are expensive and must be reserved as much as a year in advance. Call 982.3851 for more information.

July

Nambe Waterfall Ceremony Virtually every New Mexico community has its own Fourth of July celebration, but the most distinctive happening is held at an idyllic creekside site below **Nambe Falls** on the reservation land of **Nambe Pueblo** between Santa Fe and Taos. Groups from various pueblos gather to perform bow-and-arrow, buffalo, corn, harvest, and snake dances throughout the day. Admission is charged. Some pueblo arts and crafts are offered for sale. Call 455.2036 for more information.

Rodeo de Santa Fe The one major event of the summer season that is attended by more locals than tourists, this four-day rodeo, held during the first week of July, features calf roping, bucking broncos, bull riders, rodeo clowns, and lots of pageantry. It kicks off with a parade and pancake breakfast on **Santa Fe Plaza.** The rodeo is held at the **Rodeo Grounds** on Rodeo Road, near Richards Avenue, at the southern edge of Santa Fe. Admission is charged. Call 984.6760 for more information.

Taos Indian Pueblo Powwow This Native American powwow continues a tradition that began as an annual diplomatic meeting and peace celebration between Plains tribes and Pueblo Indians long before the first Europeans reached New Mexico. Held the second week of July in a large temporary dance *ramada* (framework on poles holding up a roof) constructed entirely of pine boughs and branches, the powwow features brightly costumed dancers from tribes throughout the United States and Canada competing for cash prizes. Admission is charged. Call 758.8626 for more information.

Santa Fe Chamber Music Festival From the second week of July through the third week of August, classical works are performed by ensembles of some of America's finest musicians in the **New Mexico Fine Arts Museum**'s lofty **St. Francis Auditorium.** The festival also features world premieres of new works by serious composers, as well as a sprinkling of jazz concerts. Call 983.2075 for more information.

Eight Northern Pueblos Arts and Crafts Fair Begun as an Indian pueblo–operated alternative to Santa Fe's famous **Indian Market** (see below), this fair features more than 1,100 vendors exhibiting traditional and contemporary handmade American Indian arts and crafts. The two-day event during the third week of July also features dance performances, American Indian fashion shows, and other activities. The larger pueblos north of Santa Fe, including **San Ildefonso,**

Santa Clara, San Juan, and **Taos Pueblos,** take turns hosting the fair in successive years. Call 852.4265 for more information.

Spanish Market This market fills Santa Fe Plaza the last weekend of July with more than 200 vendors of handmade, traditional Spanish arts and crafts such as tinwork, woven goods, quilts, and wood carvings. Long a minor-league stepchild of the **Santa Fe Indian Market** (see below), in recent years the **Spanish Market** has begun attracting more viewers and buyers. It has a long way to go, though, before it draws a crowd as sizable as the **Indian Market.** Call 983.4038 for more information.

August

Fiesta de Santo Domingo Corn dances (sometimes called "rain dances") are held at all New Mexico Indian pueblos during the summer months to ensure successful crops. On 4 August the largest corn dance of all takes place at the **Santo Domingo Pueblo.** Thousands of dancers in identical ceremonial dress take part in a procession through the streets of this very traditional pueblo located between Santa Fe and Albuquerque. Call 843.7270 for more information on this free event.

Santa Fe Indian Market The largest of all American Indian arts-and-crafts markets fills the downtown plaza and radiates into side streets for blocks around. More than 2,000 juried artisans show their work, and more than 100,000 people from all over the world come to see what's offered. Most participating Indian artists and craftspeople sell more of their work this weekend (the third of the month) than the entire rest of the year. Serious buyers line up hours before the show opens, and the best pieces are sold first thing in the morning. Call 984.6760 for more information.

Los Alamos County Fair and Rodeo Held yearly on 4-14 August, this fun-filled week kicks off with "Family Night," a carnival atmosphere for children of all ages. English and Western horse shows, a parade, and a kids' pet show dominate the rest of the time at the fair. Call 662.6374 for more information.

September

New Mexico Wine & Vine Festival Samples from New Mexico's wineries are the central attraction at the popular community festival in **Bernalillo,** north of Albuquerque. Live music and dancing round out the festival in early September. Admission is charged. Call 867.3311 for more information.

Santa Fe Fiesta Santa Fe's community fiesta—the only large event in town that is mainly for locals rather than tourists—is unique. Part religious and historical observance, part citywide block party, and part drunken orgy, **Fiesta** starts at dark on Friday evening the first weekend after Labor Day with the burning of Zozobra. This 40-foot-high papier-mâché marionette represents *Old Man Gloom* who has been burned at the stake each year since the ceremony was created in 1926 by early Santa Fe painter Will Shuster. As Zozobra hurls curses and verbal abuse over the loudspeakers at the onlookers packing **Old Fort Marcy Park** (near the *Cross of the Martyrs*), fire dancers taunt him and finally put him to the torch, igniting the cache of fireworks in his head. The crowd then spills out onto the plaza for all-night street dancing. Other fiesta weekend events include religious processions, a historical/hysterical parade, and a pet parade. Call 984.6760 for more information.

Taos Fall Arts Festival and San Geronimo Feast Day A mirror image of the **Taos Spring Arts Festival** (see page 13), this end-of-the-season blowout during the last two weeks of September features a kaleidoscope of visual and performing arts. The closing days of the arts festival coincide with the feast day for **Taos Pueblo**'s patron saint, San Geronimo. The events are celebrated with all-day and evening dances, foot races, pole climbs, and an arts-and-crafts market at the pueblo. Call 758.3873 or 800/732.8267 for more information.

New Mexico State Fair and Rodeo One of the largest in the nation, this state fair lasts for most of September and features livestock contests, arts-and-crafts shows, a carnival, nightly country-and-western concerts, replicas of old Indian and Spanish villages, and a Professional Rodeo Cowboy Association rodeo. Admission is charged. Call 265.1791 for more information.

Old Taos Trade Fair Held at the historic **Martinez Hacienda** during the third weekend of September, this fair reenacts the early days when Taos was a trading center for Pueblo and Plains Indians, Spanish settlers, and Anglo mountain men. Costumes and lifestyle demonstrations are featured. Admission is charged. Call 758.0505 for more information.

October

Harvest Festival at El Rancho de las Golondrinas This historical re-creation at the Spanish Colonial hacienda southwest of Santa Fe features as many as 200 volunteers in period costume. The staff at **El Rancho de las Golondrinas** raise crops using 18th-century farming methods, and this festival coincides with the harvesting of fields of blue maize. Lifestyle demonstrations include dyeing and spinning wool and grinding flour at the old waterwheel mill. Folk dancing rounds out the weekend program. Admission is charged. This celebration takes place the first weekend in October, coinciding with the **Albuquerque Balloon Fiesta.** Call 471.2261 for more information.

Albuquerque Balloon Fiesta Since 1972, when this event got its start as a 13-balloon race from an Albuquerque shopping mall parking lot, it has grown to become the largest event in New Mexico, with about 1.4 million spectators and nearly 850 hot-air balloons from all over the United States and a dozen foreign countries. Held at the **Balloon Fiesta Park,** a hot-air balloon airport specially built for the event on the north edge of the city, the events take place the first two weekends of October and feature races, contests, balloon rides, and such dramatic events as mass ascensions (when all participating balloons lift off at once) and a "balloon glow," in which illuminated, tethered balloons light up the night sky. Because of the tremendous crowds and the fact that ballooning conditions are best soon after dawn, attending the

spectacular mass ascensions means getting up at 3AM to wait in a very long line of cars. Admission is charged. Call 821.1000 for more information.

Cowboy Symposium Four days of cowboy poetry, storytelling, and music are offered in Lincoln County near **Ruidoso.** Arts and crafts, gospel music, a chuck-wagon cook-off, and daily/overnight trail rides are also on the agenda. Call 378.4142 for more information.

November

Dixon Arts Association Studio Tour Of the many annual fall studio tours that enliven Northern New Mexico's village artists' communities, the one at **Dixon** (a few miles off NM 68 south of Taos) was the first and is still the best. About two dozen local artists and craftspeople open their homes and studios to the public the first weekend in November, while others show their works at booths in the village community center. Call 753.2831 for more information.

Southeast Arts and Crafts Festival The state's most prestigious arts-and-crafts fair, a juried invitational event featuring works by the finest artisans of New Mexico, Texas, Colorado, and Arizona, is held in mid-November at the **New Mexico State Fairgrounds** in Albuquerque. Call 262.2488 for more information.

Indian National Finals Rodeo Prize winners from the many rodeos held on American Indian reservations around the United States and Canada come to Albuquerque during the third week in November to compete for the title of National Indian Rodeo Champion in this four-day extravaganza of roping, racing, and bronco and bull riding at **Tingley Coliseum,** at the **New Mexico State Fairgrounds.** Admission is charged. Call 265.1791 for more information.

December

Christmas This holiday is particularly beautiful in Santa Fe, Taos, and several areas of Albuquerque, especially Old Town. Most of the adobe-style buildings in the historic districts, the plaza walkways, and many residential areas of all three communities are lined with lanterns called *farolitos* (in Santa Fe and Taos) or *luminarias* (in Albuquerque), made from altar candles set in sand inside brown paper bags. The lanterns are in place from the first week of December until New Year's Day. Conventional Christmas decorations such as colored lights and plastic Santas are rarely seen around Santa Fe and Taos. Instead, the plazas and other public areas are hung with fresh evergreen boughs and adorned with large wooden plaques hand-painted in Christmas designs. On Christmas Eve, Santa Fe residents by the thousands stroll along Canyon Road, stopping to warm themselves by bonfires and sing Christmas carols, while local businesses provide hot cider and other refreshments along the way.

With 300 sunny days a year, Santa Fe gets only about 14 inches of rain annually. However, underground wells, aquifers, and spring runoff from the Sangre de Cristo Mountains provide a plentiful water supply.

Santa Fe

Santa Fe is a city with a split personality that works to the delight of the visitor. One persona of Santa Fe is that of a *tía,* a warm and embracing old aunt, somber and religious. That is the Santa Fe of history: muted colors, such ancient places of worship as the **Santuario de Guadalupe** and the **San Miguel Mission**, narrow and twisting streets lined with old adobe buildings, and the part of arty **Canyon Road** where the pavement ends, and you can continue walking into a simpler world resembling a quiet corner of Mexico or Spain. It is a city of inexpensive New Mexican restaurants that include **Josie's Comidas, Tia Sophia's,** or **Diego's Cafe,** where the bean and the tortilla still reign, and the chile comes in three hallowed flavors—hot, hotter, and why-can't-I-feel-my-tongue? It is a metropolis that was built by the old Spanish-speaking men who sit in the sun on white wrought-iron benches in the centuries-old **Plaza,** a city where the smell of piñon smoke from a thousand Indian-style fireplaces fills the evening air in fall and winter. It is the place where Indians from the nearby pueblos sell silver and turquoise jewelry on blankets in front of the **Palace of the Governors,** which was built when Santa Fe was founded in 1610. It is the city of the traditional Western art of Frederic Remington and Charles Russell and of the painters who came at the turn of the century and transformed the remote village into a budding art colony (their work is prominently displayed in **Nedra Matteucci's Fenn Galleries** and others).

Santa Fe's modern persona offers a different fulfillment, but it, too, is a sensual joy. This is a city where you'll discover excellent American fare at **Double A** and first-rate East Indian food at the **India Palace;** mythical contemporary art at the **Peyton-Wright Gallery,** whimsical art at **Lightside,** and classic American paintings at the **Wyeth Hurd Gallery;** and country western gone **MTV** at the **Old Santa Fe Music Hall.** It is a city where mineral water and Champagne are rapidly surpassing Coors as the drinks of choice, where a contemporary art gallery has replaced an abandoned Spanish Baptist church, the huge and expensive **Eldorado Hotel** has displaced the Big Jo Lumber Company, and nationally known designer ice-cream parlors have taken over local drugstores. These changes, made in the name of progress and tourism, irritate many residents who

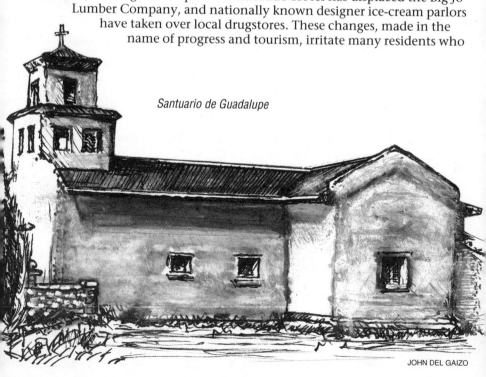

Santuario de Guadalupe

JOHN DEL GAIZO

liked things the way they were but who also realize that the local economy thrives on tourists.

The best part is that the two personae are not geographically separate. The old and the new are intermingled in the same neighborhoods, on the same blocks—BMWs are parked right beside low-riders, new restaurants waft their enticing smells across the entryways to ancient churches. This is true in each of the three areas to explore on foot—the **Downtown Plaza, Canyon Road,** and **Guadalupe Street.**

Allot at least a full day to walking the downtown area. (Serious shoppers and museumgoers can easily spend three days here.) The wall-to-wall art galleries of Canyon Road—a mixed bag of every kind of art and craft—will fill another day and Guadalupe Street several more hours, not counting a hearty lunch at **Zia Diner** or **El Cañon** and dinner at the fine **Santacafe**. And don't miss the *Girard Collection* of thousands of folk-art toys, dolls, and masks at the **Museum of International Folk Art**, about 1.5 miles from the Plaza. Also take at least one day trip, which could include hiking in **Bandelier National Monument**, where Anasazi cliff dwellers lived; sight-seeing at **San Ildefonso Pueblo**, a contemporary Indian pueblo; and breathing the air of the past at **Chimayó**, a traditional Hispanic village whose weavers embody a tradition dating back to the 17th century and whose ancient **Santuario de Chimayó** is venerated, a place still free of style and chic, where the atmosphere still speaks—regardless of your faith—of a more spiritual time.

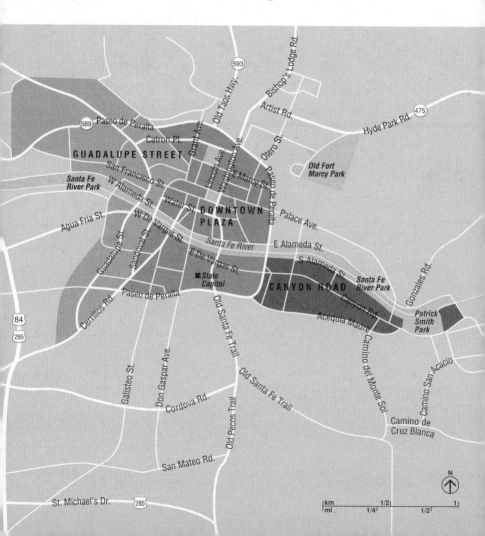

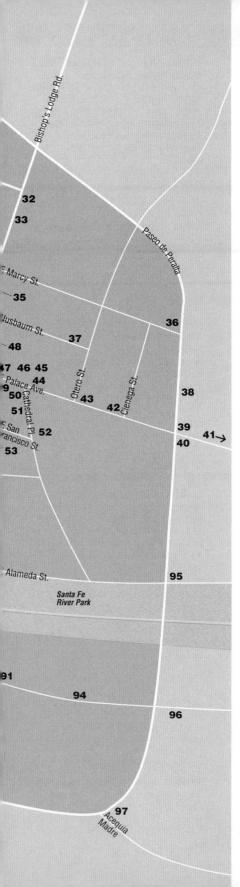

(Map labels: Bishop's Lodge Rd., 32, 33, Paseo de Peralta, Marcy St., 35, Nusbaum St., 36, 37, 48, 47 46 45, 44, Palace Ave., 9, 50, Otero St., 43, 42, Cienega St., 38, 51, Cathedral Pl., San Francisco St., 52, 39, 41→, 40, 53, Alameda St., 95, Santa Fe River Park, 91, 94, 96, 97, Acequia Madre)

Downtown Plaza

Laid out when the city was built in 1610, Santa Fe's Plaza is a square block of trees, grass, and walkways, fronted on four sides by museums, art galleries, Indian jewelry shops, an old hotel, and restaurants. For three centuries, just like the plaza of an old Mexican village, this was the place where the locals came to gossip, buy shoes, party, or just sit quietly and watch the passing parade of neighbors. And for decades it was the block that teenagers cruised in their low-riders in the evenings. But over the past almost 25 years most of that has changed. Rising downtown rents have driven the local shops to malls at either end of town, and the Plaza has become the trendy focus of the tourist trade; automobile traffic is even banned on two of the four sides during the summer to create the feel of a visitor-friendly shopping arcade. Teenagers now meet their friends across from **Häagen-Dazs**, but most local residents have little reason to come here anymore. No change in Santa Fe has caused more bad feeling among the natives than the loss of their Plaza as a locally held treasure.

The Plaza is the literal center of the downtown area, a cultural and credit-card bazaar that radiates in four directions and encompasses about 30 square blocks of restaurants, galleries, shops, churches, hotels, and bed-and-breakfasts, all crammed side by side. Explore this area on foot; there is no other way. And if you want to make friends with the locals, always call this "the Plaza"—not, as many visitors do, "the square."

1 Plaza Tree-shaded grassy areas crisscrossed by walkways make up the center of Santa Fe's downtown Plaza. For centuries locals congregated here to visit and promenade with strolling musicians on Saturday nights. During the 19th century, horse-drawn wagons that had been loaded with goods in Missouri and traveled over the Santa Fe Trail would come roaring into the Plaza at breakneck speed, circling round and round, as the drivers showed their elation at reaching the end of a long journey. Merchants would gather to see what was available to buy, while prostitutes loitered and offered their own wares.

Today, except for a few old men and in-line skating teens, the Plaza is largely a venue for visitors. White wrought-iron benches provide spots for resting and people watching, though the backs of the benches slope away so sharply they offer little comfort. In the exact center of the Plaza is an obelisk erected in 1868 to commemorate fallen Civil War soldiers. A smaller monument marks the end of the Santa Fe Trail in the northeast corner.

In late July the Plaza is the scene of a Spanish crafts market, and, on the third weekend in August, Indian Market, the city's busiest attraction, is held here. Arts-and-crafts fairs fill the Plaza on sporadic weekends. During the three-daylong September Fiesta, the Plaza is filled with food booths and dancing in the streets (not to mention some public drunkenness). For more information on these activities, see "Main Events" on page 13. ◆ Bounded by Washington and Lincoln Aves, and E San Francisco St and E Palace Ave

2 Palace of the Governors One of the oldest public buildings in the country, this blocklong pueblo-style adobe structure occupies the entire north side of the Plaza. Spanish settlement of New Mexico began in 1598, when Juan de Oñate led a group of 130 families from northern Mexico into the Rio Grande Valley. In 1610 Spanish officials established the capital of the province of New Mexico at Santa Fe, laid out the Plaza, and built this structure, facing south toward Mexico City, which was the capital of New Spain. When the Pueblo Indians revolted in 1680 and attacked Santa Fe, several thousand villagers, along with their cows and goats, occupied the palace until they were forced south to El Paso. The palace and the town were occupied by the Indians until they were retaken by the Spanish in 1692 in a peaceful conquest led by Don Diego de Vargas. The Spanish departmental governors ruled from the palace, and the territorial governors presided here after New Mexico was ceded to the US in 1848 following the war with Mexico.

The best known of the palace's occupants was Governor Lew Wallace, who served from 1878 to 1881 and wrote parts of his novel *Ben Hur* here. Working to suppress the violent desperadoes who roamed the region in those days, Wallace numbered among his enemies Billy the Kid, who once boasted, "I mean to ride into the plaza at Santa Fe, hitch my horse in front of the palace, and put a bullet through Lew Wallace."

Since 1909 the palace has been a museum, now housing more than 17,000 historical objects belonging to the **Museum of New Mexico.** Numerous permanent exhibits illustrate the state's multicultural heritage, ranging from ancient Indian pottery to artifacts from Civil War fighting in the region. The **Museum Shop,** entered from Washington Avenue, offers a large selection of Southwestern literature and silver and turquoise jewelry. ◆ Admission; children under 7 free. Tu-Su. E Palace Ave (between Washington and Lincoln Aves). 827.6483

Under the portal of the Palace of the Governors:

Indian Craft Vendors Facing the Plaza, dozens of Indians from nearby pueblos sit in front of blankets covered with hand-crafted jewelry for sale. To many visitors, this sight offers the first sharp impression of what is called "The City Different." Only Indians can sell here, and they have to certify that the wares were made by themselves or their families. The jewelry—much of it silver and turquoise—is of high quality. Bargaining is an acceptable practice with some of the artists. ◆ Daily

3 Roque's Carnitas ★★★$ In the warm months you'll be lured by the appetizing aroma of meat sizzling on the grill of Roque Garcia, a regional local, and Mona Cavalli, who emigrated from New York years ago. This is literally a moveable feast—a pushcart parked on the northeast corner of the Plaza. There's no menu, just homemade lemonade and delicious *carnitas*—strips of prime beef or chicken, marinated in a "secret" sauce, grilled with onions and green chile, and served in a tortilla topped with homemade salsa. Doctors, lawyers, and Indian vendors have been popping over here for a quick, tangy lunch to take away since 1984. In the winter Roque and Mona head south to Mexico. ◆ New Mexican ◆ Daily lunch Apr-early Nov, weather permitting. Washington and E Palace Aves

4 Catron Building A lawyer and political power, Thomas B. Catron was a member of the infamous "Santa Fe Ring," which controlled the New Mexico Territory in the second half of the 19th century. He was appointed district attorney in 1866 and elected as one of the state's first two senators in 1912, amid much wheeling and dealing in the Hall of Representatives. In 1891 he contracted for a half-million bricks to construct this office building on the Plaza, where the post office once stood. The building now houses shops and galleries. ◆ Daily. 53 Old Santa Fe Trail (east side of the Plaza, between E San Francisco St and E Palace Ave)

Within the Catron Building:

Taylor A. Dale Gallery Museum-quality Native American artifacts are featured here. Also sold are tribal art pieces from Africa, Oceania, and Indonesia, including masks and textiles. ◆ M-Sa. Second floor. 988.1487

Channing Gallery A wide range of art is offered in this gallery, including American Indian crafts (textiles, bead work, baskets, and pottery), American folk art (furniture and old forged tools mounted as sculptures), and outsider art (works by unschooled artists from such institutions as correctional and psychiatric facilities). ♦ M-Sa. Second floor. 988.1078

Dewey & Sons Trading Co. The screen door reads "Welcome," and at this shop they really mean it—the staff is exceptionally friendly and ready to help. Santa Fe–style furniture, Pendleton wool blankets woven in Native American designs, fabulous one-of-a-kind stuffed horses, buffaloes, bears fashioned from Indian trade blankets, and interesting accessories are all offered here. Another popular item, the well-made Rand's Hat, tops the heads of celebrities who appear in TV shows such as "Dr. Quinn, Medicine Woman." There's also great country music to shop by. ♦ M-Sa; Su 11AM-4PM. Ground floor. 983.5855, 800/444.9665

5 Eagle Dancer The pieces sold here range from the sublime to the ridiculous, as they do in many Indian art shops—from pueblo Storyteller dolls and Hopi kachinas to the biggest Santa Fe cliché of all, the seated wooden coyote howling at the moon (it's a fact of nature that coyotes howl standing up). The balcony contains the best Hopi kachinas, pottery, and jewelry. On the main floor is a room featuring high-quality, finely woven Navajo rugs and a vault containing Old and New Indian Pawn (Indian-owned jewelry sold to raise money). The cheap stuff, including "Navajo kachinas"—which are tourist schlock—is in the basement. The owners also operate **Wind River Trading Co.** (113 E San Francisco St, between Old Santa Fe Trail and Cathedral Pl, 989.7067), **Wind River West** (Plaza Market, on the Plaza, 982.6232), and **Turquoise Trail** (84 E San Francisco St, at Old Santa Fe Trail, 983.5230). ♦ Daily. 57 Old Santa Fe Trail (east side of the Plaza, between E San Francisco St and E Palace Ave). 986.2055

6 Packard's Indian Trading Co. Known for its top-quality Indian crafts since 1925, this store's highlights include exquisite contemporary Indian bracelets by Don Lucas, contemporary inlaid *concho* belts by Benny and Valerie Aldrich, and the finest Zuni needlepoint turquoise (carved into fine slivers and set in silver) around. Helpful employees will fit the entire family, including infants-in-arms, with Indian moccasins; kachinas are sold here, too. Owned by the Packard family for more than 50 years, the place continues to

be reliable and first-rate under the aegis of the Cannon family, who bought it in 1978. ♦ Daily. 61 Old Santa Fe Trail (at E San Francisco St). 983.9241, 800/648.7358

7 La Fonda $$$$ The oldest hotel in Santa Fe dominates the southeast corner of the Plaza. Records indicate that somewhere in the city there was a *fonda* (Spanish for "inn") to accommodate travelers early in the 1600s. The old hotel this was modeled after, also called **La Fonda,** existed on this site when it became the end of the Santa Fe Trail in 1821. Among the hotel's guests in the early days were Kit Carson, General William Tecumseh Sherman, and General and Mrs. Ulysses S. Grant. Billy the Kid is rumored to have washed dishes in the hotel kitchen. Sheriff Pat Garrett, the man who shot him, checked in just two days after Billy's death.

The diverse list of visitors in recent decades has included Errol Flynn, Senator John F. Kennedy, and Ross Perot. During the Second World War, when the atomic bomb was being built in nearby Los Alamos, scientists would often visit the hotel's bar on their day off to drink and relax. Some of the bartenders at the time reportedly were army intelligence men who kept their ears open in case the physicists, their tongues loosened by booze, began to discuss their work.

The lobby, with its high ceilings and dark vigas (wooden supporting beams), tile floors, oversized armchairs, and paintings by Gerald Cassidy, which date to 1922, remains a popular meeting place because of its convenient location. The 170 rooms and suites are furnished in traditional Spanish style; some have adobe fireplaces. Guests can relax in the indoor pool. In the summer the **Bell-Tower Bar,** the rooftop open-air lounge that overlooks downtown Santa Fe, is one of the city's most frequented rendezvous spots. ♦ 100 E San Francisco St (between Cathedral Pl and Old Santa Fe Trail). 982.5511, 800/523.5002; fax 988.2052 &

Within La Fonda:

La Plazuela ★$$$ Situated in the hotel's enclosed courtyard, this restaurant features traditional but high-priced New Mexican tacos and enchiladas, as well as steaks, chops, and seafood. These local treats are a lot cheaper elsewhere. Potted trees provide an outdoorsy touch, but the skylit roof creates a soft light that, while pleasant, gives one the feeling of being underwater. ♦ New Mexican ♦ Daily breakfast, lunch, and dinner. Reservations recommended for dinner. Main floor. 982.5511

Photogenesis Stunning black-and-white photographs—including many exquisite Southwestern landscapes—are available in this basement gallery. The works here feature images by such outstanding regional photographers as Eileen Benjamin, Peter Sahula, Mark Nohl, Ann Mason, and Nicholas Trofimuk. Browse among these prints for their sheer beauty, even if you can't afford to buy them. ◆ M, Th-Su. Basement level. 989.9540

Things Finer Robert M. Pettus's shop offers fine antique and contemporary jewelry, crystal, silver, and objets d'art. The romance of bygone eras—18th century, Victorian, Art Deco, Retro—pervades every last inch of this store. Russian icons and enamels are a specialty. ◆ M-Sa. Ground floor. 983.5552

Señor Murphy Candy Maker This long-established Santa Fe candy store offers an irresistible selection of temptations that visitors won't find back home. The emphasis is on New Mexican ingredients. One of the most popular items is red chile piñon nut brittle—a novel and surprisingly delicious snack. The factory (1904 Chamisa St, at Llano St, 988.4311), which offers guided tours to groups (generally children on school trips, no individuals), also has a retail store. ◆ Daily. Main floor. 982.0461. Also at: 1904 Chamisa St (at Llano St), 988.4311; Villa Linda Mall (4250 Cerrillos Rd, at Rodeo Rd). 471.8899

French Pastry Shop ★$ Pastries, crepes, croissants, and cappuccino are available in this crowded coffeehouse. ◆ Coffeehouse ◆ Daily. Main floor. 983.6697

8 Rio Grande Gallery The work of popular Taos artist R.C. Gorman, whose stylistic line drawings of Indian women are regarded by some as high art and by others as motel-room art, is sold here. Also showcased are the mystical abstractions of Tom Perkinson. ◆ Daily. 80 E San Francisco St (south side of the Plaza, between Old Santa Fe Trail and Don Gaspar Ave). 983.2458

9 Dewey Galleries Housed in the historic Spiegelberg building (a 19th-century mercantile store listed on the National Register of Historic Places), this gallery carries a fine selection of Navajo textiles, Native American jewelry and pottery, and contemporary fine art by American artists. ◆ M-Sa. 76 E San Francisco St (south side of the Plaza, between Old Santa Fe Trail and Don Gaspar Ave). 982.8632, 800/327.7721

9 Simply Santa Fe In 1881 this building was erected atop an older foundation to house one of the largest mercantile establishments in the region. It is now home to a three-level shop filled with some of the best work by local craftspeople. Visible in the basement is the bricked-off entrance to an underground tunnel that led to the **Palace of the Governors** (see page 20), the city's most fortified building. The merchandise, all distinctive and handmade, runs the gamut from jewelry to clothing to home furnishings. A particular joy is a steel bed frame made by Lloyd Kreitz, in which you'd wake up under a canopy of metal stars. ◆ Daily June-Christmas; M-Sa 26 Dec-May. 72 E San Francisco St (south side of the Plaza, between Old Santa Fe Trail and Don Gaspar Ave). 988.3100

10 Shalako Owners Frank and Marcia Kahlbau have spent over 25 years amassing this shop's collection—one of the largest in New Mexico—of vintage Native American crafts and Old West antiques. One artist featured here is WhiteGhost, a Minneconjou Sioux who served in Vietnam and is now a leader of his tribe and a respected artisan. There's also an unusual selection of bowie knives, and turquoise stones. ◆ M-Sa. 66 E San Francisco St (south side of the Plaza, between Old Santa Fe Trail and Don Gaspar Ave). 983.8018

10 F.W. Woolworth This may be the most revered five-and-dime in America because of its nostalgic symbolism. It's a reminder to Santa Feans of the days when the Plaza was filled with pharmacies, shoe stores, and inexpensive clothing shops, all patronized by locals. Most of these businesses are long gone to the malls, forced out of downtown by rising rents and lack of parking. **Woolworth's** is the last holdout; and at press time there were rumors that it too would be leaving. ◆ Daily. 58 E San Francisco St (south side of the Plaza, between Old Santa Fe Trail and Don Gaspar Ave). 982.1062

10 Plaza Bakery/Häagen-Dazs The former **Zook's Pharmacy** became a Häagen-Dazs outlet in the late 1970s, an event that marked the point of no return in remote Santa Fe's headlong dive into the modern yuppie world. The **Häagen-Dazs** people claim that more of their ice cream is sold in this crowded shop in a year than at any other location in the US. ◆ Daily. 56 E San Francisco St (south side of the Plaza, between Old Santa Fe Trail and Don Gaspar Ave). 988.3858

Restaurants/Clubs: Red   **Hotels:** Blue
Shops/ ⑨ Outdoors: Green   **Sights/Culture:** Black

11 Glenn Green Galleries Though it displays the works of about 25 contemporary artists, including the sculptures of Paul Moore, this gallery is primarily an outlet for renowned Indian sculptor Allan Houser (who died in 1995). Recipient of the National Medal of the Arts in 1992 and the Prix de West in 1993, Houser's work is shown throughout the country. His *Offering of the Sacred Pipe* is in the courtyard of the US Mission to the United Nations in New York City, and at press time his 12-foot-high *May We Have Peace* was temporarily sitting on the Vice President's lawn awaiting the opening of the Smithsonian Museum for the American Indian in Washington, DC at the end of the century; the maquette for the sculpture was presented to President Clinton in 1994. ◆ Daily. 50 E San Francisco St (south side of the Plaza, between Old Santa Fe Trail and Don Gaspar Ave). 988.4168

12 Ore House ★$$$ Sit on the balcony overlooking the Plaza, sip one of 80 kinds of margaritas, and feel immune to the bustle below. By the time you've sampled a few, you may not care that the food—which includes standard New Mexican fare, steak, a salad bar, and a daily seafood special—is ordinary. ◆ New Mexican/Steak/Seafood ◆ Daily lunch and dinner. Reservations recommended for dinner. 50 Lincoln Ave (at E San Francisco St). 983.8687

13 Plaza Cafe ★★$ A downtown fixture, this place opened in 1918 as the **Plaza Restaurant** and has been owned by the Razatos family since 1947. It is now operated by a new generation—brothers Len and Dan and sister Belinda—who modernized the interior and changed the name to its current moniker. The grill has remained simple, unpretentious, and family-oriented and is definitely not a bar—alcohol is served only with meals. The food includes huge hamburgers, New Mexican specialties, and Greek dishes. Boxed lunches can be made up for day trips. ◆ New Mexican/American/Greek ◆ Daily breakfast, lunch, and dinner. 54 Lincoln Ave (west side of the Plaza, between E San Francisco St and W Palace Ave). 982.1664

14 Palace Avenue In the 19th century the stretch of this road that fronts the north side of the Plaza was the rowdiest street in town. West Palace was home to gambling halls and to many of the "fancy women" who entertained trail-weary traders and love-starved soldiers. Most prominent among the painted ladies was Doña Tules Barcelo, owner of the most lavish gambling hall, a brothel, and a bank. She was eagerly accepted in prominent society, to the despair of a few local bluenoses. Her story was fictionalized by Ruth Laughlin in the novel *The Wind Leaves No Shadows.* Today the street is home to a variety of galleries and shops. ◆ From Grant Ave to Canyon Rd

The Historic Santa Fe Trail

Debt-ridden William Becknell left Franklin, Missouri on 1 September 1821 looking for adventure and wealth. He got both. Arriving in Northeast New Mexico on 16 November 1821, he was welcomed by the Spanish New Mexicans with open arms. Starved for goods from the east, they eagerly purchased his merchandise—yard goods, hardware, and cutlery; it was cheaper than European articles and of better quality than Mexican materials. They paid in silver, furs, and mules, making a risk-taker like Becknell rich.

Thus the Santa Fe Trail between Franklin and **Santa Fe** was born, and a new era of prosperity began in the West. With traders traveling with goods secured in covered wagons, this 900-mile road of commerce spanning five states—Missouri, Kansas, Oklahoma, Colorado, and New Mexico—played a crucial role in the westward expansion of the United States.

At the beginning, the primitive thoroughfare attracted adventurers and mountain men—traders and merchants desperate enough to endure hardship for profits. Tons of goods were hauled behind slow-moving ox and mule teams that rarely advanced more than 12 miles daily. There were rivers to ford and blizzards that froze the animals, leaving people stranded with no way to move forward or back. The pioneers suffered from disease, starvation, and attacks. One notably vicious incursion against white traders occurred on the Cimarron River in 1828. Men were tortured and killed, women and children kidnapped, and goods, wagons, and livestock destroyed.

But despite such hardships, the trail continued to be a major artery to the west. When the US declared war against Mexico in 1846, General Stephen Watts Kearny took to the thoroughfare. His goal (realized four years later) was to win New Mexico as a US territory. As trade grew in the 1850s, forts were built along the trail to protect the flourishing traffic.

In 1866, when traffic peaked at 5,000 freight wagons, the **Atchison, Topeka, and Santa Fe Railroad** had already reached eastern Kansas. As its tracks crept westward, trail traffic dwindled, and in 1879, when the first locomotive steamed into Lamy, 20 miles from Santa Fe, the Santa Fe Trail became history. Years of hardship and death, success and wealth, blurred into distant memory.

For some, it is very much still alive: Two Santa Fe Trail Association chapters are in New Mexico: **End of the Trail** in Santa Fe (473.3124) and the **Corazón de los Caminos** in **Wagon Mound** (666.2262). Both chapters host field trips along the trail and welcome visitors.

15 Museum of Fine Arts At the end of the 19th century, traditional adobe architecture was giving way to brick construction in Santa Fe; more than six million bricks were ordered by local builders in that year alone. In 1916 a local artist, Carlos Vierra, spearheaded a movement to return to the traditional adobe style. This museum, one of his early victories, was built in 1917 on the site of a former army barracks to ease overcrowding in the **Palace of the Governors.** Designed by architects **I.H. Rapp** and **William M. Rapp,** the structure has soaring curves, breathtakingly beautiful against the bright blue sky. The building helped inspire the Pueblo Revival–style (now known as Santa Fe–style) architecture that has held sway in the city ever since. A 1982 renovation by **Edward Larrabee Barnes** and **Antoine Predock** increased the exhibit space. The influence of Spanish mission churches, most notably the one at **Acoma Pueblo,** is visible in the **St. Francis Auditorium** at the west end of the building (chamber music concerts are held here).

This is one of the few museums in the world that was created specifically for local artists to display their own work; no attempt was made to gather a collection of European old masters. In time, however, the open-door policy ended, and curated exhibits of contemporary art were balanced with shows featuring New Mexico's own old masters— early painters of the Santa Fe and Taos art colonies, including Joseph Sharp, Ernest Blumenschein, Irving Couse, Victor Higgins, John Sloan, and Andrew Dasburg, and such photographers as Eliot Porter, Laura Gilpin, and Edward Weston. The permanent collection includes 13 works by Georgia O'Keeffe. ♦ Admission; children under 17 free. Tu-Su. 107 W Palace Ave (between Lincoln and Sheridan Aves). 827.4455

16 Contemporary Southwest Galleries Owners Cliff Phelps and Frank Howell display works in a variety of media, all in contemporary Southwestern style. They're the local representatives of Miguel Martinez of Taos, painter of a thousand faces, all of them haunting Hispanic women. Also striking are the imaginative ceramic sculptures of Gene and Rebecca Tobey, derived from Indian fetish motifs. ♦ Daily. 123 W Palace Ave (at Sheridan Ave). 986.0440. Also at: 203 Canyon Rd (at Paseo de Peralta). 988.7271

16 Horwitch LewAllen Gallery Under Horwitch family ownership and LewAllen management, this space exhibits the works of top artists. Among those works featured are massive stone-slab sculptures by Jesús Bautista Morelos; mixed-media painting/construction by Roy De-Forest; colorful landscapes by John Fincher; and the unique paintings of dalmatians by the late Dick Mason. ♦ M-Sa. 129 W Palace Ave (between Sheridan and Grant Aves). 988.8997

17 Montez Gold Personable owner Rey Montez—whose roots here date back to the Spanish conquistadores—carries contemporary jewelry by about 50 local artists, as well as hand-painted leather and silk clothing. Catch Rey when he isn't busy, and he'll be happy to discuss the family tree. A specialty of the shop—75 percent of the business, in fact—is custom-made wedding rings. ♦ M-Sa. 135 W Palace Ave (at Grant Ave). 983.9449

THE PALACE

18 Palace Restaurant and Saloon ★★$$$ Doña Tules ran her saloon, gambling hall, and bawdy house on this site until she died in 1853. In 1959 excavation began for the present restaurant, whose rich red interiors and saloon-type doors retain the Old West flavor of the original. Popular with local politicians and real estate agents, this after-work drinking spot serves continental and Northern Italian cuisine. The menu, which changes seasonally, includes homemade pasta, seafood, free-range poultry, and meats, transformed into dishes such as *tagliarine di mare* (wide pasta with scallops, shrimp, and sun-dried tomatoes in a light pesto sauce), sautéed sweetbreads, and *petto di pollo al formaggio* (grilled chicken breast with goat cheese, herbs, and red lentils). ♦ Continental/ Northern Italian ♦ M-Sa lunch and dinner. Reservations recommended for dinner. 142 W Palace Ave (at Burro Alley). 982.9891 ♿

19 Grant Corner Inn $$ Tucked behind a pretty weeping willow, this Colonial-style manor was built in the early 1900s as a home for a wealthy ranching family. Today it's a first-rate bed-and-breakfast, renovated and owned by Pat Walter, wife Louise Stewart, and daughter Bumpy. The atmosphere here is Old World, with an assortment of four-poster beds, quilts, gooseneck lamps, and other antiques that makes each of the 12 rooms a gentle visit to another century. An extraordinary breakfast is served before a large fire in winter, outdoors in summer. Guests can also stay at a nearby Southwestern-style hacienda. ♦ 122 Grant Ave (at Johnson St). 983.6678 ♿

20 Riva Yares Gallery For more than 25 years Riva Yares ran a gallery in Scottsdale before she moved to Santa Fe. The roster of artists whose work she has exhibited includes Milton Avery, Hans Hoffman, Alex Katz, Alexander Liberman, Larry Poons, Elias Rivera, and George Segal. ♦ Tu-Sa. 123 Grant Ave (between W Palace Ave and W Marcy St). 984.0330

21 Pickney R. Tully House This adobe house is an architectural curiosity: Built in 1851, it is painted to look like brick. Tully eventually deeded the place to his son-in-law, Oliver P. Hovey, who in 1848 had begun publishing *The Santa Fe Republican,* New Mexico's first English-language newspaper, using a printing press he had shipped from Missouri. ♦ 136 Grant Ave (at Griffin St)

22 Homewood Suites $$$$ This all-suite hotel offers 105 spacious units decorated in soft Southwestern rose-and-turquoise hues. All have full kitchens with stoves, refrigerators, and microwaves. Living rooms feature sofa beds, TVs with VCRs, gas fireplaces, and balconies. Amenities include an exercise room, outdoor swimming pool, two hot tubs, a 24-hour convenience store, and an executive center with a copy machine, fax machine, typewriter, and computer for guests' use. The hotel provides free shuttle service to the Plaza (five blocks away) and any other desired destinations in the downtown area. Rates include a continental breakfast and evening social hour (fruit and cheese or light dinner, no cocktails). ♦ 400 Griffin St (between Paseo de Peralta and Rosario Blvd). 988.3000, 800/225.5466; fax 988.4700 ♿

23 First Presbyterian Church In a region that is predominantly Catholic, this church has held strong since opening its doors in 1867; it's the oldest Protestant church in New Mexico. ♦ 208 Grant Ave (at W Marcy St). 982.8544

24 Sweeney Convention Center When this was Santa Fe's mid-high school, Dolly Parton and other touring singers would perform here in the **Sweeney Gym.** In the early 1970s the city converted the school into a convention center that now hosts gatherings of up to several hundred people. At press time there was talk of constructing a larger, more modern facility, but it won't happen for years, if ever. The **Santa Fe Convention and Visitors Bureau** is located inside. ♦ 201 W Marcy St (at Grant Ave). 984.6760

25 Federal Courthouse A beautiful piece of Greek Revival stonework, this building stands out in adobe Santa Fe like a goddess in a sandbox. In 1850 the US Congress authorized the construction of a "capitol building" here, but appropriated a mere $20,000. Four years later, $50,000 more was added, but funds still ran out after only 1.5 stories had been built above the basement. The building stood without a roof for the next 25 years, falling into increasing dilapidation. In 1883, when the site was selected for a large territorial fair, a temporary roof was added so that Indians participating in the six-week celebration could stay inside. A racetrack about one-third of a mile long was laid out in an oval around the grounds, and horse and burro races were held. A year later a stone monument to frontiersman Kit Carson was erected at the main entrance by his comrades in the Grand Army of the Republic. The building was finally completed in 1889—36 years after construction began. Rough stone for the walls was quarried in the Hyde Park region of the hills above the city. Dressed stone came from the village of Cerrillos, to the south. The building, however, never did become the capitol. On the east side of the courthouse is **Grant Park,** a tree-shaded oasis that looks like a bit of New England, and to the west is the nondescript **Main Post Office.** ♦ M-F. ♦ S Federal Pl (at Lincoln Ave). 988.6610

26 City Hall A bronze statue of St. Francis, the city's patron saint, stands in front of this modern building—his back to the goings-on inside—where the mayor's office and a host of other city agencies are located. The eight-member city council normally meets every other Wednesday at 4PM and 7PM. When a new development project is listed on the agenda—as it often is—the room gets crowded and tempers hot. ♦ M-F. 200 Lincoln Ave (between W Marcy St and S Federal Pl). 984.6500

27 Piccolo Cafe ★★$ This tiny corner hideaway is a refreshing place to take a break. Assorted pastries and bagels are available in the morning, and at lunch and dinner there's a large assortment of sandwiches, as well as Greek and garden salads. Coffees, cakes, soft drinks, nonfat frozen yogurt, sundaes, and floats are on tap well into the evening. Bag lunches can be provided. ♦ Cafe ♦ Daily breakfast, lunch, and dinner. 142 Lincoln Ave (at W Marcy St). 984.1709

28 Lincoln Place For many years locals shopped at **Sears** in what was then called the **Old Sears Building,** until the huge department store moved out to **Villa Linda Mall.** Now renovated, this edifice houses shops on the ground floor—with maroon awnings that look as if they belong in Beverly Hills—and three restaurants upstairs. To get to the restaurants, ride on the only escalator in the entire city. But it only goes up; take the stairs or the elevator down. ♦ 130 Lincoln Ave (between W Palace Ave and W Marcy St). No phone

Within Lincoln Place:

Garduño's of Santa Fe $$ The Garduño family has been serving regional food to New Mexicans for over a quarter of a century. Unfortunately, the line out the door is a testament only to their reputation, not the food. But the margaritas are the size of swimming pools, and the Fajita Express lunch buffet features chicken fajitas, enchiladas, burritos, tostadas, salads, and desserts for $6.95, which might explain the line. The family also owns four restaurants in Albuquerque. ♦ New Mexican ♦ M-Sa; lunch and dinner; Su brunch and dinner. Reservations recommended. 983.9797

Cafe Escalera ★★★$$$ This clean, well-lighted place with a cloth ceiling is a favorite with locals. The small menu changes daily, but always includes a beef, chicken, fish, and vegetarian selection. Locally grown organic produce is used in all the dishes, making the best use of seasonal offerings. ♦ American/Mediterranean ♦ M-Sa breakfast, lunch, and dinner; Su dinner. Reservations recommended for lunch and dinner. 989.8188

Babbo Ganzo Trattoria ★★★$$$ Classic Tuscan food as well as New Mexican specialties are prepared by chef Giovanni Scorzo, who claims his pizza—baked in a wood-burning oven—is the best in the world. Many people agree: His ultrathin crust is exactly what you would eat in Florence. The pastas are uniformly good, and the antipasto and daily seafood specials, such as halibut with mushrooms, are excellent. ♦ Italian/New Mexican ♦ M-Sa lunch and dinner. Reservations recommended Friday and Saturday. 986.3835

Kent Galleries/Contemporary Craftsman One of the finest craft galleries in town, this place features the longtime favorite—droll pottery covered with rabbits made by Rabbit Art Works. Beautifully wrought ceramics range here from the functional to the purely artistic. The outstanding jewelry collection includes contemporary gold and silver works, many with semiprecious stones, by regional and local artists. The gallery walls, which zigzag for an entire block, feature popular local landscapes in oil pastel by Maggie Muchmore. ♦ M-Sa; Su noon-5PM. 988.1001

29 **Davis Mather Folk Art Gallery** Coiled, brightly colored wooden snakes glare out from the walls and shelves of this tiny, jam-packed shop, along with assorted sheep, roosters, families of cats, and folk-art buses filled with animal passengers. The town's first folk-art shop opened in the mid-1970s, caught the Santa Fe wave, and is still going strong. Hang around, and you might meet the owner's wife, Christine Mather, a former museum curator who coauthored the hugely successful book *Santa Fe Style*. ♦ M-Sa. 141 Lincoln Ave (at W Marcy St). 983.1660

30 **Paul's** ★★★$$ Santa Feans consider this elegant hole-in-the-wall restaurant decorated with international folk art a local secret. Among its variety of interesting menu items, chef Paul Hunsicker features a baked salmon with a pecan-herb crust in sorrel sauce. Another mouthwatering dish is roasted duck with a chipotle-tomato-orange sauce. Save room for the pièce de résistance—chocolate ganache. It's a delicious confection of white and dark chocolate mixed together like a marble cake and served on a pecan crust. Breakfast features *migas* (eggs scrambled with tortilla strips). ♦ Continental/Southwestern ♦ M-Sa breakfast, lunch, and dinner. Reservations required. 72 W Marcy St (between Washington and Lincoln Aves). 982.8738

31 **Il Piatto** ★★★$$ Under the same ownership and chef as **Bistro 315** (see page 38), this rustic dining spot with collages of old cooking utensils on the walls recently opened to mixed reviews. The menu features Italian fare, including several pasta selections from gnocchi to *orechiette* (ear-shaped pasta) to *pappardelle* (broad noodles). Curiously, couscous and curried dishes are also offered. ♦ Italian ♦ M-F lunch and dinner; Sa-Su dinner. 95 W Marcy St (between Washington and Lincoln Aves). 984.1091

32 **Padre Gallegos House** This Territorial-style adobe home was built in the 1850s by Padre José Manuel Gallegos a few years after he was defrocked as a priest by Archbishop Lamy, who had taken a dim view of the padre's gambling, dancing, and political activities. According to some historians, Padre Gallegos was a ringleader of the 1847 Taos revolt against the American occupation of the New Mexico Territory, in which Governor Charles Bent was assassinated. During the Civil War the building was used as a rooming house. Beginning in 1868, part of the north tier of rooms where **Santacafe** (see below) is located served for a time as an Episcopalian chapel; it is believed that the former padre wed the widow Candelaria Montoya there. Gallegos died in 1875 and was

buried in Rosario Cemetery a few blocks away. ◆ Free. Daily. 231 Washington Ave (at S Federal Pl). No phone

Within the Padre Gallegos House:

Santacafe ★★★★

$$$ One of Santa Fe's finest, this restaurant offers beauty at every turn: in the soft white adobe interiors of the small rooms, in the boulder-studded courtyard where lunch and dinner are served in the warm months, and, under the watchful gaze of co-owners Bobby Morean and Judith Ebbinghaus, in the way every appetizer and entrée is presented. The menu changes with the seasons, and the combinations of ingredients are novel and usually delicious. Crab egg rolls are a traditional favorite appetizer, and the flash-fried calamari is crisp yet tender, as is an entrée of Oriental duck breast in Velarde sweet-and-sour cherry sauce. One variety of pizza is made with fresh peppers, chiles, tomatoes, basil, and Sonoma jack cheese. The pleasant staff always offers impeccable service. On occasion the taste of a subtle dish, such as scallops, may be too subtle for complete satisfaction, or crab cakes a bit too spicy. But overall, dining here is a lovely experience. ◆ New Southwestern ◆ M-Sa lunch and dinner; Su dinner. Reservations required. 984.1788

33 Territorial Inn $$ Just a short jaunt from the Plaza, this 11-bedroom bed-and-breakfast is set back from the street behind a well-kept lawn and large cottonwood trees, giving it a nice secluded feeling. The building itself, constructed in the 1890s by **George Shoch**, a Philadelphian, is a blend of stone and adobe architecture with an unusual pitched roof. Levi Hughes, a prominent local merchant, lived here in the 1920s with his wife and threw lavish society parties. In the public living room a large fire blazes on cool evenings. Two of the rooms have their own fireplaces, and eight have private baths. In the back garden, a hot tub is enclosed in a gazebo. Eat breakfast in the garden in summer or in your room. ◆ 215 Washington Ave (between E Marcy St and S Federal Pl). 989.7737; fax 986.1411

34 Bull Ring ★★★$$$ Formerly located next to Santa Fe's capitol building, this restaurant recently moved to this elegant but informal setting with high ceilings, burgundy accents, and a shady patio. As the name connotes, beef is the star attraction. The prime rib here is perfectly cooked with a salty crust and pairs well with the garlic mashed potatoes drenched in butter. At lunch try the blackened prime rib sandwich with horseradish mayonnaise. Be sure to save room for the dense, moist, chocolate torte. ◆ American ◆ M-F lunch and

dinner; Sa-Su dinner. 150 Washington Ave (at W Marcy St). 983.3328 &

35 Santa Fe Public Library Once the main fire station, then converted into **City Hall,** this two-story Territorial-style building is now the main branch of the local library. Visitors cannot check out books without a local address, but they are welcome to use the **Southwest Reading Room,** which houses a distinguished collection of works on the region, both fiction and nonfiction. The periodicals' reading room offers a modest selection of current newspapers and magazines. ◆ M-Sa; Su 1-5PM. 145 Washington Ave (at E Marcy St). 984.6780

36 Josie's Casa de Comida ★★$ This popular luncheonette serves delicious, quintessential Santa Fe fare. Josie retired once but was called back to active service by the entreaties of her hungry regulars. Come here for homemade burritos and enchiladas, but be sure to save room for one of the savory pies or cobblers. ◆ New Mexican ◆ M-F lunch. No credit cards accepted. 225 E Marcy St (between Paseo de Peralta and Otero St). 983.5311

37 Peyton Wright Gallery Artists who dip their brushes in dreams and myths dominate John Wright Schaefer's boldly evocative contemporary gallery. Over 30 local, regional, and international painters and sculptors are shown here. Orlando Leyba's mixed-media works and Miguel Zapata's bronze sculptures represent the cutting edge of contemporary Hispanic art. The Indian visions of Darren Vigil Gray churn with an inner fury. Also featured are Spanish Colonial silver, paintings, and furniture, as well as Navajo and Rio Grande textiles and weavings. ◆ M-Sa; Su by appointment. 131 Nusbaum St (between Otero St and Washington Ave). 989.9888

38 Dancing Ground of the Sun $$ David and Donna McClure gave up careers in Honolulu to run this bed-and-breakfast whose name comes from an old Indian name for Santa Fe. All five of the units are casitas (bungalows), each with its own kitchen. Three have fireplaces for those cool Santa Fe evenings. A continental breakfast and afternoon refreshments are provided. ◆ 711 Paseo de Peralta (between E Palace Ave and E Marcy St). 986.9797, 800/645.5673

39 Wyeth Hurd Gallery This gallery is dedicated to paintings and prints by what may be America's foremost family of artists: patriarch N.C. Wyeth, who died in 1945; his son Andrew Wyeth, the most famous; his daughter, Henriette Wyeth, whose strong still lifes may make her the most enduring painter of the lot; Henriette's late husband, Peter Hurd, who is best known for watercolors of the New Mexico landscape; Jamie Wyeth, Andrew's son, whose portraits of celebrities are well known nationally. The new generation continues to carry on the family tradition. ♦ Daily. 301 E Palace Ave (at Paseo de Peralta). 989.8380

39 Dumont Maps and Books of the West Interested in reading *Dodge City—The Cowboy Capital, Cattle Trade of the West,* or *Six-Guns and Saddle Leather?* These and hundreds of other rare, used, and new volumes about the Southwest are available in this unpretentious shop run by André and Carol Dumont. Antique maps, prints, and collectibles from the American West are also featured here. ♦ M-Sa; Su noon-5PM. 301 E Palace Ave (at Paseo de Peralta), Suite 1. 988.1076

40 La Posada $$$ One of the most pleasant hotels in town, this six-acre spread of grass, fruit trees, and casitas offers 119 rooms and 40 suites—all just an easy three-block walk from the Plaza. The Victorian-style main building was constructed in the 1880s by Abraham Staab, a German immigrant who made a fortune in the mercantile business. The ghost of Staab's wife, Julia Shuster Staab, is said to be a permanent nonpaying guest in **Room 256.** Surrounding the main house are rows of casitas, both old and new, many of which contain Native American fireplaces, flagstone floors, vigas, and skylights. There's also an outdoor pool, rose garden, and a lovely patio with wrought-iron tables shaded by umbrellas, as well as the **Staab House** restaurant and bar. ♦ 330 E Palace Ave (between Delgado St and Paseo de Peralta). 983.6351, 800/727.5276; fax 982.6850 &

The first groups of travelers on the Santa Fe Trail reported that the woods were full of game, the plains and canyons full of antelope and buffalo, and the streams teeming with fish. There were more beavers than people, and wolves were so numerous that burial sites had to be covered with rocks.

Maria Benitez, considered Queen of Flamenco, dances worldwide. But visitors to Santa Fe can see her perform all summer long at the Picacho Plaza Hotel.

Within La Posada:

Staab House ★$$$ This restaurant has a nice rustic feel to it, enhanced by a large fireplace. The breakfasts are excellent; in the summer the superb, though expensive, all-you-can-eat Sunday brunch buffet features about 40 items. Lunch and dinner, however, rarely excite. ♦ American ♦ Daily breakfast, lunch, and dinner. Reservations recommended for dinner. 986.0000 &

41 Alexander's Inn $$ After a hard day's shop at the Plaza, nothing could be more relaxing than a bubbling hot tub soak under the stars. A stay at this quiet and intimate 1903 Craftsman-style inn offers myriad luxuries, such as deep, footed bathtubs, rooms with fireplaces, and a garden of lilacs and apricot trees, a lovely setting for breakfast outdoors. Owner Carolyn Lee bustles about seeing to the happiness and comfort of her guests, including baking chocolate chip cookies and offering restaurant recommendations. There are six rooms in the main house, each beautifully outfitted with antiques and collectibles, and two cottages with kitchens and spiral staircases leading to very romantic bedrooms. ♦ 529 E Palace Ave (between Rodriguez and Armijo Sts). 986.1431

42 Palace Design Copper lamps and shades that look like tall pyramids are leading attractions in this designer variety store, along with exotic mirrors, wrought-iron tables, candlesticks, and wall sconces. Owner James Aumell has traded here since 1970. ♦ Daily. 217 E Palace Ave (at Cienega St). 988.5204

43 Nicholas Potter, Bookseller The oldest used bookstore in town was started in 1969 by Chicago-born Jack Potter, whose son Nick took over in 1975. It's a bibliophile's heaven. If Nick doesn't have a book, he'll try to track it down. The shop stocks more than 8,500 volumes, all hardbacks, of predominantly literary and scholarly works. ♦ Daily. 203 E Palace Ave (at Otero St). 983.5434

43 Palace Avenue Books If nothing old strikes your fancy at **Nick Potter's,** try something new next door at Judy Dwyer's bookshop, which is strong in current works of history and philosophy. The space is small, but the selection of Southwestern scholarly works may be the largest in town. Also stocked are books on Native American history, myths, culture, and art, as well as general fiction and nonfiction. ♦ M-Sa. 209 E Palace Ave (between Cienega and Otero Sts). 986.0536

Tales from the Land of Enchantment

Northern New Mexico is a region where the human spirit has sometimes battled the ruggedness of the land and sometimes lived with it in fragile harmony, and where different cultures have responded to the trials of life in different ways. These conditions have attracted many writers, some who come to live, others merely to visit and record what they have discovered. The following books are noteworthy for the way they evoke and illuminate the people and the land.

Alburquerque by Rudolfo Anaya (University of New Mexico Press, 1992) In this historical novel, Anaya—one of New Mexico's most celebrated literary figures—traces the growth of Albuquerque and the role of Hispanic culture there from the 17th century to the present.

Brave Are My People—Indian Heroes Not Forgotten by Frank Waters (Clear Light, 1993) Nominated five times for the Nobel Prize in literature, Waters illuminates the humorous and heartbreaking lives of 15 heroic Native American leaders of the past, including Sitting Bull and Chief Seattle. The author has lived among the Ute and Navajo and was closely associated with the Hopi and Taos Indians.

Canyon of Remembering by Lesley Poling-Kempes (Texas Tech University Press, 1996) A novel of miracles, including flying sheep, and about life in New Mexico.

Dance Hall of the Dead by Tony Hillerman (Harper & Row, 1973) This Albuquerque author won the Edgar Award for his mystery set at **Zuni Pueblo** and has since written about 10 more mysteries steeped in the lore of the Navajo and Pueblo Indians. Many of Hillerman's latest books—including *Talking Gods* and *Coyote Waits*—have become huge best-sellers. Every detail is authentic, as attested to by the fact that Hillerman was made an honorary Native American by the Navajo nation.

Death Comes for the Archbishop by Willa Cather (Vintage, 1990) First published in 1927, this is a classic anecdotal novel of the life and deeds of Archbishop Lamy, whom Cather has named Father Latour.

The Delight Makers by Adolf F. Bandelier (Harcourt Brace Jovanovich, 1971) A novel about the prehistoric Pueblo Indians, in which the foremost archaeologist of the region blends fact and fiction.

Georgia O'Keeffe In the West edited by Doris Bry and Nicholas Callway (Alfred A. Knopf, 1980) An oversized book of plates containing many of the artist's most distinctive paintings of the region.

Great River by Paul Horgan (Farrar, Straus & Giroux, 1984) A monumental biography of the Rio Grande that won the Pulitzer Prize for history.

It Happened in New Mexico by James A. Crutchfield (Falcon Press, 1995) A collection of the most provocative episodes and characters in the history of New Mexico, including stories of Billy the Kid, Pancho Villa, and Smokey the Bear.

Kokopelli—Fluteplayers Images in Rock Art by Dennis Slifer and James Duffield (Ancient City Press, 1994) Richly illustrated and well researched, this guide describes the 300 rock art sites of Kokopelli in the Southwest. Also included is a sampling of Native American myths and stories about this mysterious sacred figure.

Lamy of Santa Fe by Paul Horgan (Noonday Press, 1975) A detailed biography of the archbishop who helped shape the city, this book won Horgan the first of his two Pulitzers.

Laughing Boy by Oliver La Farge (Signet, 1971) This novel about a Navajo boy first published in 1929 won the Pulitzer Prize for fiction.

Mayordomo by Stanley Crawford (University of New Mexico Press, 1988) The author, who lives on a garlic farm between Santa Fe and Taos, elegantly conjures up nature and the land along one of Northern New Mexico's *acequias* (irrigation ditches).

The Milagro Beanfield War by John Nichols (Holt, Rhinehart and Winston, 1974) This novel, set in a village near Taos where the author lives, is long, wonderful, and folksy. (Robert Redford's movie version, while pleasant, is not an adequate substitute.) Nichols wrote two subsequent books in a New Mexico trilogy, *The Magic Journey* and *Nirvana Blues.*

Red Sky at Morning by Richard Bradford (Harper & Row, 1968) This coming-of-age story is set in Northern New Mexico during World War II and was later made into a movie.

River of Traps by William deBuys and Alex Harris (University of New Mexico Press, 1990) Words and photographs are used to depict life in a small Hispanic village in Northern New Mexico in this widely acclaimed book.

Santa Fe Recipe by Joan Stromquist (Tierra Publications, 1992) Easy recipes from some of Santa Fe's famous restaurants—**Santacafe, Guadalupe Cafe, Zia Diner,** and **Celebrations**—and **Wild Oats Community Market,** complete with anecdotal quotes from its chefs. Part of a series that includes *Taos Recipe* and *Santa Fe Lite & Spicy* by the same author.

Taos by Irwin R. Blacker (Brooke House, 1959) This huge historical novel is set in the early days of the Indian and Spanish settlements.

This Dancing Ground of Sky—The Selected Poetry of Peggy Pond Church edited by Kathleen Church (Red Crane Books, 1993) Best known for her heartwarming *The House at Otowi Bridge: The Story of Edith Warner and Los Alamos,* in this deeply moving collection of poems, Church reveals her passion for the people and landscape of her home state, New Mexico.

44 Frank Patania Masks from Bali, tribal art from New Guinea, and carvings from Indonesia offer a welcome break from the Southwestern bazaar. Frank Patania also sells silver and gold jewelry he designs himself, as well as Navajo jewelry. ♦ M-Sa. 119 E Palace Ave (between Otero St and Washington Ave). 983.2155

45 Sena Plaza Stop in this courtyard, one of the prettiest and most serene spots in Santa Fe, and relax on benches amid the profusion of day lilies, hollyhocks, roses, and large shade trees; let the gurgling fountain blot out the traffic noise. This was once the courtyard of the residence of Doña Isabel and Don Jose Sena. Starting with a small house, Sena little by little built a hacienda of 33 rooms to house their 11 children, the servants, horses, and chickens. Part of the second story was added when the building was restored in 1920. Now owned by prominent local art dealer and real estate mogul Gerald Peters, it houses shops, galleries, and a restaurant. But the lovely courtyard still conveys the feeling that time itself has paused to rest. ♦ 125 E Palace Ave (between Otero St and Washington Ave)

Within Sena Plaza:

Montez Gallery All his life, Santa Fe native Rey Montez watched his father, Ramon, carve traditional Hispanic *retablos* (renderings of the saints on wooden plaques), as well as animals and flowers, out of sugar pine. An electrician by trade, Ramon gave his artwork to friends but never tried to sell it. In 1989 Rey opened a gallery to display the art of his father and other traditional Hispanic folk artists of the area, whose work had been largely overlooked amid the seemingly endless number of Indian art stores. Today there are two shops near each other, filled with *bultos* (wood carvings of saints), *retablos,* appliquéd straw crosses, and assorted objects of tin. Both are considered the most authentic Hispanic galleries in town. ♦ M-Sa. Suite 10A and Suite 3. 982.1828

La Casa Sena ★★★$$$$ This elegant and formal dining room occupies a 19th-century Territorial-style adobe house and serves wonderful local and continental fare. Eat under the stars in warm weather. Highlights on the full New Mexican menu include an exquisite black bean soup served with a cruet of sherry, *pollo en mole* (chicken in a red chile-mole-sesame sauce), and *truchas en terracotta* (trout cooked in clay). Delicious whole-wheat sopaipillas are served at lunch, and the wine list is outstanding. ♦ New Mexican/Continental ♦ Daily lunch and dinner. Reservations required. 988.9232

Cantina ★★★$$$ Adjacent to **La Casa Sena** (and under the same ownership), this laid-back eatery provides one of the most enjoyable dining experiences in town. The talented staff sing excerpts from Broadway musicals past and present, while serving and in a nightly show. Sounds corny, but it's fun. The best local ingredients are always used in the gourmet fare here. A red-chile pasta with scallops, shrimp, and salmon is wonderful, as is the avocado cheesecake (yes, avocado—try it!) with a piñon nut crust. Reservations are not taken, and since the room is L-shaped, it's best to show up a half-hour before show time for a good view and an enchanted evening. ♦ New Mexican ♦ Daily dinner. Shows: daily 6, 8PM. 988.9232

Soap Opera

Soap Opera Santa Fe's bathers have been stopping by this aromatic shop for more than two decades to pick up exotic soaps scented with cedar and sage, piñon pine, avocado, lavender, sandalwood, and patchouli. ♦ Daily. 982.8066

46 The Shed ★★$ A few steps through a passageway off Palace Avenue, Prince Plaza—a small courtyard—houses one of downtown's busiest lunch spots. The line forms early as patrons queue up for typical New Mexican fare, including tacos and enchiladas. ♦ New Mexican ♦ M-W lunch; Th-Sa lunch and dinner. 113 1/2 E Palace Ave (between Otero St and Washington Ave). 982.9030

47 Trujillo Plaza In 1942 nuclear physicist J. Robert Oppenheimer chose a boys' ranch (an outdoor-oriented private school) in Los Alamos, New Mexico, as the site of the Manhattan Project—the effort to design and build an atomic bomb that would end World War II. Scientists were recruited from across the US, but the project was so secret that the only address and destination they were given was 109 East Palace Avenue in Santa Fe. When their trains were met in Lamy, the nearest rail stop, they were brought here to check in, then driven in military jeeps or buses the 40 miles to Los Alamos. Here, too, their mail arrived, so their location would remain unknown to the outside world. Today the historic address houses shops. ♦ 109 E Palace Ave (between Otero St and Washington Ave)

47 Rainbow Man In business since 1945, this eclectic shop is housed in the rebuilt remains of a building wrecked during the Indian uprising of 1680. Owners Bob and Marian Kapoun display everything from historic photographs to railroad memorabilia and old dining-car china, vintage Indian blankets, and Old Pawn jewelry. There's also a collection of miniature kachina dolls, including one-inch-high wonders by Bess Yanez. ♦ Daily. 107 E Palace Ave (between Otero St and Washington Ave). 982.8706

48 Inn of the Anasazi $$$$ Of all the hotels in town, this hostelry is the only true work of art. Built in 1991 by the **Robert D. Zimmer Group,** it tucks 59 rooms into a small space only a half-block from the Plaza and looks as if it has been here forever—exactly the intended effect. The outside is dark adobe with protruding vigas that cast the afternoon shadows like a sundial. Heavy wood and leather furniture fill the interior, which has the allure of a cozy private hideaway. All of the rooms have ceilings constructed of vigas and *latillas* (cross beams), along with four-poster beds, gaslit fireplaces, Indian rugs, and hand-carved cabinets that hide the modern TVs and VCRs. Service is prompt and first-rate, except for the valet parking in the underground garage, which may take some time because of the narrow property site. ♦ 113 Washington Ave (between E Palace Ave and Nusbaum St). 988.3030, 800/688.8100; fax 988.3277 &

Within the Inn of the Anasazi:

Anasazi Restaurant ★★★$$$ The same dramatic Southwestern ambience that characterizes the hotel permeates this 96-seat restaurant. The tables are made of rough-hewn wood, and the *bancos* (adobe banquettes) are upholstered with handwoven textiles from Chimayó. Up to 12 guests can dine together in the private wine cellar. The menu, created primarily from food grown in the region, features such exotic combinations of New Mexican and Native American dishes as organic tenderloin of beef with white cheddar, mashed potatoes, and mango-red-chile jelly and wood-grilled natural chicken with country-style corn pudding, garlic, sage, and organic vegetables. Although the food usually tastes quite good, its richness may tax the digestive system. The wine cellar is extensive. ♦ New Mexican/Native American ♦ Daily breakfast, lunch, and dinner. Reservations recommended. 988.3030

48 Hotel Plaza Real $$$ Right next door to the **Inn of the Anasazi** and built about the same time, this hotel strives for a brighter atmosphere. The Territorial-style architecture features brick trimwork and white-painted columned porticoes extending out from the pale beige walls. Many of the 56 rooms and 40 suites contain wood-burning fireplaces, and some have balconies. Continental breakfast is

included, and underground parking is available. Guests are invited on complimentary Santa Fe walking tours, Tuesday through Saturday at 11AM. ♦ 125 Washington Ave (at Nusbaum St). 988.4900, 800/279.7325 &

49 James Reid Ltd. James Reid has been showcasing his own silver work—especially buckles and belt-tip sets—as well as that of other local artists since 1980. In an unusual concept, the artisans he employs work together and collaborate on the design and creation of all sorts of excellent silver jewelry. ♦ Daily. 114 E Palace Ave (between Cathedral Pl and Washington Ave). 988.1147

50 Gusterman's Silversmiths Unusual for downtown Santa Fe, the jewelry found here has the simple clean lines of Scandinavian design. Co-owners and sisters Britt and Kerstein Gusterman learned the trade from their father, a master silversmith from Sweden. The family emigrated to Colorado where the elder Gusterman owned several successful silver shops. Kerstein manages the business, while Britt continues the family smithing tradition. Two local smiths help her craft the exquisite earrings, necklaces, bracelets, and pins of gold and silver that are all created on site. Custom-made pieces are also available. ♦ Daily. 126 E Palace Ave (at Cathedral Pl). 982.8972

51 Institute of American Indian Arts Museum In a classic juxtaposition of church and state, the blocklong structure across from the **St. Francis Cathedral** (see below) used to be the **Federal Building.** Local residents would come here to pick up their tax forms from the Internal Revenue Service, among other things. When the feds vacated the place, the **Institute of American Indian Arts (IAIA),** an art school for Indian students, took over and converted the building into a museum, which opened in 1992. Today the *National Collection of Contemporary Indian Art*—more than 8,000 pieces of sculpture, pottery, basketry, beadwork, and paintings—is housed here. At press time, however, the **IAIA** school was operating out of temporary quarters at another location while planning and raising money for a new campus on privately donated land south of the city.

The museum's goal is to entice people to view Indian art the way Indians do, in a meditative, quiet mood. Toward that end, the main entrance opens into the **Lloyd Kiva New**

Welcoming Circle, a space for quiet contemplation with a fire pit in the center. Visitors are urged to meditate here before continuing on. Inside, one permanent exhibit features the works of graduates of the institute since its founding in 1962, including Earl Biss, Kevin Red Star, Dan Namingha, and others. Another exhibit, *Early Innovators,* traces the development of Indian art in this century through the sculpture of Allan Houser, the paintings of Pablita Velarde, the jewelry of Charles Loloma, and much more. The **Allan Houser Art Park** is a lovely outdoor sculpture garden with changing exhibits. ♦ Admission. M-Sa; Su noon-5PM. 108 Cathedral Pl (between E San Francisco St and E Palace Ave). 988.6281

52 St. Francis Cathedral Built in the 1800s, this was the seat of the Archdiocese of Santa Fe until 1974 when the current archbishop, Roberto Sanchez (the first Hispanic to hold that position), moved the headquarters to Albuquerque after his elevation to the post. One of the most historically interesting buildings in town, the cathedral (pictured below) is still used for regular church services, weddings, and funerals.

In 1851, when New Mexico was one of the wildest outposts of the Wild West, the pope sent French bishop Jean Baptiste Lamy to Santa Fe to try to tame it with culture and religion. Lamy believed a dominant religious symbol was needed, so he laid plans for a huge cathedral; the cornerstone was set in 1869. Huge blocks of yellow stone were mined at quarries about 20 miles south of town, loaded onto wagons, and brought to the site. (Lamy, a village not far from the stone quarries, was named after the bishop.) His French Romanesque–style cathedral was built around an older parish church dating from 1714. Stained-glass windows imported from France were installed in 1884, and the cathedral was dedicated to St. Francis, the patron saint of Santa Fe, two years later. Its twin towers were supposed to be topped with steeples 160 feet high, but these were never added.

The old Spanish-style parish church was incorporated into one corner of the cathedral, where it remains as a chapel dedicated to the oldest wooden Madonna known to exist in North America. This statue was carved in Mexico and brought to Santa Fe around 1625; it was taken with the populace driven into exile by the Pueblo Revolt from 1680 to 1692. The legions of Don Diego de Vargas, who retook the city from the Indians, returned it to the church. Originally called *Our Lady of the Assumption,* it was renamed *La Conquistadora* (Our Lady of the Conquest) after the city was reconquered. The most venerated religious object in Santa Fe went by that name until the summer of 1992, when Archbishop Sanchez agreed with Indian protestors that the moniker was offensive and

St. Francis Cathedral

JOHN DEL GAIZO

formally dubbed it *Our Lady of Peace.* A local woman dresses the statue in different clothing every day. Each June it is carried through the streets in a solemn procession that symbolizes the retaking of the city.

Archbishop Lamy, a scholar with European tastes, profoundly influenced the taming of Santa Fe and is commemorated by a bronze statue, which stands in front of the cathedral. When Willa Cather began to spend time in Santa Fe in the 1920s, seeking inspiration for a novel to be set here, she found it in the story of Lamy, told in her classic *Death Comes for the Archbishop.* A wonderfully readable tale, it is stocked by all the local bookstores. **Cathedral Park,** alongside the church, provides a fine, shady resting place. In summer don't miss the free afternoon concerts performed in the cathedral by artists from the **Santa Fe Opera.** ♦ 213 Cathedral Pl (between E Alameda St and E Palace Ave). 982.5619

53 Tom Taylor With almost 50 years of experience, Tom Taylor creates hand-crafted boots and custom-made belts that are stunning (except perhaps to animal activists). He uses 15 types of leather, including ostrich, Italian calf, snakeskin, and alligator. His wife, Jean Taylor, crafts the buckles and other silverwork. Boots made to order take four to six months. ♦ M-Sa May–early Sept; M-W, F-Sa mid-Sept–Apr. 108-110 E San Francisco St (between Cathedral Pl and Washington Ave). 984.2231

54 Fourth World Cottage Industries Owned by Lydia and Marines Perez, these two second-floor shops keep whole families in Guatemala employed turning out handicrafts, from clothing to jewelry. The shops also sell crafts from Indonesia, Thailand, China, Japan, India, Peru, Ecuador, and Morocco. ♦ M-Sa; Su noon-5PM. 102 W San Francisco St (between Don Gaspar Ave and Galisteo St), Second floor. 982.4388

54 Alla In 1980 James J. Dunlap and Barbara A. Sommer opened a business that seemed most unlikely to succeed—a second-floor bookstore limited almost exclusively to books in Spanish. Not only are they still going strong, they've added more space across the hall and now also carry works in French and Portuguese, as well as some books in English dealing with Latin America and CDs and cassettes from Latin America. The store recently added an art gallery that displays the works of two Mexicans—painter Antonio Alvarez Morán and photographer Manual Alvarez Bravo. ♦ M-Sa. 102 W San Francisco St (between Don Gaspar Ave and Galisteo St), Second floor. 988.5416

54 Nambé Foundry Outlet Cast at a foundry in the southern part of Santa Fe, Nambéware consists of dishes, bowls, plates, and platters made of a secret metal alloy that contains no silver, lead, or pewter, though its silver color suggests all three. It can be used for cooking, yet the metal still glows. Some of the designs have been displayed by New York City's Museum of Modern Art. Seconds are also sold here at reduced prices. ♦ Daily. 104 W San Francisco St (between Don Gaspar Ave and Galisteo St), First floor. 988.3574. Also at: 924 Paseo de Peralta (between E De Vargas St and the Santa Fe River). 988.5528

55 Plaza Mercado Spanning half a block, this three-story collection of shops and restaurants was created in the mid-1980s and expanded in 1991 by Gerald Peters on the site of older, humbler businesses. Enter from either San Francisco, Water, or Galisteo Streets. ♦ 112-122 W San Francisco St (between Don Gaspar Ave and Galisteo St)

Within Plaza Mercado:

Eclectica Wonderful Mexican works—tin bird cages, hand-carved and hand-painted full-size altarpieces, Talavera pottery, Zapotec rugs—as well as replicas of Mexican antiques pack this tiny shop. Owner Efrain Aguirre-Prieto is an artist from Mexico who designs a lot of the tin and wrought iron. If you want a dozen matching tin candelabras, he'll design them, have them crafted in Mexico, and ship them off to you. ♦ Daily. 112 W San Francisco St, First level. 988.3326

Downtown Day Spa Dip your body in mud right in the heart of town. Or how about trying a cellulite herbal wrap, seaweed body facial, aromatherapy, or a paraffin manicure? Half-hour foot massages are also available. ♦ M-Sa. 112 W San Francisco St, Third level. 986.0113

BAR & GRILL

San Francisco Street Bar & Grill ★★★$ The best hamburger in town (try it with green chile) is served at Robert C. Day's convenient, casual restaurant, one of the few downtown where you can eat late. The Santa Fe sausage plate with black beans is a special treat at dinnertime. Despite its basement location, this place, more of a grill than a bar, has a spacious feel. A **Patio Grill** pushcart in the rear courtyard is open summer afternoons. ♦ American/New Mexican ♦ Daily lunch and dinner. 114 W San Francisco St, Downstairs. 982.2044

Restaurants/Clubs: Red   **Hotels:** Blue
Shops/🌳 Outdoors: Green   **Sights/Culture:** Black

Santa Fe School of Cooking For those who fall in love with New Mexican food and want to learn how to prepare it, this school offers a two-hour cooking class. At the end participants eat the meal prepared. An adjacent market sells all the foodstuffs needed to make the dishes at home. ◆ Group rates are available. Call for schedules. 116 W San Francisco St, Third level. 983.4511 ఉ

Jane Smith Exquisite handmade Western wear for men and women—including doeskin leather cowboy gloves complete with beadwork, Plains Indian–style leather tunics with shells and beads, handmade boots, and broomstick skirts—are all offered here. ◆ Daily. 122 W San Francisco St, First level. 988.4775

Blue Corn Cafe ★★$ The Southwestern-style space at this dining spot is attractive; the mood is youthful and lively; and the food is consistently good—homemade tortilla chips, fresh, light tortillas kept warm at the table, and excellent burritos and *chiles rellenos*. Best of all, the moderate lunch prices don't go up a penny at dinner: most entrées are in the single digits, amazing for the Plaza area. ◆ New Mexican ◆ Daily lunch and dinner. 133 W Water St, Second level. 984.1800

56 Evangelo's This used to be a macho local bar where outsiders feared to tread. But since Nick Klonis took over from his father in 1984, it draws a fashionable and eclectic crowd. No food is served, but nearly 300 imported beers are offered. The South Seas decor is a shock here in the high desert. There are pool tables downstairs. ◆ Daily. 200 W San Francisco St (at Galisteo St). 982.9014

57 Andrew Smith Gallery Santa Fe native Andrew Smith's photography gallery is one of the best in the city. Classic early American pictures by Edward S. Curtis, who recorded Indian life throughout the West; Ansel Adams, who traveled widely in New Mexico; Eliot Porter, who captured nature in color close-ups while based in nearby Tesuque; and Laura Gilpin, who called Santa Fe home while recording the lifestyle of the Navajos, are among the works showcased here. A large selection of contemporary photography includes pictures by W. Eugene Smith and other international stars. ◆ M-Sa; Su noon-4PM. 203 W San Francisco St (at Galisteo St). 984.1234

58 Collected Works Bookstore This independent bookstore is owned by Dorothy Massey, who does a good job of stocking literary backlists, such as the complete works of Hemingway, but the emphasis here is on Southwest regional books. ◆ M-Sa until 9PM; Su. 208/B W San Francisco St (between Galisteo and Sandoval Sts). 988.4226

58 Tia Sophia's ★★$ Three siblings in the Maryol family, who grew up in Albuquerque, now run New Mexican restaurants in Santa Fe. This one is Jim Maryol's, and it's strong on *huevos rancheros* (fried eggs served on corn tortillas, smothered in red- or green-chile salsa) and bacon-and-egg rolls. Breakfast burritos, a house specialty that has become popular in many parts of the country, were supposedly invented here. ◆ New Mexican ◆ M-Sa breakfast and lunch. 210 W San Francisco St (between Galisteo and Sandoval Sts). 983.9880

59 Lensic Theatre Built in 1930 and dedicated to the people of Santa Fe, this is one of the few old-fashioned movie palaces in the country that hasn't been carved up into a hundred-plex. It's worth catching almost any film on the huge screen under the soaring roof just to recapture the special feeling that movie-going once provided. ◆ 211 W San Francisco St (at Burro Alley). 982.0301

60 Eldorado Hotel $$$$ Santa Fe's largest hotel (219 rooms) is located in the building most hated by locals. Built in 1986 on the site of a former lumberyard, its massive, square-block, five-story bulk exceeds the human scale that the city has tried to preserve. The structure is bathed in the requisite fake adobe color, the windows painted blue, and the lounges and rooms are decorated in trendy Southwestern style, and the rates are designed to keep out the riffraff. You'll feel as if you never left the big city. There's an indoor swimming pool as well as shops on the premises. ◆ 309 W San Francisco St (at Sandoval St). 988.4455. 800/955.4455; fax 982.0713 ఉ

Within the Eldorado Hotel:

Eldorado Court ★★$$ The hotel lobby doubles as a restaurant. The small menu includes sandwiches and salads, and several hot entrées are featured at lunch and dinner. An expensive but sumptuous all-you-can-eat brunch featuring eggs Benedict, pheasant medaillons, and kiwifruit salad is served on Sunday. ◆ New Southwestern ◆ M-Sa breakfast, lunch, and dinner; Su brunch and dinner. Reservations required for Sunday brunch. 988.4455 ఉ

Old House ★★★$$$$ The **Eldorado Hotel** was built around an old adobe house that the developers did not dare demolish in the face of local opposition. Instead, they covered it over and turned it into an upscale restaurant. Inside this elegant dining spot a festive ambience features whimsical carved rabbits and winged horses, a stunning kachina wall mural, and a cozy lounge with hand-carved circular bar tables and upholstered chairs. No beans and *posole* (corn-based stew) are served here, although the emphasis is on the region's produce and spices. Instead, there's usually a rattlesnake appetizer, roasted rack of lamb with a mustard-and-cracked-pepper crust, grilled veal with shiitake mushrooms and hazelnut sauce, a pasta, and a seafood special. ◆ Continental ◆ Tu-Su dinner. Reservations required. 986.1864 ♿

61 Hilton of Santa Fe $$$ Unlike the developers of the **Eldorado Hotel,** this worldwide chain was satisfied with designing what is probably the world's shortest **Hilton** a two-story, Territorial-style building with 159 guest rooms. In the early 1700s this was the site of the home of a prominent and notorious local family named Ortiz. The house later became a large mercantile establishment, then, rumor has it, a brothel. The hotel was built around the old home, whose courtyard was preserved as the **Chamisa** restaurant, where breakfast is served. Southwestern style—with a huge wood-burning fireplace in the lobby—predominates, of course. One reason for the fealty to local customs may be that Conrad Hilton was born in the tiny New Mexico village of San Antonio, about 150 miles to the south. ◆ 100 Sandoval St (at W Water St). 988.2811, 800/336.3676 ♿

Within the Hilton of Santa Fe:

El Cañon ★★★$$ A cozy, inviting room with stucco banquettes, cowhide chairs, and a warming fire, this self-serve counter offers a variety of simple but tasty meals all day. From 7 to 11AM there are decadent homemade cinnamon buns, muffins, scones, and croissants. From 11:30AM to 2PM, choose a smoked turkey, pork, or beef rib-eye hand-carved sandwich on homemade bread; or select a soup (one is always vegetarian), stew, or Caesar salad. From 2 to 5PM, the stews and soups continue, along with cocktails and coffees, and from 5PM to midnight there are sensational margaritas to wash down the tapas. ◆ American ◆ Daily 7AM-midnight. 988.2811 ♿

PIÑON GRILL

Piñon Grill ★$$$ More formal than **Chamisa** (see above), this dining room is set with white cloths and flower bouquets. Assorted beef, chicken, wild game, and seafood dishes are available, including Chimayó marinated rack of lamb, smoked duck breast, piñon salmon, blue corn quail, and the winner: Southwestern blackened elk

on baby greens. Vegetarians will enjoy the platter of fire-roasted seasonal vegetables topped with portobello mushrooms. ◆ New Western ◆ Daily dinner. Reservations recommended. 988.2811 ♿

62 Alpine Sports On winter mornings the parking lot of Harvey Chalker's establishment is jammed with skiers renting skis before heading out to the slopes. In the afternoon they return with their brightly colored lift tickets hanging from their clothes as if they're for sale. Skis are also sold here, as are all the requisite ski equipment and clothing. A full line of hiking and mountain-climbing gear takes care of the summer months. ◆ Daily Dec–mid-Mar; M-Sa mid-Mar–Nov. 121 Sandoval St (at W Water St). 983.5155

63 Santa Fe Weaving Gallery Want to put on the dog, literally? Nancy Paap creates lush coats and jackets from the hand-spun hair of pedigreed chow and Samoyed show dogs. (The prices are pedigreed, too.) Paap and 19 other fiber artists, most from New Mexico, are represented. Victoria Rabinowe shows fine hand-painted silk garments, and Kate Boyan, a designer from Alaska, creates exquisite beaded bags in jewel and earth tones using elk and deer skins. ◆ Daily Apr-Oct; M-Sa Nov-Mar. 124½ Galisteo St (at W Water St). 982.1737

64 Montecristi Custom Hat Works Row after row of hats line the walls of this offbeat shop. Each chapeau is custom designed and tailored to fit its new owner perfectly. Step inside to see hats being steamed into the proper size and shape. Since 1978 Milton Johnson and his workers have been crafting exquisite Panamas and fine fur felts, as well as unusual hat bands. ◆ M-Sa. 118 Galisteo St (between W Water and W San Francisco Sts). 983.9598

65 Foreign Traders Established in 1927 as **The Old Mexico Shop** by Tony Taylor, the brother of Lady Bird Johnson, this business is now owned by Taylor's grandson, Alex Tschursin. A direct import store, it is filled with heavy wooden tables, chairs, and cabinets, as well as ceramic dishes and tiles. Most items hail from Mexico. ◆ Daily Memorial Day-Labor Day; M-Sa the rest of the year. 202 Galisteo St (at W Water St). 983.6441

66 Artesanos Mexican designs entice browsers and collectors in this huge family-run import shop owned by Polo Gomez. There are 170 styles of Talavera tile alone, as well as lead-free dishware, UL-approved Mexican lights, pigskin furniture, hand-blown glass, traditional Mexican folkloric art, and the largest selection of Mexican artifacts in Santa Fe. Most of the tiled kitchens in town probably were born here. A private shipping department will mail chilegrams—chile *ristras* (strings) or wreaths—to friends back home. ♦ M-Sa. 222 Galisteo St (between W Alameda and W Water Sts). 983.1743. Also at: 1414 Maclovia St (off Cerrillos Rd). 471.8020

67 Overland Sheepskin Sheepskin coats hanging high grab the eyes, and the pungent smell of leather infuses the nose in Jerry and Marge Leahy's sprawling shop. Also sold here are leather and canvas coats, luggage, and accessories. ♦ Daily. 225 Galisteo St (between W Alameda and W Water Sts). 988.5387

68 Galisteo News ★$ Locals and visitors alike enjoy coffee, cakes, and sandwiches indoors or out at this combined newsstand and coffee bar. It was the first of its kind in town when it opened in the early 1980s. A large selection of magazines is for sale. ♦ Sandwiches/Pastries ♦ Daily. 201 Galisteo St (at W Water St). 984.1316

69 Coyote Cafe ★★★$$$$ You might think that the decor of Mark Miller's trendsetting place-to-be-seen—the staircase is painted in a surreal mix of colors and a menagerie of carved wooden animals peers down from a desert scene on the balcony overlooking the dining room—is a tough act to follow in the kitchen. Just wait for the food (the menu changes monthly). The restaurant's forte is the elevation of New Mexican regional food into an upscale cuisine—buttermilk corn cakes with chipotle shrimp and rib chops with ancho-chile onion rings and blackened tomato salsa are highlights. When it works, it's great, and it works fairly often. Dinner is restricted to a fixed-price, three-course meal, which can be a bit too much. For a better bargain and less food, come for lunch or head upstairs to the **Rooftop Cantina**. Here, similarly exotic combinations—such as a very spicy barbecued duck and jack-cheese quesadilla or mild soft tacos stuffed with sea bass—are available under an outdoor canopy at much lower prices. ♦ New Mexican ♦ Coyote Cafe: M-F dinner; Sa-Su lunch and dinner. Rooftop Cantina: daily lunch and dinner Apr-Oct. Reservations recommended at Coyote Cafe. 132 W Water St (between Ortiz and Galisteo Sts). 983.1615

In the street level of the Coyote Cafe:

Coyote Cafe General Store In addition to the souvenir T-shirts, aprons, and mugs, this shop offers a mélange of Southwestern food products, including dried chiles, fresh organic produce, and wild game—enough items to pretend to be Mark Miller at home (and the cookbooks to show you how). For those who want a little spice in their life, there's a wide array of *hot* sauces. ♦ Daily. 982.2454

70 American Country Collection As jam-packed as a country attic, this shop features reproductions of antique furniture (and some actual antiques), as well as lamps, rugs, and collectibles with a down-home motif. The company's larger store, where much of the furniture is made, is located at 620 Cerrillos Road, between Don Diego Avenue and Paseo de Peralta (984.0955). ♦ Daily. 129 W Water St (between Don Gaspar Ave and Galisteo St). 982.1296

71 Arius Santa Fe Art Tile This shop offers tiles, painted with every design imaginable, from traditional Southwestern and Indian scenes to Jewish themes surrounding the word *shalom* (peace). In 1972 Roberta Goodman began experimenting with hand-painted tile art in a small studio. Soon after, she opened this shop downtown and built it into a worldwide business. All the tiles are still hand-painted locally. A popular specialty is custom-painted tile murals to set into the outer wall of homes, surrounding the house number. But all sorts of custom murals and individual tiles are possible. These tiles make tasteful, inexpensive souvenir gifts. ♦ Daily. 114 Don Gaspar Ave (between W Water and W San Francisco Sts). 988.1196. Also at: La Fonda Hotel, 100 E San Francisco St (between Cathedral Pl and Old Santa Fe Trail), Lobby. 988.1125

71 Lindee's Original Santa Fe Fiesta Fashions For three days every September, the city indulges in an orgy of food, drink, and dancing known as Santa Fe Fiesta. Traditional fiesta costumes led Lindee Shaw in 1969 to spin off an entire line of locally produced fashions for both sexes and all ages, which have since been featured in some of the nation's leading department stores. Broomstick skirts in cotton or taffeta form the basic line; up to 10 yards of fabric are used per skirt. But fiesta fashion also includes handmade Navajo velvet shirts, ribbon shirts, and peasant blouses. ♦ M-Sa. 118 Don Gaspar Ave (between W Water and W San Francisco Sts). 986.5078

72 Hotel St. Francis $$$ A hotel built on this spot in 1880 was destroyed by fire. The current structure, which opened in 1924 as the **De Vargas Hotel,** often was alive with the wheeling and dealing of local politicians. Falling into disrepair, it became Santa Fe's cheapest hotel in the 1970s, offering run-down, $12-a-night rooms two blocks from the Plaza and just around the corner from the old bus station (now a parking lot). It was renovated in the mid-1980s and given its present name. High ceilings and casement windows lend the 83 rooms Old World charm and are reminders of the hotel's long history. Afternoon high tea is served in the now high-class (though overstuffed) lobby that suggests a British boarding house. The outdoor veranda with wrought-iron tables is a convenient spot to have a drink and watch the passing parade. The building is a National Historic Landmark. ♦ 210 Don Gaspar Ave (at W Water St). 983.5700, 800/529.5700 &

Within the Hotel St. Francis:

The Club ★★$$$ Formerly **On Water,** this restaurant was completely renovated by new owners Patricia and Goodwin Taylor to reflect their love for horses, dogs, and the chase. Plum-colored leather armchairs, forest-green walls, and fox-hunt tapestries create a hunt club theme, finished with a fireplace paneled in dark wood. Chef Paul Bach offers such hearty fare as roasted beef tenderloin, grilled lamb chops with mango chutney, and roasted duck breast. The patio, with a fountain, green wrought-iron tables, and shade trees, is lovely in summer. ♦ American ♦ M-Sa lunch and dinner; Su brunch and dinner. Reservations recommended. 983.5700

73 **Pasqual's** ★★★$$ Some people swear by this place—decorated in a Southwestern motif and one of the few downtown restaurants open for breakfast. Many favor the large center table where single diners can find company. Others swear *at* the place because of its uncomfortable cane-backed chairs. The homemade muffins and scones are great ways to start the day. Lunch and dinner selections include gourmet sandwiches, soups, and salads. ♦ Sandwiches/Salads ♦ M-Tu, Th-Su breakfast, lunch, and dinner; W breakfast and lunch. 121 Don Gaspar Ave (at E Water St). 983.9340

73 **Chile Shop** Everything you ever wanted to know about Southwestern food, the ingredients to prepare it, and the requisite wares for setting a Southwestern table is available in one fascinating shop owned by SuAnne Armstrong. This is headquarters for china and pottery, cookbooks, more than a dozen varieties of chile and chile powder, red-and green-chile salsas, blue cornmeal, blue corn chips, and the wonderful *posole*—in short, the stuff that makes life in Santa Fe worth living. Gift boxes can be made to order and shipped. ♦ M-Sa; Su noon-6PM. 109 E Water St (between Don Gaspar Ave and Old Santa Fe Trail). 983.6080

74 **El Centro** This two-story adobe-colored building was one of the first downtown structures to be subdivided to house a cluster of stores. A half-dozen small artsy-craftsy shops operate within, but the only ones worth noting are **Joe Wade Fine Arts** and **Prairie Edge.** ♦ Daily. 102 E Water St (at Shelby St)

Within El Centro:

Joe Wade Fine Arts There are three Western art galleries here run by Joe Wade. By far the most interesting is **Wade Contemporary,** which features a kind of Western impressionist art—adobe churches and other subjects presented in bright colors and dancing brush strokes. Among the most pleasing works are the pastel landscapes by Victoria Taylor-Gore. ♦ M-Sa. 988.2727

Prairie Edge In a city where Pueblo and Navajo arts and crafts dominate the shopping scene, this bright, spacious Native American gallery offers an intriguing counterpoint: an array of contemporary Lakota and Oglala Sioux works using traditional materials of the Plains tribes—bone, leather, fur, feathers, and beads. From traditional and contemporary Plains Indian jewelry to ceremonial pipes and elaborately beaded buckskin fashion wear, Indian crafts enthusiasts will find out-of-the-ordinary gift items and collectibles here. The owners also run the **Sioux Trading Post** (1428 Cerrillos Rd, across from the Santa Fe Indian School, 820.0605), which specializes in such supplies as beads, hides, and animal horns. ♦ Daily. 984.1336

74 **India Palace** ★★★$$ An appendage to the rear of **El Centro,** this restaurant is housed in a renovated building painted deep pink. Inside, white stucco walls are adorned with elephant tapestries, camel batiks, and a mosque stencil. There's also a simple outdoor patio with a roof and hanging flower pots. But the real reason to come here is the superb East Indian cuisine prepared by chef Bal Dev Singh—the kitchen is hailed as first-rate not only by the *New Mexican* and *Albuquerque Journal,* but by world-traveled gastronomes as well. A variety of excellent curries tops the menu. The breads, including spinach *paratha,* are memorable. ♦ Indian ♦ Daily lunch and dinner. Reservations recommended for dinner. 227 Don Gaspar Ave (in El Centro, enter through the Water St parking lot). 986.5859

Years before adopting the motto "Land of Enchantment," New Mexico was known as the "High and Dry" state. Wheeler Peak, the highest point in the state, stands at 13,161 feet near Taos. Fruitland, a rural town in San Juan County, receives a mere 6.76 inches of rain each year.

75 Julian's ★★$$$ Another Italian restaurant that has joined the ever-growing Italian presence in Santa Fe, this dining spot caters to a smartly dressed crowd. Lovely Italian glass fixtures hang from the ceiling next to vigas, casting a wonderful glow on the myriad pasta dishes. Although the menu is basically Northern Italian, there are a few surprises, such as duck with blueberries and balsamic vinegar. ♦ Northern Italian ♦ Daily dinner. 221 Shelby St (between E Alameda St and E Water St). 988.2355

76 Old Santa Fe Trail From 1821 to 1880—when the railroad linked the Midwest to the Pacific Coast—a steady stream of goods flowed over this trail, which circled to the south of the Sangre de Cristo Mountains. The city was a welcome sight to traders as they raced down the hill after weeks or months of driving goods in covered wagons over rugged terrain occupied at times by hostile Indians. Ahead lay good profits, warm meals, and women that money could buy. ♦ From E Palace Ave to E Berger St, where it becomes the Old Pecos Trail

76 Char Char Vasquez has been designing suede (made mostly from lamb) and leather clothing since 1977, and her creations are produced locally. The shop also includes a nice selection of hats, jewelry, and other one-of-a-kind specialty items. ♦ Daily. 104 Old Santa Fe Trail (between E Water and E San Francisco Sts). 988.5969

JOHN DEL GAIZO

77 Loretto Chapel The first Gothic structure built west of the Mississippi, this chapel (pictured above) was constructed from 1873 to 1878 near **St. Francis Cathedral** for the Sisters of Loretto, the first nuns to come to New Mexico. In 1853 they had established **Loretto Academy,** a school for young women, in Santa Fe. The chapel was designed after Ste-Chapelle, Paris's Gothic jewel. Most attention today focuses on what is called the **Miraculous Staircase.** Legend has it that the chapel's French architect was killed by John Lamy, the archbishop's nephew, because he was suspected of adultery with Lamy's wife. He left no plans for the stairway that would have to be built to reach the choir loft; indeed, there was not even enough room left for a conventional staircase. The sisters prayed for help to St. Joseph, the patron saint of carpenters, and an unknown carpenter soon appeared. He built an amazing spiral staircase with two 360-degree turns, using no nails and giving it no central or visible support. His only tools were a T-square, saw, and tub of water for softening the wood. He left without taking money and without even leaving his name. Whether or not its construction was a miracle, the staircase is very real (and marvelous) and can be viewed within. The chapel is now a private museum owned by the **Inn at Loretto.** ♦ Admission. Old Santa Fe Trail (between E Alameda and E Water Sts). No phone

78 Inn at Loretto $$$ Santa Fe's most picturesque architectural addition in years is this hotel whose tiered design was inspired by the **Taos Pueblo.** Managed by the Nobe House Hotels and Resorts, it stands on the site of the **Loretto Academy.** The inn, decorated in Southwestern style throughout, has 143 rooms and suites, an outdoor swimming pool, and a routine restaurant/coffee shop. Assorted shops can be found in the lobby. ♦ 211 Old Santa Fe Trail (between E Alameda and E Water Sts). 988.5531, 800/727.5531; fax 984.7988 ₺

79 Garrett's Desert Inn $$ While this may just be an ordinary motel, it boasts a convenient location only two blocks from the Plaza. Rates for the 88 guest rooms are lower than at most of the downtown hotels but higher than similar standard accommodations on Cerrillos Road's motel strip. **Le Café on the Trail,** located in the motel's lobby, serves breakfast, lunch, and dinner. ♦ 311 Old Santa Fe Trail (just south of the Santa Fe River). 982.1851, 800/888.2145; fax 989.1647

80 Bistro 315 ★★★$$$ Located along busy Old Santa Fe Trail, this tiny European-style dining spot plays 1940s big band music at lunchtime—a welcome way of drowning out the traffic noise. But the food more than makes up for the lack of tranquillity. Chef Matt Yohalem's eclectic menu changes daily and is presented on a tableside blackboard. Appetizers might include arugula salad, country pâté, or crab cakes with exotic slaw. Continue with such flavorful entrées as steak *frites* (with french fries), barbecued lamb, or grilled tuna niçoise, with sides of corn pudding or garlic mashed potatoes. Be sure to leave room for one of the delicious desserts:

crème brûlée, lemon tart, or flourless chocolate cake. Dine outdoors year-round on the patio with a tent roof; it's heated in winter. ◆ Continental ◆ Daily lunch and dinner. 315 Old Santa Fe Trail (between E De Vargas St and the Santa Fe River). 986.9190 ♿

81 Pink Adobe ★★$$$ Called "the Pink" by many locals, this is the closest thing to an institution among Santa Fe restaurants. An old adobe building with many small rooms, all with fireplaces, this dining spot has been serving hearty fare since the end of World War II. Rosalea Murphy, the owner and chef, hails from New Orleans, and gives an occasional nod to her native city (try the chicken marengo). The steaks, smothered in fresh mushrooms or green chile, are as good as anywhere in the land and huge. The rest of the menu, including a small selection of shrimp, lamb, pork, and New Mexican dishes, is undistinguished. The adjacent **Dragon Room**, in which a tree grows through the roof and free popcorn is served, is one of the most popular bars in town, both among local residents and visiting movie stars. ◆ Steak ◆ Daily lunch and dinner. Reservations recommended. 406 Old Santa Fe Trail (between Paseo de Peralta and E De Vargas St). 983.7712

81 Act 2 Fashion designer Gayle McDonald is the owner of Santa Fe's premier shop for vintage clothing and jewelry, filled to overflowing with tempting creations from Hollywood feature films. The shop—designed by local painter Deborah McNaughton, whose work is shown in London, New York, and Santa Fe—offers a vast collection of Bakelite jewelry, and the merchandise changes weekly. You may find yourself trying on some divine number alongside a celebrity, so keep an eye out. ◆ Daily. 410/B Old Santa Fe Trail (between Paseo de Peralta and E De Vargas). 983.8585

81 Guadalupe Cafe ★★★$ Recently relocated here from Guadalupe Street, this informal dining spot was part of the Santa Fe scene years before nouvelle New Mexican cuisine came to town and will be here long after that fad passes. Chef and co-owner Isabel Koomoa serves consistently good hearty fare, whether it be a cooked-to-order hamburger with excellent fries, any of a half-dozen enchiladas—from the standard chicken to a nontraditional (for landlocked New Mexico anyway) seafood version—spaghetti, breast of chicken relleno (stuffed with cheese and rice), or a variety of overstuffed sandwiches. Try the half-sandwich with soup or salad, and be sure to leave room for one of the fine desserts. Breakfast delights include *migas* or fresh raspberry pancakes. Pleasant and casual, the place also features an outdoor patio with white wrought-iron tables and umbrellas. ◆ New Mexican ◆ Tu-Sa breakfast, lunch, and dinner; Su brunch. 422 Old Santa Fe Trail (between Paseo de Peralta and E De Vargas St). 982.9762

The story of New Mexican furniture began after 1598, when Juan de Oñate's Spanish expedition arrived. With him came the first *carpinteros*, skilled Spanish woodworkers, who fashioned furniture for the colonists. Bringing tools and techniques from Spain and Mexico, they created a new Spanish Colonial style.

Child's Play

When talk of visiting yet another gallery elicits groans from the little ones, what's a parent to do? Here are ten tips for keeping the kids entertained in Northern New Mexico:

1 Visit the more than 10,000 handmade toys and dolls from around the world at the **New Mexico Museum of International Folk Art** in **Santa Fe.**

2 Ride a burro and see a living prairie dog village at **Jackalope Pottery** in Santa Fe.

3 Learn to make pottery or weave on a Navajo loom in the activities area of the **Museum of Indian Arts and Culture** in Santa Fe.

4 Walk (or run) around the park filled with huge sculptures at **Shidoni Foundry** in **Tesuque,** then watch molten bronze being poured to make a statue.

5 Listen to Indian storytellers such as Joe Hayes and Pablita Velarde who frequently appear at various Santa Fe locations, including the **Wheelwright Museum of the American Indian,** the **Santa Fe**

Children's Museum, and the **Old Santa Fe Trail Bookstore & Coffeehouse.** Check for times in local newspapers and the free *Santa Fe Kids,* available throughout the city.

6 Climb wooden ladders up to the cliff dwellings at **Bandelier National Monument** where Indians lived 800 years ago.

7 Make a stop in the Wild West at the **Kit Carson Home** in **Taos** and see the leather outfits mountain men wore and the guns and knives they carried.

8 Tour the home of a Native American at **Taos Pueblo** or at any of a dozen other Indian pueblos between **Albuquerque** and Taos.

9 Stand inside the glowing, rumbling volcano simulation at the **New Mexico Museum of Natural History & Science** in Albuquerque.

10 Look at (but don't touch) the live baby rattlesnakes in the **American International Rattlesnake Museum** in Albuquerque's **Old Town.**

82 Roundhouse The seat of the state government, this round building supposedly was modeled after a Pueblo kiva, a ceremonial structure where the Indians meditate with their gods. Whether the same sort of wisdom passes inside, in the offices of the governor and the legislators, is debatable. Territorial-style motifs—brick trim and white columns—were added to give the building a more official look. From the air, the walkways emanating from four sides help create the shape of the Zia sun sign, which is the state symbol. Works by New Mexican painters adorn the interior walls, and large bronze sculptures by several local artists grace the grounds. The interior is a modern and functional cylinder of offices and meeting rooms. No one ever uses the official name: **Capitol Building.** ◆ Tours M-F 10AM, 2PM. Old Santa Fe Trail (at Paseo de Peralta). 986.4589

83 Four Kachinas Inn $$ A perfect haven for relaxation, this five-room bed-and-breakfast in a quiet historic neighborhood offers serenity and privacy. Guest rooms are simply decorated with handmade furniture, weird and wonderful kachina dolls, and unusual art, like Hopi head pieces used in ceremonial dances. Some rooms have pitched ceilings, and all have private garden patios. The pleasant adobe guest lounge is stocked with travel books, magazines, soft drinks, and tasty brownies. Breakfast is light—fresh baked pastries, fruit, coffee, and juice—beautifully presented and served in the room. Ask innkeeper John Daw for a slice of his superb coconut pound cake, which wins the blue ribbon every year at Santa Fe's County Fair. ◆ 512 Webber St (between Santa Fe Ave and Paseo de Peralta). 982.2550, 800/397.2564

84 New Mexico State Library There is a larger collection of books on the Southwest and a more complete reference room here than at the city library. Old magazines in the upstairs stacks date back to the early part of the century. Visitors can make arrangements at the circulation desk to check out books. ◆ M-F. 325 Don Gaspar Ave (between Paseo de Peralta and E De Vargas St). 827.3800

85 Real Burger ★★$ Very good hamburgers and sandwiches are ordered at a wooden counter in this little barn filled with wooden booths and wonderful cooking smells. Be sure to order the crinkle-cut fries, which come with

a bit of chile in the flavoring. ◆ American ◆ M-Sa breakfast, lunch, and early dinner. 227 Don Gaspar Ave (between E Alameda and E Water Sts). 988.3717

85 Santa Fe Village An adobe-style shopping mall built in the 1970s, this sprawling structure is a dark catacomb filled with gift stores and several sandwich/coffee shops. ◆ 227 Don Gaspar Ave (between E Alameda and E Water Sts). No phone

86 Inn of the Governors $$$ Two blocks from the historic Plaza, this charming hotel features 100 bright and airy rooms and an outdoor heated pool. The lobby is a comfortable place to relax, as is the outdoor terrace; there's alfresco dining in warm weather under pastel umbrellas. ◆ 234 Don Gaspar Ave (at W Alameda St). 982.4333, 800/234.4534; fax 989.9149

Within the Inn of the Governors:

Mañana Restaurant and Bar ★$$ The food here is varied and decent—char-grilled ahi tuna, duck fajitas, and linguine with chicken and bell peppers. The cozy kiva bar is a popular local meeting place and features live music at night. ◆ New Mexican/American ◆ Daily breakfast, lunch, and dinner. 982.4333

87 Alameda Street One of the prettiest streets in town, this east-west passage runs along the north side of the Santa Fe River, which is a river only in the spring when the snow on the Sangre de Cristo Mountains is melting and running off. The rest of the time it is a dry ditch. But **Santa Fe River Park,** a narrow strip of grass running along both sides of the river, is a peaceful venue of tall shade trees—a nice place for a respite from sight-seeing. Picnic tables are spotted along the park, which totals 19 acres and is shaped like a long ribbon. ◆ From Rim Rd to Calle Nopal

88 Bataan Memorial Building This sprawling government office building was the state capitol before its dome was removed when the **Roundhouse** opened in 1951. Today it houses, among other things, the attorney general's office and its consumer fraud division. The building was named in honor of those who survived the infamous Bataan Death March in the Philippines during World War II and those who did not. As a result of this march, New Mexico sustained the most casualties of any state in the country. ◆ M-F. 460 Galisteo St (between S Capitol and W De Vargas Sts). No phone

89 East De Vargas Street Though the Santa Fe River is dry about 10 months of the year, this area, just south of the river, is believed to have been the first part of Santa Fe to be settled. The Indians named it *analco* (the other side of the water). In the early Spanish colonial period of the 1600s, it became the other side of the tracks. Spanish soldiers and priests resided on the Plaza side of the river, which is close to the safe haven of the **Palace of the Governors;** their Mexican and Indian servants lived here in what was then called the Barrio de Analco. During the 1680 Pueblo Revolt, the barrio was the most vulnerable area and was totally destroyed. The barrio, however, was rebuilt early in the 18th century. At first, the social divisions still prevailed, and primarily laborers lived here; later, more prominent residents moved into some of the same houses, often adding rooms. A walk along this narrow street affords a peaceful escape, away from the bustle of shopping and into history. Most of the buildings are still private residences and can be viewed—except for the **Oldest House** (see below)—only from the outside. Those listed below have been designated by the Historic Santa Fe Foundation as worthy of preservation. ♦ From Paseo de Peralta to Don Gaspar Ave

90 Roque Tudesqui House The exact age of this building is not known, but at least one wall was built partially of puddled adobe, indicating Indian construction from the pre-Spanish period. Puddled adobe is made with poured mud, rather than adobe bricks. Many of the walls are three feet thick. By 1841 it was the residence of an Italian trader, Roque Tudesqui (the only thing recorded about him is that he was 38 and single). In late spring, beautiful and ageless wisteria vines bloom on the patio. This is a private house. ♦ 129-135 E De Vargas St (between Old Santa Fe Trail and Don Gaspar Ave)

91 Oldest House Maps dating to 1882 label this the "oldest building in Santa Fe," and it may appear on an earlier map from 1768 that shows a structure at this approximate location. The house, a good example of early adobe construction, is made of puddled adobe, and tree-ring

cuts taken from some of the vigas indicate a cutting date of from 1740 to 1767. Visible inside are dirt floors, very low log ceilings, a corner fireplace, and puddled mud walls. ♦ Donation requested. Daily. 215 E De Vargas St (between Paseo de Peralta and Old Santa Fe Trail). 983.8206

92 San Miguel Mission Believed to be the oldest church in the US, this chapel (illustrated below) dates to the earliest years of the Spanish settlement, around 1625. It was originally used as a mission church for the Tlaxcalan Indian servants in the Barrio de Analco, who had been brought from Mexico by the Spaniards. Much of the church was destroyed during the 1680 Pueblo Revolt, but some walls were left standing. When the Spanish rebuilt the chapel in 1710, they put up new walls outside the old ones. The restoration turned the church into a kind of fortress, with the windows high up and adobe battlements on the roof. The current square tower was added around 1887. Inside the chapel is an altar screen dating to 1798, which displays a statue of St. Michael, the patron saint of the chapel. The paintings on the screen were created in Mexico in the 18th century. Colonial paintings on buffalo hide are also on display. The interior was restored in 1955. The chapel and a gift shop are owned and run by the Christian Brothers. ♦ 401 Old Santa Fe Trail (at E De Vargas St). 983.3974

93 Old Santa Fe Trail Books & Bistro A high-ceilinged, two-story Victorian building (1903) houses this popular bookstore that is a hangout for Santa Fe's lively literary subculture. With quality titles in all categories, the store has especially good selections of Judaica and women's topics. Poetry and prose readings, book signings, and kids' storytelling hours are presented several times a week. The indoor-outdoor bistro in the back offers exceptional green salads, plus soups, daily specials, gourmet coffees, good margaritas, and a decent wine selection. Live folk music is performed

San Miguel Mission

M. BLUM

some evenings—call ahead for a schedule.
♦ Daily. 613 Old Santa Fe Trail (between E Buena Vista St and E Santa Fe Ave). 988.8878

94 Boyle House Another of Santa Fe's oldest houses, this adobe was built of walls more than four feet thick in some places. Ceilings of *rajas* (split wood overlaid with straw and earth) are further evidence that it dates to the early period of Spanish settlement. At various times it belonged to US soldiers, the Catholic church, and Spanish landowners. It was acquired by the Boyle family in the 1800s and is still a private residence. ♦ 327 E De Vargas St (between Paseo de Peralta and Old Santa Fe Trail)

95 Inn on the Alameda $$$$ Across from Santa Fe River Park, this lovely small hotel built in Pueblo style blends in nicely with its surroundings. The 66 tasteful rooms and suites are individually decorated with local crafts; some have private balconies. The old harmonizes pleasantly with the new, as in a year-round outdoor Jacuzzi. Although it's just a short walk from both the Plaza and Canyon Road, the inn is removed from the downtown bustle. A complimentary breakfast buffet includes bagels, pastries, fruit, and cheese. ♦ 303 E Alameda St (at Paseo de Peralta). 984.2121, 800/289.2122 ♿

96 Adolph Bandelier House Adolph Bandelier, the archaeologist who conducted many of the original studies of pueblo sites in New Mexico, Arizona, and Mexico (and for whom **Bandelier National Monument** is named), lived in this house with his first wife, Josephine Huegy, from 1882 to 1892 and used it as his headquarters. Despite its designation, he never owned the house but rented it. In 1919 Santa Fe merchant Henry S. Kaune, whose wife, Elizabeth Carol Bandelier, was Bandelier's second cousin, purchased the house. A private residence, it is still owned by the Kaune family. ♦ 352 E De Vargas St (between Garcia St and Paseo de Peralta)

97 Nedra Matteucci's Fenn Galleries This gallery feels almost like a museum, partly because it occupies its own building on the Paseo, partly because of the dim adobe interior, and partly because most—though not all—of the artists represented are dead. Established in the early 1970s by Forrest Fenn and purchased in 1988 by Nedra Matteucci, the gallery is a great place to roam among the buffalo—and other paintings and bronzes reminiscent of the Old West—created by Charles Russell and Frederic Remington. All of the Taos founders are exhibited, as are more modern painters such as John Marin and Marsden Hartley of the old Alfred Stieglitz school. There is also a fine collection of paintings by the late artist/architect **Nikolai Fechin.** Out beyond the gallery building is a lovely pond and a sculpture garden of spirited works in bronze and stone by Glenna Goodacre and Doug Hyde, among others. The owner also has another gallery, **Nedra Matteucci Fine Art** (555 Canyon Rd, between Camino Escondido and Delgado St, 983.2731). ♦ Daily May–mid-Sept; M-Sa mid-Sept–Apr. 1075 Paseo de Peralta (at Acequia Madre). 982.4631

Custom Made: Indian Arts and Crafts

The first-time visitor to New Mexico is likely to be boggled by all the Indian merchandise that seems to be marketed everywhere. Most Indian arts were developed hundreds of years ago for practical, religious, or decorative uses. Kachina dolls (carved from dried cottonwood root) were created for religious instruction, pots and baskets were used to store grain and cornmeal, rugs were designed to warm and decorate hogans (a Navajo dwelling made of logs and mud), and jewelry was created for aesthetic purposes and to indicate status within the tribe. Today the same items are made primarily to sell to the public; it is one of the few ways Indians can live on the reservation and still earn a living.

Three variables determine the price of Indian art. The first is age; truly old pots and baskets created for practical use generally cost much more than new ones. The second, as in any art form, is the quality of the work. And the third is the nature of the materials. The following is a very brief guide to the more popular art forms:

Baskets
Nomadic Indians developed portable vessels made of straw or similar materials to transport goods. However, most Indian baskets for sale in Northern New Mexico come from Arizona or California—the Pueblo Indians live in stable villages and have no need for baskets. The Jicarilla Apache near the Colorado border make some baskets, mostly for the tourist trade.

Jewelry
Indian jewelry runs the gamut from bracelets and necklaces to rings, earrings, and *concho* belts (made of a series of silver ovals, known as *conchas,* strung on leather). Different tribes are associated with different specialties. The Zuni are best known for inlaying fine turquoise and other stones in silver; the

Hopi specialize in silver overlay techniques; the Santo Domingo Indians string finely carved shell beads—*heishi*—into necklaces and earrings; and for centuries the Navajo have been creating elaborate pieces with silver and turquoise.

Turquoise is the stone most frequently used in Indian jewelry because it is indigenous to the area. But the quality of the stone varies greatly, from natural turquoise to treated. It is often difficult to tell if turquoise is natural or treated; your best bet is to buy from a reputable dealer or bring a knowledgeable friend along when you shop. (See "Turquoise Treasure" on page 50). Other stones the Indians trade for, such as coral or jet, are not treated. Old Pawn jewelry—made for the Indians' own wear decades ago and then pawned for cash—costs more than the new pieces made for tourist trade. (Beware of dealers who sell new jewelry as "Old Pawn," for it's usually junk.)

Kachina Dolls

These dolls are a form of religious art created primarily by the Hopi and to a lesser extent by the Zuni. They are small, elaborate wooden carvings that represent the men who dance in costume as kachina spirits during Hopi celebrations, and were initially used to teach Hopi children about the spirits. A dried cottonwood root is carved, then sanded and painted. The best dolls are chiseled from a single root, using no joints or glue, except to fasten on the symbolic items the dolls are holding. The Hopi have more than 400 kachina spirits, each with its own costume. Artistry varies greatly, and prices range from several hundred to several thousand dollars.

In recent years other tribes, particularly the Navajo, have begun making kachina dolls that tend to be larger, more brightly colored, and decorated with leather skirts. These particular dolls have no religious significance to the Navajo and are made strictly to sell to tourists. Some of the best kachinas can be found in Santa Fe at the **Kachina House** and at **Packard's Indian Trading Co.**

Pottery

Many different tribes use similar techniques to create the pottery found throughout New Mexico. Clay is gathered by hand and carefully rolled into coils, and the coils are shaped into pots. The pots are then fired in outdoor kilns. Some modern Indians buy commercially made pots and paint them with tribal designs, and these, of course, are worth less than the handmade pots. **Acoma Pueblo** specializes in distinctive black and white pottery designs that are often complex and exquisite. **San Ildefonso** and **Santa Clara Pueblos** are especially renowned for their solid black pottery.

The most famous Indian potter was Maria Martinez of **San Ildefonso Pueblo,** who began making black pottery in 1919. She revived an old style of pottery found in the ruins on the nearby **Parajito Plateau.** Experiments to reproduce this style were encouraged by the **School of American Research** in Santa Fe; they were very successful, and the pottery became a good source of income for the pueblo. Pots made by Maria Martinez, who died in 1980, sell for thousands

of dollars. Her descendants, as well as many others at **San Ildefonso,** continue to make the distinctive black pottery. Other types of pottery often feature animal designs and may include clouds, rain, the sun, and flowers. The most common design is the rainbird, because birds were considered carriers of prayers to the gods, and survival depended heavily on rainfall. Since pottery originated for the purpose of holding food and water (see the Zuni water vase illustrated above), all pots were made with prayers to the gods for rain, sunshine, and good crops.

Rugs and Blankets

The Navajo are weaving specialists, in part because they have been shepherds for centuries and have access to plenty of wool. Their intricate and brilliantly colorful designs, such as "Two Gray Hills" (named after the site of a trading post), are famous. The finer the weaving, the better the rug or blanket and the higher the price. Many stores sell rugs with Navajo designs that are actually made by the Zapotec Indians in Mexico. These are of coarser quality and should cost much less. Two Gray Hills rugs in their best form have no dyed colors—only the natural colors of white, black, and gray. The "Chief's Blanket" has broad black and white stripes with three bands of contrasting color, usually blue or red, at each end. "Diamond Twill" or "Double Saddle" blankets feature a diamond pattern with variations, usually in red, white, black, and gray. Often there is a slight break in the border design of a blanket. This is created intentionally, so spirits don't get trapped inside the pattern. Navajo *yei* (divinities) are represented in the designs of the *Yei-bichai* blankets, also known as *Yei* blankets. They are typically made from brightly colored yarns and may be touted by dealers as Navajo ceremonial blankets. In fact, they are often made by Anglos or Anglicized Indians; most Navajos regard the blankets as a parody of their religion and find them offensive.

From the ancient civilizations of Mexico and Central and South America, the Pueblo Indians inherited the ancient method of preserving corn—adding lime to keep it fresh. Corn was the fiber of their diet, and chiles supplied the variety or personality.

Canyon Road

For those who like the earthy cachet of adobe architecture, Canyon Road may well be the most sensually pleasing street in America. Once an Indian trail leading to the distant **Pecos Pueblo**, the ruins of which are now a National Historical Site, the road begins at **Paseo de Peralta** and winds for more than a mile on a slight incline toward the **Sangre de Cristo Mountains**. In late afternoon, the clarity of light makes the mountains appear closer than they are. The narrow, curving street is lined on both sides with old adobes, many with their doors and window frames painted bright turquoise. Some were built in past centuries by local families, others around the turn of this century by such early members of the Santa Fe art colony as Fremont Ellis. For many years Canyon Road was the focal point of the local art colony. A trailblazing group of artists, "Los Cinco Pintores" (the five painters), all lived along the road or on the intersecting **Camino del Monte Sol**. As recently as the early 1970s, painters, potters, sculptors, and glassblowers could be seen working in their studios here, their doors open to the public.

Today much of that scene has changed. Some of the homes are still private residences, but nearly all of today's painters have been driven farther afield in search of cheaper rent. The old adobes are now filled with art galleries and jewelry shops.

Stroll leisurely along the street and enjoy the sensual experience. The eye is pleased by the brightly colored contemporary and primitive paintings at the **Cline Fine Art Gallery**, housed in one of the most exquisitely wrought of all the adobes, and the sense of touch delights in the bronze outdoor sculpture at the **Meyer Gallery**. The sixth and perhaps most important sense, the sense of humor, is served by the whimsical ceramic teapots in all manner of shapes and personas at **Off the Wall**. Canyon Road satisfies all the other senses as well. With only a single lane of one-way, slow-moving traffic, the relative

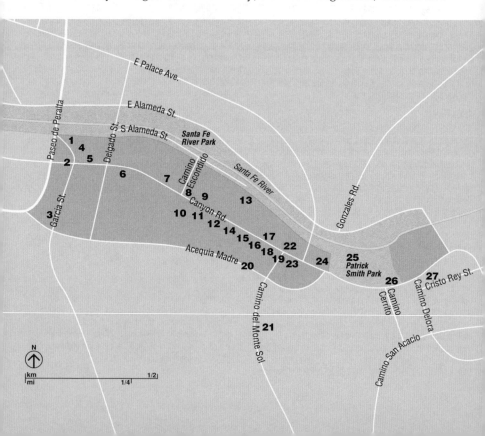

silence is an old-fashioned pleasure. And for fine taste sensations, have a light lunch at **Celebrations** and dinner at **Geronimo.**

Art and commerce end where **Palace Avenue** enters Canyon Road. But keep walking and you'll experience a bit of silent time travel into the Santa Fe of centuries past—the street narrows even more, the walls and homes are made from brown mud, the sidewalks disappear, and all sense of hucksterism fades.

1 Shops at 225 Just a block from Paseo de Peralta is this cul-de-sac of stucco buildings with 12 galleries. Park in the private parking lot on busy weekends. ♦ Daily. 225 Canyon Rd (between Garcia St and Paseo de Peralta)

Within the Shops at 225:

Munson Gallery This establishment traces its ancestry to a gallery on the East Coast that opened in 1860, making it one of the oldest in the country. It has been operating in Santa Fe since 1979, but one of the most notable painters who exhibits here is originally from New York. A realist, Richard Segalman tends to isolate women on beaches and in open fields or at the window of uncertain rooms, lending them the evocative sadness of a lonely life. After the glut of Western clichés in many local galleries, Segalman offers a welcome taste of genuinely emotional art that transcends the commercial horde. Melissa Zink's abstract collages, a blend of painting and sculpture, also leave the buck-chasing herd in the dust. Another artist worth viewing is Elmer Schooley, who paints large-scale close-ups of New Mexican landscapes in a style reminiscent of pointillism. Local painters Tom Berg and Douglas Atwill are also shown here. ♦ Daily. 983.1657

Meyer Gallery Sculptor Dave McGary displays his realistic Native American figurative bronzes at this gallery, complete with braves and warriors outfitted in full ceremonial regalia. Kent R. Wallis uses rich colors to paint impressionistic landscapes of the forests and valleys of Utah and northern California. William C. Hook's acrylic landscapes, done in broad, confident strokes, come alive with the vividness and vitality of oils. ♦ Daily. 983.1434

Leslie Flynt Gallery Hand-crafted and -painted fine furniture are offered here at reasonable prices. Wooden mirrors painted in pastels, bookcases, chests, tables, and cabinets are just some of the unique pieces on display. ♦ Daily. 982.5178

Gallery 10 An outstanding collection of jewelry, pots, and tapestries by Native American artists are exhibited at this gallery. Master potter Al Qöyawama's wares, with their distinctive corn-ear motif, are prominently displayed, as are the works of Jackie Stevens. A Winnebago artist, Stevens's pottery is characterized by mica-flecked beige clay, rather than the usual terra-cotta tones typical of the region. The jewelry presented is world-class. ♦ Daily. 983.9707

New Trends Gallery Featured at this gallery are animal carvings handcrafted by Mexican Indians. These ironwood pieces—porpoises, whales, and birds—are surprisingly inexpensive. Also offered are alabaster sculpture by Native American artists and collages made by Anglos. ♦ Daily. 988.1199

DREAMTIME GALLERY
AUSTRALIAN ABORIGINAL ART

2 Dreamtime Gallery This is the only gallery in the US that features Australian Aboriginal art exclusively. Clifford Possum's geometric paintings, slithering wood-carved reptiles by Maruko artists from the Central Desert in Australia, batik scarves hand-painted by the Kngwarreye family (also from the Central Desert), and canvases by Emily Kngwarreye, a New Territory artist in her eighties, are some of the highlights. Exhibits change monthly, and some pieces are priced under $25. Owner Heather Harbour will gladly show you her didgeridoo horn, which she says is 50,000 years old. Aborigines often visit the gallery to give lectures and workshops. ♦ M-Sa. 223 1/2 Canyon Rd (between Garcia St and Paseo de Peralta). 986.0344

2 Gary Mauro Gallery The molded female form is the primary subject matter of artist Gary Mauro, whose works are featured here. He's best known for his bas-reliefs, in which he draws forms on muslin, then sculpts the contours into them with a quiltlike textile, over which he applies strokes of color. Sometimes he makes molds from the bas-reliefs and casts them in bronze or aluminum. His drawings and paintings are also on display. ♦ Daily. 233 Canyon Rd (between Garcia St and Paseo de Peralta). 988.3048

3 Garcia Street Books The feeling in the Canyon Road area's only general-interest bookstore is that each title has been carefully handpicked. The travel and arts sections are especially good. The shop shares the building with **Downtown Subscriptions** (983.3085), a magazine store and cafe with a spacious patio where many Santa Fe authors hang out when they're not writing—and sometimes when they are. ♦ Daily. 376 Garcia St (at Acequia Madre). 986.0151

PROJECT TIBET

4 Project Tibet Carrying a fascinating collection of Tibetan jewelry, art, crafts, and clothing, this nonprofit shop is the only store in the Southwest that features products made by Tibetan refugees. Director Paljor Thondup fled Eastern Tibet as a child and later settled in Santa Fe, where he attended **The College of Santa Fe.** Profits are channeled back to Tibetan refugee camps. ♦ M-Sa. 403 Canyon Rd (at Garcia St). 982.3002

4 Leaping Lizard Several local artists, with tongues in their cheeks, show brightly colored yet sophisticated drawings and sculptures of anthropomorphic animals and mystical creatures of their own divining. Max Lehman's hilarious ceramics are "neo-Maya"—Maya Minnie and Queenie Quark are just two of the characters. Whimsical animal silkscreens are offered by children's book illustrator Tom Ross, the gallery owner, whose earth-loving dinosaur, It Zwibble, has starred in children's books and on **HBO.** ♦ Daily. 409 Canyon Rd (at Garcia St). 984.8434

5 William Vincent A rarity in Santa Fe, this gallery features impressionist art. Works by William Vincent, Alfred Morang, Tommy Macaione, Louis Tedesco, Mary Dolph Wood, and Gene Gonzales are featured. Mr. Vincent, Santa Fe's leading impressionist, has been painting on Canyon Road for almost 40 years. ♦ Daily. 415 Canyon Rd (between Delgado and Garcia Sts). 982.9500

CLINE ⑨ GALLERY

6 Cline Fine Art Gallery This rambling structure of classic adobe brown with turquoise trim was at one time a ranch house that belonged to the Sena family. Now owned by Geoff and Helen Cline, former residents of Tulsa, Oklahoma, the gallery features the work of fellow Tulsan and octogenarian Alexandre Hogue, known for his Dust Bowl paintings. The wonderful flowing landscapes of K. Douglas Wiggins are also shown here. The better-known Taos and Santa Fe founders are also on display as are contemporary bronze sculptures by Bill Barrett. ♦ Daily. 526 Canyon Rd (between Camino Escondido and Delgado St). 982.5328

7 El Zaguán Two towering chestnut trees, a lovely garden, and a sprawling hacienda make up one of Santa Fe's cherished locations. A prominent local merchant, James Johnson, purchased the property in 1849 when it was just a small mud house. Johnson added many rooms, converted the house to Territorial style, planted an orchard and a cornfield out back, and built corrals for the oxen and horses that hauled goods over the Santa Fe Trail to be sold in his general store on the Plaza. One of the new additions was the "chocolate room," where chocolate was ground and served in the afternoons. He also built a private chapel and a large library. The name comes from the Spanish word, *zaguán*, a covered passageway that runs the length of the house in the rear.

The Victorian garden west of the house was designed in the 1880s by Adolph Bandelier, the renowned anthropologist. Bandelier imported the peony bushes from China; the two chestnut trees were already here. The building was threatened with destruction in 1927 but was saved by Mrs. Charles H. Dietrich. A private school for girls was housed in the building in the 1930s. Today it is owned by the Historic Santa Fe Foundation (983.2567), an organization dedicated to preserving the historic architecture of Santa Fe; its offices are in apartment No. 3. The rest of the place is made up of rental apartments, but the garden is open to the public. On any given day you might find an artist painting there. To enter the garden use the courtyard entrance and bear left under the portal. ♦ 545 Canyon Rd (between Camino Escondido and Delgado St)

8 Ernesto Mayans Gallery Established in 1977 by writer Ernesto Mayans, this has consistently been one of the most noteworthy galleries in town for contemporary representational art. A special highlight is the stunning black-and-white photography of André Kertész. Local painters represented include David Barbero, Ralph Leon, Joel Greene, Cathy Folk-Williams, Keith Crown, and Arthur Haddock. ♦ Tu-Sa. 601 Canyon Rd (at Camino Escondido). 983.8068

9 Celebrations ★★$ A stroll up Canyon Road can be tiring and thirst-making, especially in the heat of a New Mexico summer. This is the best place to break for a light lunch; eat on one of two pleasant patios or indoors. The menu features imaginative seafood presentations, including crawfish étouffée and seafood fettuccine, as well as traditional New Mexican dishes. Breakfast, including cholesterol-free omelettes, is served all day. ♦ Continental/New Southwestern ♦ M-Tu, Su breakfast and lunch; W-Sa breakfast, lunch, and dinner. Reservations recommended. 613 Canyon Rd (between E Palace Ave and Camino Escondido). 989.8904

10 David Ross Studio/Gallery Step into this shop and enter a magical mystery zoo populated by sly and seductive wooden dalmatians, zebras, tigers, and rabbits. This sweet folk art is carved and painted by David Ross, a former scenery designer, who'll be glad to talk while working. Ross had a studio in Florence until he was driven out by the 1966 flood. Soon after arriving in Santa Fe in 1972, he started his brightly colored menagerie, whose most prominent denizens are hand-carved dalmatians (pictured above), painted with tempera, that adorn the sides of portable library stairs. Bring a picture, and Ross will carve your favorite animal to order. More practical items include chests and headboards in the shape of animals. ◆ Daily. 610 Canyon Rd (between Camino del Monte Sol and Camino Escondido). 988.4017

11 Off the Wall This is a great place to shop for gifts—the prices are reasonable, and owners Therese Bisceglia and Tom Martin don't take anything too seriously. Featured here is Santa Fe's largest collection of contemporary teapots and Judaica created by US artists. A wide variety of ceramics, metal, wood, and jewelry by such artists as Michael Lambert, Susan Garson, and Jackson Medford is on display. The owners also like to introduce eligible singles to each other, so you might walk out of here with a date. ◆ Daily. 616 Canyon Road (between Camino del Monte Sol and Camino Escondido). 983.8337

12 Running Ridge Gallery Abstract, nonfunctional pieces in sculptured glass and ceramics, as well as modern paintings, fabric art, and jewelry, are featured in this airy space run by Barbara G. Grabowski and Ruth Farnham. ◆ M-Sa. 640 Canyon Rd (between Camino del Monte Sol and Camino Escondido). 988.2515, 800/584.6830

12 Martha Keats Gallery Recently expanded, this gallery in a century-old adobe building features paintings by Santa Fe–based and internationally established artists who work in oil, watercolor, pastel, monotype, and mixed media, as well as their collages and sculptures. New works by Sarah Bienvenu, Paul Canfield, Jon Carver, Ani Fraser, Thomas Freund, Ron Fundingsland, Mallory Lake, Melinda Miles, Dan Newmann, Luis Orozco, Stephen Poling, Dorlies Schapitz, Irene Schio, and Barbara Wagner are represented. ◆ M-Sa. 644 Canyon Rd (between Camino Escondido and Camino del Monte Sol). 982.6686

13 The Compound ★★$$$$ One of the priciest restaurants—and certainly the most formal—in town is situated down a sloping driveway off Canyon Road. Whether this formality is justified by the continental food (pâté de foie gras, caviar, and rack of lamb are among the menu selections) is a matter of opinion, and opinion varies. However, the surroundings, mostly in white, are a visual delight designed by **Alexander Girard,** who converted a 19th-century hacienda into several dining areas. ◆ Continental ◆ Tu-Sa dinner. Reservations required. No infants or small children allowed. 653 Canyon Rd (between E Palace Ave and Camino Escondido). 982.4353

14 Helen Hardin Estate/Silver Sun The renowned Indian painter Pablita Velarde is from Santa Clara Pueblo and now lives in Albuquerque. Her granddaughter, Margarete Tindel, is a young artist who also lives there. Sadly missing is the middle generation: Pablita's daughter and Margarete's mother—Helen Hardin. As a child Helen would hear her mother get up in the middle of the night to paint under naked bulbs while the family slept. After becoming an artist, Helen did the same thing. Her work was less traditional than Velarde's; Hardin combined sacred Indian mythology with a more modern sensibility and a subtle sense of humor. Her fame rivaled her mother's when she died of cancer in 1984 at the age of 41. The true cause of her death, her mother has been quoted as saying, was that she made public the Indian spirit world that is supposed to remain private. For seven years after her death, her work remained in storage, until her heirs, including husband Cradoc Bagshaw, a photographer, decided her legacy of etchings and acrylics should be available to the public, and this gallery was opened in 1991. Cheryl Ingram, who had owned **Silver Sun** at this spot since 1976, became the estate representative and gave Hardin's work a place of honor and a room of its own in her store. Ingram also shows small Navajo sculptures and delicate miniature pottery from **Acoma Pueblo** and Native American handmade jewelry. There's a wide variety of turquoise and silver earrings ranging in price from affordable to high-end traditional. ◆ Daily. 656 Canyon Rd (between Camino del Monte Sol and Camino Escondido). 983.8743

14 Tresa Vorenberg Goldsmiths Unique gold and silver jewelry by local and national jewelry designers adorns the showcases of this store, including work by the owner. The contemporary designs range from inlay to diamonds. Also offered are abstract, landscape, and figurative paintings by local artists. ♦ M-Sa; occasionally Su. 656 Canyon Rd (between Camino del Monte Sol and Camino Escondido). 988.7215

15 Fletcher Gallery This gallery is committed to exploring the latest developments in contemporary realism. Nationally and internationally recognized realist artists featured here include Scott Frazer, Patrick Faulhaber, John Nava, P.S. Gordon, Stephen Fox, and David Hines. ♦ M-Sa. 668 Canyon Rd (between Camino del Monte Sol and Camino Escondido). 983.9441

Graphics House Gallery

16 Graphics House Gallery Two fine craftspeople share this studio space: Anne Sawyer, who has an etching press on one side of the building, and David E. Brighton, who keeps an art-engraving workshop on the other. Sawyer's miniature etchings are among the most affordable art in town. ♦ Daily. 702 Canyon Rd (between Camino del Monte Sol and Delgado St). 983.2654

16 Gypsy Alley More than a dozen shops and galleries await down this quaint, narrow alley. Paintings, folk art, jewelry, photography, and Mexican rugs are all available. Shop owners here are friendly and helpful. ♦ 708 Canyon Rd (between Camino del Monte Sol and Delgado St)

As the wandering hunchback of myth and legend, Kokopelli traveled the ancient Southwest. His fluteplaying served both to announce his friendly intentions as a trader and to woo the maidens he encountered with his music of love. He became recognized as a humorous symbol of fertility, with his pack full of seeds, trading old songs for new among the native peoples.

Within Gypsy Alley:

Gentle Spirit Gallery Owner/artist Estella Loretto bills her shop as one of New Mexico's only galleries owned and operated by Native Americans. Her clay and bronze sculptures and raku pieces show her training in Japan and Italy, but she says her real education came from her grandmother and mother who raised her in the **Jemez Pueblo.** Loretto is best known for her contemporary "monumental art pieces," such as *No Wa Mu Stio* (Offerings for Good Life), which stands eight feet high in front of the **Capitol.** Other Native American artists shown here include Ricardo Rojas, Jacque Stevens, and Maralyn Rikel. ♦ M-Sa. 6 Gypsy Alley. 989.4793

'OOT'Í

OOT'Í Gallery Stroll farther down the alley for a look at the cowboy and Pueblo photographs of Janis Schwartz. While based in New York, Schwartz roamed the world shooting in color. Then she moved to New Mexico and switched to black and white. It was an inspired choice; her pictures are simply luminous. The name of the gallery is the Navajo word for vision. ♦ Daily; by appointment at artist's gallery/home (455.2127). 7 Gypsy Alley. 984.1676

17 Moondance Gallery The focus at this gallery is on works with mythological, ecological, and ceremonial themes. Especially noteworthy is the exquisite jewelry crafted by Nomi Green in 14-karat gold, sterling silver, and bronze. On the lighter side are the whimsical ceramic animal totems, guardians, and allies created by Kathy Lostetter. ♦ Daily. 707 Canyon Rd (between E Palace Ave and Camino Escondido). 982.3421

17 Artisans This is one of the most complete art supply stores in the Southwest, stocking every major brand (plus some minor brands) of oil paints, watercolors, acrylics, and pastels, as well as brushes, canvas, paper, inks, pens, pads, erasers, and how-to books—supplies for everyone from the beginner to the accomplished master. ♦ M-Sa. 717 Canyon Rd (between E Palace Ave and Camino Escondido). 988.2179

Restaurants/Clubs: Red   **Hotels:** Blue
Shops/ ♥ Outdoors: Green   **Sights/Culture:** Black

18 Geronimo ★★★$$$ The setting for this restaurant is **Borrego House,** an adobe whose history can be traced to a smaller structure that stood here in 1753 on a farm that extended back about a hundred yards to the *Acequia Madre,* the "mother ditch" that supplied the farm's water. In the 19th century it was owned for 75 years by the Borrego family, who added the large front room and the front portal for entertaining. From then until 1939 the house was willed to various children and heirs room by room, a fairly common local practice in those days; at times even parts of a room were bequeathed. Between 1928 and 1939, all the rooms were purchased individually from the heirs by Mrs. Charles Dietrich, who then restored the house. But the inside, with its uneven floors and walls, retains the essence of true Santa Fe style. The building has changed hands and restaurant incarnations several times since.

Today owner Cliff Skogland and Chefs Kristin and Stephen Jarrett serve such first-rate food as a chipotle chile and marinated duck quesadilla and mesquite-grilled black angus rib-eye steak. Also delicious is the crispy red corn relleno—the filling is chicken smoked on the premises. ◆ Continental ◆ M dinner; Tu-Sa lunch and dinner; Su brunch and dinner. Reservations recommended. 724 Canyon Rd (between Camino del Monte Sol and Camino Escondido). 982.1500

19 Camino del Monte Sol Beginning in the 1920s, this street, which intersects Canyon Road just past the **Borrego House**, was the home of Los Cinco Pintores, five painters who banded together by that name and came to symbolize the vitality of the Santa Fe art colony. They were Fremont Ellis, Walter Ufer, Joseph Bakos, Willard Nash, and Will Shuster. The group bought a tract of land together and built their homes and studios here. Other painters, and writers such as Mary Austin, also built in the area. The street was previously called Telephone Road because it followed the main telephone line into town, but artist and resident William Penhallow Henderson and his wife, Alice Corbin, a poet, preferred something more literary and renamed it after a nearby mountain. For the most part the homes remain private residences. About a half-mile up the road is **St. John's College,** where the curriculum is designed around the "Great Books" program advocated by educator R.M. Hutchins, and connected to the older college of the same name in Annapolis, Maryland. ◆ From Old Santa Fe Trail to Canyon Rd

20 Acequia Madre In the days before piped-in water and deep wells, *acequias* (ditches) were the vessels of life; after rainfall and during the spring runoff, they carried the water that made farming, and survival itself, possible in this region. Ditch irrigation in the Indian regions began as much as a thousand years ago. Water rights belonged to all those who own property along the ditch, according to the size of their property. The landowners all had to help maintain the *acequias,* clearing the winter's debris in spring so water could flow through. Each ditch had a *mayordomo* (steward) who supervised the cleanings. The practice still exists today, though the water here is used more for maintaining gardens than for growing food. Running alongside the ditch is a quiet residential street bearing the same name. Walk down Acequia Madre to Garcia Street, then turn right; one block will bring you back near the base of Canyon Road. On Acequia is **Acequia Madre Elementary School,** whose walls feature a mural painted by a prominent local artist, Frederico Vigil. ◆ From the Santa Fe River at the upper end of Upper Canyon Rd, along Upper Canyon Rd to Acequia Madre St, to Don Gaspar Avenue just south of downtown

21 Mary Austin House This refurbished old adobe has long been a focal point of the local art scene. Austin, an early Santa Fe writer and feminist, built the house in the 1920s with the help of architect **John Gaw Meem** and artist William Penhallow Henderson. Painter John Sloan created the decorative windows in the rear of the building, and photographer Ansel Adams lived here when he and Austin were working on books together. Willa Cather wrote much of her novel *Death Comes for the Archbishop* in the house library. And photographer Laura Gilpin lived just to the north. ◆ 439 Camino del Monte Sol (between Camino Santander and Acequia Madre)

Within the Mary Austin House:

Gerald Peters Gallery A former student at St. John's College, Gerald Peters created one of Santa Fe's most successful art galleries, specializing in classic 19th- and 20th-century American and European art. Featured here are works by prominent painters of the American West (Miller, Russell, Bierstadt); Taos artists Sharp, Ufer, and Blumenschein; New Mexico modernists Dasburg, Bisttram, and Los Cinco Pintores; and particularly O'Keeffe. ◆ Daily May-Sept; M-Sa Oct-Apr. 988.8961

22 Imperial Wok ★★★$$ This dining establishment—perhaps the best of Santa Fe's half-dozen Chinese restaurants—is owned by Benny and Marta Hung. The specials are priced a bit high for Chinese food, but they are extremely good, especially the seafood dishes. Don't miss the Club Seafood—king crabmeat, shrimp, and scallops sautéed with Chinese vegetables in a white wine sauce. Lunch is less expensive, but the chef's specials are not available. In the evening the covered courtyard has a dark, romantic air that's found in few Santa Fe restaurants. There's also a parking lot. ◆ Chinese ◆ M-Sa lunch and dinner; Su dinner. Reservations recommended. 731 Canyon Rd (at Camino del Monte Sol). 988.7100

Turquoise Treasure

A phosphate of aluminum that contains small quantities of copper and iron, turquoise has been prized throughout the centuries as a medical wonder, ornament, and religious symbol. Aristotle wrote in 300 BC that it "prevents death by accident and is beneficial for scorpion and reptile stings." A European alchemist in 1618 lauded the stone as having "the virtue of soothing the mind and the heart, of guarding against all external dangers and accidents. It brings happiness and prosperity to its wearer."

The tombs of Egyptian pharaohs have yielded gold jewelry inlaid with turquoise from the Sinai Peninsula. Central Asian and Middle Eastern cultures valued turquoise mined from the Nishapur deposits near the Caspian Sea. European royalty once adorned themselves lavishly with the exotic stone, which came to them from Turkey. Mexican Aztecs used turquoise in their religious ceremonies, creating intricate mosaics now on display in museums throughout the world.

During the 16th century, New Mexico's Tano Indians excavated large amounts of turquoise that were then used in prayer ceremonies before hunting and fighting and for trading. When the first successful Spanish colony was established in New Mexico under Juan de Oñate at the end of that century, colonists turned their attention to mining the cherished stone, forcing the Indians to be their laborers.

Up until the 1960s, New Mexico mined a greater quantity of turquoise than any other state; its total retail value exceeded $5 million at that time. The most important deposits were from the Cerrillos mining district of Santa Fe County, which yielded the highest-grade stones. But by the 1960s, most of New Mexico's mines had been exhausted. Today huge amounts of the stone are brought in from other states—mostly Nevada—and countries to meet the demands of Native craftspeople for their jewelry.

One of the largest private collections in the world was amassed 1930-60 by J.C. Zachary and his son, New Mexican miners and traders. Together they created the **Turquoise Museum** in **Albuquerque** (see page 104) to educate the public on turquoise; featured are various stones from 60 mines in four continents and six countries. There are many degrees of turquoise— natural is the most valued, and "treated" is a low-grade stone that has been impregnated with resin to stabilize it so it doesn't crumble; in some cases the resin is also dyed to give the stone a brighter color. Be aware when purchasing turquoise that most stones for sale on the commercial market are only 10 percent pure. Consider asking the seller the following questions: Is it natural? Is it authentic Indian handmade? Can you give me a letter of authenticity? Rest assured, once you've seen the real thing, you won't settle for anything less.

23 El Farol ★★★$$$ One of the city's longest-running restaurants, housed in an atmospheric, centuries-old adobe with many small rooms, this dining spot features tapas, those wonderful small dishes that originated in Spain. The problem here is choosing among the wide array of dishes, such as baby squid fried in beer butter; scallop seviche; chorizo (sausage) with green peppercorn and mustard sauce; sautéed wild mushrooms with spaghetti squash; or hickory-smoked chicken breast with cucumber. The hosts suggest three or four tapas per person, but two might fill you up unless you're really hungry; you can always order another later. The extremely popular bar, which is decorated with murals painted by Alfred Morang, features live blues, jazz, and folk entertainment. ♦ Tapas ♦ Daily dinner. Reservations recommended. 808 Canyon Rd (between E Palace Ave and Camino del Monte Sol). 983.9912

24 Platinum Gallery Billing itself as the first gallery in the world to specialize in hand-printed photographs made with platinum materials, this beautiful place offers museum-quality platinum prints by Stieglitz, Weston, Curtis, Evans, Kasebier, Kuhn, and Bravo. The gallery also represents 30 photographers, including Thomas Harding, who uses a lensless "pinhole" camera; and Tony Hauser, whose camera requires a sheet of 12" by 20" film. Platinum prints are ten times more difficult and costly to make than traditional silver prints, but the result is an image with astonishing tonal ranges and a lifetime of thousands of years. Just walking through this gallery is a fascinating education. ♦ Tu-Sa; or by appointment. 943 Canyon Rd (between Acequia Madre and E Palace Ave). 982.8920

25 Patrick Smith Park A few steps past 943 Canyon Road is a small entryway into this park, more commonly known as "Canyon Road Park." The lovely 5.4-acre patch of greenery has a softball field, soccer field, and basketball hoops but is also used for tossing a football or Frisbee, picnicking, or reading a book in the shade of a tall tree. The park's far side, bordering the Alameda, offers more parking space.

Beyond this point on Canyon Road are just a few shops and old adobe buildings—many have not been restored in a long time—that are private residences and a few artists' studios. The sidewalks disappear here, and the slope toward the mountains becomes steeper. But this narrow, curving stretch of road retains much more the European feel that once permeated all of Santa Fe than does the lower part. Since most visitors don't make it this far, a walk here offers a feeling of peace and serenity. Watch out for the cars that come from both directions. ♦ Between Canyon road and the Santa Fe River (near Camino Cerrito)

26 Frederico Vigil Studio Probably the best-known Hispanic artist in Santa Fe, Frederico Vigil is a master of painting frescoes. His are colorful mélanges of Hispanic and regional imagery that often summarize hundreds of years of history in a single work. They can be found on the inside and outside walls of schools and churches throughout the area. Vigil collects and grinds his own pigments, slakes his own lime months in advance, and draws his designs in the studio before transferring them to wet plaster, where there is little margin for error. When he is not out working on a wall, Vigil draws and paints in this studio, which

is open to visitors if he is around. ♦ Call ahead as hours vary. 1107 Canyon Rd (at Camino Cerrito). 983.9511

27 Cristo Rey Church In 1540 Spanish explorer Francisco Vásquez de Coronado and his expedition blazed the first European trail through the Southwest. Four hundred years later, to commemorate that event, Santa Feans built one of the largest adobe structures in existence (illustrated below). **John Gaw Meem** designed this beautiful church in the Spanish-mission Classical style. Nearly 200,000 adobe bricks made from the soil at the site were used in the construction. Local residents performed the work under the guidance of professional builders. The church was specifically designed to contain a superb stone reredos (altar screen) that had been carved in Mexico in 1760. The reredos had been installed in a military chapel on the Plaza called **La Castrense.** Later it was placed in a parish church. Archbishop Lamy, who with his French pretensions did not like local art, had the reredos concealed behind a wall of **St. Francis Cathedral** when the cathedral was being built on the site of the parish church in 1869. Today the reredos is displayed prominently here. ♦ 1120 Canyon Rd (between E Alameda St and Camino Delora). 983.8528

Cristo Rey Church

JOHN DEL GAIZO

Guadalupe Street

Many Americans first heard of Santa Fe through the big-band tune, "On The Atchison, Topeka, and Santa Fe," the Oscar-winning theme song for the 1946 Judy Garland film *The Harvey Girls*. The irony is that the railroad that carried the same name never stopped in Santa Fe. The main rail line in 1879 reached the village of Lamy, 20 miles to the south, beyond the rugged Sangre de Cristo Mountains, and only a narrow spur line used mostly for freight cars connected the railroad with the capital city. The spur line ended on Guadalupe Street, where the old, vacant station is still visible. This was a logical spot for the line's terminus because a few hundred yards away was the end of **El Camino Real**, a 1,500-mile overland trade route from Mexico City, and debarking passengers had only a short walk to the hotels near the Plaza.

In the late 1800s, warehouses were built in this area to serve the railroad, and Guadalupe Street became a commercial hub. After the trucking business got into gear, however, the rail-shipping industry slowed down, and some of the warehouses were abandoned while others became the homes of automobile dealerships, auto repair shops, and other utilitarian businesses patronized by local residents. When tourism became a big business in Santa Fe in the late 1970s, Guadalupe Street was refurbished. The auto dealers moved to the far south end of town, and the abandoned spaces, just a few blocks from the Plaza, were renovated into shops and restaurants that today line the busy thoroughfare as well as the narrow side streets. The district has joined the Plaza and Canyon Road as one of the city's major areas in which to browse and shop.

A few good art galleries dot the district, notably **Laura Carpenter Fine Art** for world-class sculpture and installation art. Most of the shops in the neighborhood stock practical goods, selling fine cookware, luggage, and stationery—a welcome change from the glut of Indian jewelry stores near the Plaza. You can indulge in excellent hearty American dishes at **Double A**, choice Italian fare at **Pranzo Italian Grill**, sushi and other Japanese dishes at **Sakura** and **Shohko Cafe**, and fresh baked pastries and cakes at **Pásale Bakery.** You can even find New York-style bagels, bialys, and Reuben sandwiches at **Bagelmania**, and the homespun **Aztec Street Cafe** is a pleasant hideaway for a coffee break.

The street takes its name from the **Santuario de Guadalupe**, an 18th-century adobe church dedicated to the Virgin of Guadalupe, the most venerated religious figure in Mexico. The **Santa Fe River** divides the byway into South and North. For 10 months of the year, the grassy banks of this "river" enclose nothing but a dry ditch. Only in April and May, when the snows on the mountains are melting, does a small river flow. But the **Santa Fe River Park** along the banks, sprinkled with benches and picnic tables, is still a convenient place for resting or a picnic lunch.

1 Santuario de Guadalupe One of the city's most visually dramatic landmarks, this adobe church was built between 1776 and 1795 by Franciscans. The site was chosen to mark the end of El Camino Real. In the beginning, the church was a simple adobe structure with a flat roof and a tower on one side, typical elements of New Mexican churches at that time. Mass was celebrated only occasionally, by itinerant priests, until Archbishop Lamy converted the run-down building into a regular parish church in 1880. The French archbishop, ever eager to improve on local taste, had it renovated into a Romanesque, New England-style church with a pitched roof, steeple, and white picket fence. In 1961 a much larger, more modern church, **Our Lady of Guadalupe Parish,** was built behind the old chapel, which soon fell into disrepair. There was talk of tearing down the old building—whose walls are three to five feet thick—and replacing it with a parking lot. But a nonprofit

group was formed to rescue it. The arch-diocese deeded the chapel to the Guadalupe Historic Foundation, which in 1976 undertook another renovation, removed most of the external ornamentation, and restored the chapel closer to the original style. Weakness in the structure of the bell tower led to further renovation in 1991. The former church is now used for occasional concerts by the **Desert Chorale** and art exhibitions.

The chapel is dedicated to Our Lady of Guadalupe, the most revered religious figure in Mexico. Featured prominently is an oil-on-canvas reredos (altar screen) of the Virgin of Guadalupe painted in 1783 in Mexico by José de Alzibar, a prominent artist of the time. The huge canvas was brought north by mule in several sections and assembled in the church.

Alzibar's signature and the lines where the canvas was joined are clearly visible. ◆ 100 S Guadalupe St (between Agua Fria St and the Santa Fe River). 988.2027

2 Agua Fria Street This narrow street (its name is Spanish for cold water) follows the path that was the end of El Camino Real 200 years ago. Today it is the principal artery through the unfashionable west side of town. A drive along this street to its southern terminus at Airport Road (about 10 minutes away) offers a clear picture of how most native Santa Feans live, far from the upscale glitz introduced to the downtown area to serve the newly arrived millionaire set. With the renovation of Guadalupe Street, however, real estate prices have climbed at the street's northern end. ◆ From Guadalupe St to Airport Rd

3 Cookworks When renowned chef and author Julia Child comes to town, she has book signings at this outstanding kitchenware store, which occupies three storefronts along Guadalupe Street. Supplying both Santa Fe's fine restaurants and the large number of Santa Feans who enjoy cooking gourmet dishes as much as eating them, this store offers an impressive selection of pots, pans, woks, knives, espresso makers, and all manner of unusual cooking utensils—great for browsing even if you're not into baking. ♦ Daily. 316, 318, 322 S Guadalupe St (between Montezuma Ave and Agua Fria St). 988.7676

4 Aztec Street Cafe ★★$ This small coffeehouse furnished with bare wooden tables is filled with writers, painters, and other creative types who pass the time reading newspapers, playing checkers, or philosophizing over good coffee and serviceable desserts. Meals tend to be simple; sandwiches and green-chile burgers are among the typical choices. ♦ Cafe ♦ Daily breakfast, lunch, and dinner. 317 Aztec St (between Sandoval and S Guadalupe Sts). 983.9464

5 Double A ★★★★$$$$ One of Santa Fe's most innovative and exciting new restaurants (and said to have cost $2 million to build), this place offers superb decor and out-standing food. Owner Andrew Altchek mills about, chatting with well-dressed guests and movie stars like Robert Redford, who come to see and be seen. The high-ceilinged room, an auto-parts store back in 1941, gleams with imaginatively used wood, leather, metal, and fieldstone. Some of the visual delights include a stunning, gargantuan portrait of a white horse by Joe Andoe; glass cases displaying humorous Western ceramics, fishing lures, and novels by Zane Grey; pots of emerald wheatgrass adorning tables; and an elegant bar where Santa Fe glitterati sip martinis from Art Deco glasses. But it's Chef Marion Gillcrist's fare that draws raves: penne with buffalo sausage, melt-in-your-mouth barbecued short ribs, tender spicy fried calamari, woody "cowboy coffee-rubbed" quail, and irresistible horseradish mashed potatoes. Even though portions are huge, don't even consider passing up the lemon-ginger meringue pie or white chocolate crème brûlée, artistically presented by pastry chef Kathy Redford. At press time, the **A Bar** jazz club was set to open next to the restaurant. ♦ American ♦ Tu-F lunch and dinner; M, Sa-Su dinner. Bar until 2AM. 331 Sandoval St (between Montezuma Ave and Aztec St). 982.8999 &

6 Access Maps & Gear No relation to the ACCESS® Press guidebooks, this shop occupies a corner of **FrameCrafters** (988.2920), a frame shop that was opened by Mardes York and Ginny York 20 years ago. Most locals probably don't know it exists, but tourists will delight in the cornucopia of antique maps and reproductions of the same, globes in all sizes, topolopes (envelopes made from topographical maps), topographical jigsaw puzzles, and relief maps. Prints of early New Mexico are also sold. A mail-order catalog is available. ♦ Tu-Sa. 321 S Guadalupe St (between Montezuma Ave and Aztec St). 982.3330

6 Santa Fe Pottery Fourteen local potters show their work in Frank Willett's small, charming shop, which has been here since 1972, before Guadalupe Street was rediscovered. Dinnerware, cookware, stoneware lamps, and sconces line the white shelves. Potters used to work in the back room with their wheels and kilns, but the space is now used only for display. ♦ M-Sa. 323 S Guadalupe St (between Montezuma Ave and Aztec St). 988.7687

7 Zia Diner ★★$$ Meat loaf like mother never made is the unlikely standout on the menu here. It's chock-full of piñon nuts—tasty but not greasy—and you can get it with mashed potatoes and a vegetable or as a sandwich on French bread. Other old-fashioned diner items include an open-faced, hot fresh turkey sandwich. The homemade pies—especially the strawberry rhubarb—are wonderful. Daily specials at lunch and dinner are a bit more fashionable—quiches, angel-hair pasta with sun-dried tomatoes, that sort of thing. A large, sprawling, popular place enlivened by pastel walls and ceilings, this restaurant has booths and tables on two levels, a patio for warm days, as well as a soda fountain with stools. This is a favorite haunt of actor Gene Hackman. Wine and beer are available. ♦ American ♦ Daily lunch and dinner. Reservations recommended. 326 S Guadalupe St (between Montezuma Ave and Agua Fria St). 988.7008

7 Pásale Bakery ★★$ Formerly **Zia Bakery,** this eatery is a small mecca for Santa Fe's cafe culture. Come here for coffee and pastries and some down-home fun on "Cowboy Poetry Nights" (call ahead for schedule). ♦ Coffeehouse ♦ Daily. 328 S Guadalupe St (between Montezuma Ave and Agua Fria St). 988.5155

8 Sanbusco Market Center The word Sanbusco is an acronym for Santa Fe Builders Supply Company, which operated here in the late 19th and early 20th centuries out of a large warehouse and 2.5 acres of sheds and shipping docks. Shelves were stocked with lumber, nails, paint, and other supplies. By 1972 the compound was virtually abandoned and, in recent years, has been renovated into a sprawling complex of shops by builder Joe

Schepps, who retained the old name. ◆ Daily. 500 Montezuma Ave (between S Guadalupe and Dudrow Sts). 983.9136

Within the Sanbusco Market Center complex:

Jamison Galleries Opened in 1964 by Margaret Jamison, this Western gallery, now owned by Zeb and Betty Conley, is probably the longest-running gallery in town. Works by the Taos and Santa Fe old masters are usually on display, as well as early works, offered for resale, by such contemporary Indian painters as Fritz Scholder, Earl Biss, and Kevin Red Star. ◆ M-Sa. 560 Montezuma (between S Guadalupe and Dudrow Sts), Suite 103. 982.3666

Pranzo Italian Grill ★★★$$$ This lovely restaurant has soft peach walls, formal white-clothed tables, a gently curving bar, plus a roof patio that's open in warm weather. The food is usually excellent—some locals put it right up there with Santa Fe's best; others have found it a bit uneven. An assortment of pizza and pasta, ranging from spaghettini with baby shrimp, olive oil, garlic, sun-dried tomatoes, peas, and provolone to linguine with sausage and roasted bell peppers in a basil-tomato sauce, are included on the menu. Most dishes are priced a bit lower than the competition. Chicken, veal, and seafood are at the higher end of the range. There is a good selection of recent-vintage Italian, Californian, and New Mexican wines. ◆ Italian ◆ Daily lunch and dinner. Reservations recommended. 540 Montezuma Ave (between S Guadalupe and Dudrow Sts). 984.2645

The Winery This shop stocks somewhere between 800 and 1,000 labels from all over the world. ◆ M-Sa. 500 Montezuma Ave (between S Guadalupe and Dudrow Sts). 982.9463

Farmers' Market Small farmers from throughout the area bring fresh produce into town to sell at an outdoor market set up on Saturday in the **Sanbusco** parking lot. Writer Stan Crawford is likely to be here selling the garlic he grows near his home in nearby Dixon, about which he's written a book, *A Garlic Testament*. Strands of garlic or chile *ristras* (decorative dried strands of red chile strung together) are easy to transport home and make good gifts. In addition to fresh melons, fruit, and corn in season, canned and baked goods, sauces, and spices are sold. ◆ Tu, Sa-Su morning June–mid-Nov. Sanbusco parking lot

9 University Plaza In the 1880s Protestant evangelists who wanted to convert the Catholic locals, whom they looked on as heathens, constructed this unusual corner building as a school. With its mansard roof and nonadobe construction, this is an architectural oddity for Santa Fe. It was named the **University of New Mexico**—no kin to the current university in Albuquerque—and was supposed to be a center of "moral education." But the locals didn't much care for the idea, and the missionaries didn't care much for life in Santa Fe. They packed up and moved on, to no one's disappointment. The building later became the **Franciscan Hotel,** and its mansard roof was removed when a third story was added; in the 1970s the roof was restored in an attempt to recover some of the structure's old charm. Today it's an office building. ◆ 330 Garfield St (at S Guadalupe St)

10 Old Railroad Depot The **Atchison, Topeka, and Santa Fe Railroad** has been hailed in story and song, but the name was a misnomer. The main track of the railroad, which in 1880 linked the Midwest to the Pacific coast and made the Santa Fe Trail obsolete, never did touch Santa Fe, thanks to the greed of some local residents. The railroad company planned to lay tracks through a narrow pass between Glorieta and Santa Fe, but several Santa Feans bought part of it, then demanded a large price from the builders. Instead of yielding to this extortion, the railroad rerouted the tracks to Albuquerque, which became a boomtown, while Santa Fe remained off the beaten path.

After much lobbying by Archbishop Lamy, a 20-mile spur line was built along another route linking Santa Fe to the main track. Today the village of Lamy sits at the junction. In recent decades only occasional trains of a few cars each carried freight to Lamy to be transferred to the main line, and the railroad ultimately discontinued service and spoke of tearing up the tracks. A group of investors, including actor Michael Gross of television's "Family Ties," formed the **Santa Fe Southern Railway,** which carries passengers to and from Lamy either to meet **Amtrak**'s east-west trains or to go on a sight-seeing ride. These trains depart from the **Santa Fe Depot** on Tuesday, Thursday, and Saturday at 10:30AM. (See **Santa Fe Southern Railway** on page 63.)The acreage around the depot is the last undeveloped area near downtown, and its potential has been the subject of years of controversy. At press time, the city administration had submitted a plan to expand the area and in an unusual gesture was holding meetings with interested citizens to obtain their views on how the property should be developed. The construction of *Outside* magazine's headquarters just across the old tracks from historic warehouse buildings housing book publishers Bear & Co. and John Muir Publications suggests that the railroad yards may emerge as Santa Fe's "publishers' row." ◆ Off S Guadalupe St (at W Manhattan Ave)

11 Tomasita's ★$ Situated in a former rail yard warehouse, this restaurant is owned by Georgia Maryol, one of the three Maryol siblings who run local New Mexican restaurants (brother Jim heads up **Tia Sophia's,** and sister Toni runs **Diego's Cafe**). This is the most popular of the trio despite being the least pleasant. At lunch and dinner people crowd in and are willing to wait from 45 minutes to an hour to eat in a large hall that is jam-packed and noisy and to endure rude service; after all that waiting, they'll shoo you out for quick turnover. The food is no better than most New Mexican restaurants and not as good as some, but many say the margaritas are among the best in town. ◆ New Mexican ◆ M-Sa lunch and dinner. 500 S Guadalupe St (at W Manhattan Ave, in the railroad yards). 983.5721

12 High Desert Angler Probably the least publicized art form in Santa Fe is the art of tying fishing flies. If you want to learn, this is the place. Jan Crawford not only rents and sells rods and reels, flies, and all manner of fishing gear, she gives classes in every aspect of fly-fishing. She also offers classes just for women. With a ready smile, she'll teach you everything from casting to landing and releasing fish, and—according to her brochure—how to think like a trout. She'll even lead you to water in New Mexico. ◆ Daily. 435 S Guadalupe St (entrance on Read St). 98.TROUT (honest)

13 Laura Carpenter Fine Art A beautiful old house with stained-glass windows has been transformed into a stunning space and one of the few galleries in this section of town that specializes in contemporary art. Featured also is a program of lectures related to the exhibits and shows in an adjacent gallery. Among the nationally known artists shown are James Lee Bayers, Louise Bourgeois, Eric Fischl, Ellsworth Kelly, Agnes Martin, Ed Ruscha, Kiki Smith, and Richard Tuttle. ◆ Tu-Sa. 309 Read St (between Sandoval and S Guadalupe Sts). 986.9090

14 Hotel Santa Fe $$$ A novel commercial enterprise, this hotel is a partnership between a group of private investors led by builder Joe Schepps, and **Picuris Pueblo,** the smallest Indian tribe in New Mexico, which is situated near Taos. By allowing the pueblo to own 51 percent of the hotel, the investors were able to get 90 percent of their loans guaranteed by the federal government under a program aimed at encouraging Native American enterprise. The hotel is big, yet nicely designed and set back from the street. The 131 spacious, bright rooms are tastefully furnished and decorated in Southwestern style. The deli serves breakfast or sandwiches later in the day. Other amenities include an outdoor pool and hot tub. A number of the staff members are from the pueblo. Another plus is that the rates here are somewhat lower than lodgings closer to the Plaza. Complimentary shuttle service to downtown is provided. ◆ 1501 Paseo de Peralta (at Cerrillos Rd). 982.1200, 800/825.9876; fax 984.2211 ♿

15 Santa Fe Travelodge $$ This standard chain motel is remarkable only because its 48 guest rooms are the lowest-priced accommodations within walking distance of Santa Fe's downtown Plaza (even so, the rates are no bargain). There are the usual roadside amenities—air-conditioning, cable TV, and in-room phones, as well as a small outdoor heated pool (a rarity in water-scarce Northern New Mexico). Other affordable motels can be found farther east along Cerrillos Road, the commercial strip that is Santa Fe's busiest street. ◆ 646 Cerrillos Rd (between Paseo de Peralta and S Guadalupe St). 982.3551, 800/578.7878

16 Old Santa Fe Music Hall ★★★$$$ Although the dinner theater concept is a bit passé, entrepreneur Gordon Heiss has come up with a winning combination of tasty food and delightful entertainment. The servers, dressed in blue jeans and fringed denim vests, also double as the cast, and they do a great job at both. A variety of entrées is offered—cowboy chicken, Santa Fe enchiladas, Pueblo buffalo stew, and grilled Rocky Mountain trout. None is outstanding, but the show saves the evening. Hosted by Belle Carson, who offers some keen competition to Dolly Parton, the show treats the audience to 14 rollicking musical numbers consisting of cowboy torch songs, scat singing, Marilyn Monroe and Carmen Miranda lookalikes, yeehahs, cancans, and Joplin rags. Stephan Ray Swimmer is a standout in his Native American-gone-**MTV** Day-Glo hoop number, and Robert Murphy is hilarious as a lonesome cowboy who mistakenly wanders into a New York jazz bar. ♦ American ♦ Shows: M, W-Su 7PM. 100 N Guadalupe (between W Alameda and W Water Sts). 983.3311 ঙ

16 Poulet Patate Rotisserie Provençal ★★$$ Translated from the French as "chicken potato rotisserie provençal," this eatery serves exactly what its name promises—spit-roasted herbed chicken and copious portions of all varieties of potatoes. The decor is simple, yet evocative of Provence as are the cooking odors from its open kitchen. It's the only real French restaurant in Santa Fe. ♦ Chicken/French ♦ Daily lunch and dinner. 106 N Guadalupe St (between W Alameda and W Water Sts). 820.2929

17 Vanessie ★★$$$ Don't step inside these doors unless your appetite is huge. Only the basics are served—beef, chicken, rack of lamb, and fresh fish—but the portions are gigantic, and everything is à la carte. If you order a baked potato, it's likely to weigh 22 ounces. A side salad is enormous and so is dessert. The signature appetizer is a fried onion loaf that is big enough to feed a horde of hungry people. A piano bar that gets rolling around 9PM and keeps going until 1AM or 2AM is a big draw. ♦ Continental ♦ Daily dinner. Reservations recommended. 434 W San Francisco St (between N Guadalupe St and Park Ave). 982.9966

18 Sakura ★★★$$ The best sushi in town is served here at Santa Fe's second-oldest Japanese restaurant. The interior is divided into tables on one side and private tatami rooms on the other, with an outdoor patio facing a grassy courtyard in warm weather. Singles can eat on stools at a small bar and watch their sushi being prepared. The salmon teriyaki, raw tuna dishes, and California rolls are divine. This is an especially good bet at lunchtime. ♦ Japanese ♦ Tu-F lunch and dinner; Sa-Su dinner. Reservations recommended for dinner. 321 W San Francisco St (at N Guadalupe St). 983.5353

18 Fabio's Grill ★★★$$ This incarnation of Fabio Macchioni's original Tuscan restaurant downtown now calls itself a grill, but its heart is still in Northern Italy. The spinach and ricotta gnocchi are the best in Santa Fe, and the Maine lobster over pasta is more than enough to write home about. As expected, grilled meat plays a central role on the menu, but there's something for everyone here.

Fabio is always on the premises to ensure that all runs smoothly in this dining spot filled with skylights and large windows. A roaring fireplace commands center stage in the winter. ♦ Italian ♦ Daily dinner. 329 W San Francisco St (at N Guadalupe St). 984.3080

19 Shohko Cafe ★★★$$ Back in the mid-1970s, when anything but an American or New Mexican menu was risky business, Shohko Fukuda and her husband, Hiro, opened Santa Fe's first Japanese restaurant at another location. But good food conquered provincialism as the city grew more cosmopolitan. Within a few years Shohko moved to this larger site, added a sushi bar, and is now the proud ancestor of the city's Asian restaurants. The sushi is a bit tame (the rice is not pickled), but sure pleasers are the shrimp or vegetable tempura, chicken teriyaki, and the yakitori dinner. ♦ Japanese ♦ M-F lunch and dinner; Sa dinner. Reservations recommended on Friday and Saturday. 321 Johnson St (at N Guadalupe St). 983.7288

20 Georgia O'Keeffe Museum Scheduled to open in July 1997, this new museum will be dedicated to preserving and presenting the life works of one of America's most remarkable artists. The permanent collection of O'Keeffe's works here will be unequaled by any other museum in the world. ♦ Contact the tourist office for opening date and schedule. 217 Johnson St (between Grant Ave and Chapelle St). No phone at press time

New Mexico has the dubious distinction of having the highest per capita number of lightning deaths in the country. When thunderstorms develop, seek lower ground.

Although many people think of Northern New Mexico as desert country, there's water skiing, sailing, and swimming in many of the area's lakes.

New Mexico's state song, "O Fair New Mexico," was written by Elizabeth Garrett, the daughter of famed Sheriff Pat Garrett. In 1917, Governor Washington E. Lindsey signed legislation making the song official. In 1928, America's most famous march composer and conductor, John Philip Sousa, presented Governor A.T. Hannett and the people of New Mexico with an arrangement of the state song embracing a musical story about the Indians, the Calvary, the Spanish, and the Mexicans.

Restaurants/Clubs: Red   **Hotels:** Blue
Shops/ ♈ Outdoors: Green   **Sights/Culture:** Black

Adobe Abodes

Along with the desert landscapes and the mystical light of this region of the country, the adobe architecture of **Santa Fe, Taos,** the older sections of **Albuquerque,** and all of the surrounding smaller villages gives Northern New Mexico its truly distinctive look.

Most homes and commercial buildings are either constructed of adobe or painted in shades of brown to look like adobe. They typically stand a story high, the roofs are flat, and all of the structure's corners are rounded, with small windows spaced carefully around the building. The doors and windowsills are frequently painted turquoise, bright blue, or white. Adobe walls surround many homes, and larger, older residences have been built around courtyards in the traditional Spanish manner. No place else in the US looks like this—and most visitors find it a fascinating change.

In Santa Fe and Taos this adobe look is preserved by law—no building in Santa Fe can stand more than 65 feet high (about five stories), and that maximum is only permitted in a small part of the downtown area. Throughout most of the city, commercial buildings are limited to heights of 36 feet and residences to 24 feet. In the historic districts, even the trim color and the roof shape are strictly regulated to preserve the traditional style, and all buildings are painted in brownish hues to match the colors of the surrounding landscape; this follows the Indian tradition of blending in with nature rather than warring with it.

Adobe construction was initiated by the Pueblo Indians long before the Spanish arrived. Stiff, damp sections of mud, about 8 or 10 inches high, were laid one on top of another, and each layer was allowed to dry before the next was applied (this construction method is called "puddling"). The Spaniards achieved the same effect by drying

the mud in wooden molds. Details introduced to the Indians by the Spanish were the kiva-style corner fireplace, which replaced the "smoke hole" in the roof, and the *horno* (a beehive outdoor oven of Moorish origin). Some homes also have garden areas that are enclosed by coyote fences (unpainted vertical tree limbs used to keep animals in or out).

Most early adobe homes in the region were built around a central courtyard in the Spanish tradition. Windows often were small to keep heat in during the winter and out in the summer, and the roofs were supported by protruding vigas (wooden beams).

In the 19th century many structures were designed in the squarer-looking Territorial style, in which brick was placed atop adobe walls, and more decorative woodwork was added to the doors and windows. Though builders today still use handmade adobe bricks, many modern structures are constructed of cheaper cinder block covered with adobe-colored stucco instead.

The architect best known for adapting ancient adobe building methods to modern needs was **John Gaw Meem,** who died at the age of 88 in 1983. Born in Brazil to American parents and raised there and in the eastern US, **Meem** came to Santa Fe on doctor's orders at the age of 26 because he had contracted tuberculosis and needed to live in the clean environment found in the West at that time. For six decades thereafter he designed quite a bit of the adobe architecture of Northern New Mexico. Among his best-known buildings are the **Cristo Rey Church** (see page 51) and the **Santa Fe Public Library** (see page 27).

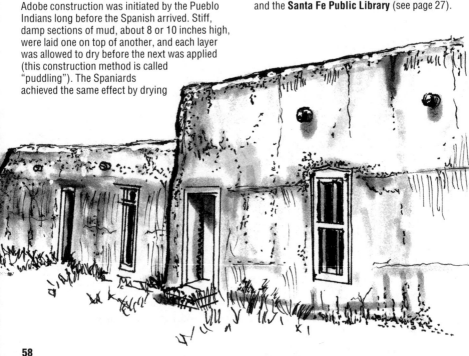

21 **Adobe Abode** $$ Although owner Pat Harbour's first career was in advertising, it was her flair for design that attracted her to the bed-and-breakfast business. Her guests gush over the imaginative and witty rooms she has created, leaving notes in the guest book like "your whole place is like a warm embrace." Each of the six rooms has a different personality and decor, reflected in names like **Casita de Corazón, Bronco,** and **Provence Suite.** The **Cactus Room** is especially romantic, with hand-loomed Mexican fabrics, a wood-burning fireplace, and an art-tile bathroom with a skylight and soft pinkish-coral walls. Some rooms have private patios. Amenities include color TVs, telephones with answering machines, terry-cloth robes, and mini coffeepots. It's conveniently located four blocks from the Plaza in a quiet residential neighborhood. ♦ 202 Chapelle St (at McKenzie St). 983.3133; fax 986.0972 ᪥

22 **Bagelmania** ★★$ A bright spot located in a converted auto-body shop, this bagel emporium is a very popular downtown hangout, and, for the most part, owners Jeff, Faurest, and Gary Schwartzberg are doing things right. (They should; the family has been in the business in New York since 1932.) Bagels and bialys are baked daily on the premises. The fish is smoked, the corned beef is lean, the chopped liver is the real thing—made fresh every day from chicken livers—and the atmosphere is casual and pleasant, the walls filled with black-and-white photos of the Big Apple and old-time movie stars. If the place is a bit noisy, well, that's New York for you. ♦ Deli ♦ Restaurant: M-Tu breakfast and lunch; W-Su breakfast, lunch, and dinner. Bakery: daily. 420 Catron Pl (between Griffin and N Guadalupe Sts). 982.8900

23 **Diego's Cafe** ★★★$ This is the newest of the three New Mexican restaurants run by one of the Maryol siblings, in this case sister Toni Hill, who is co-owner with husband John Hill. It's also the best. The New Mexican food, while not original in concept, is consistently excellent. Toni is one of the most cheerful hostesses in town, the prep work in the kitchen is careful, and the ingredients are top quality. The nacho appetizer is a meal in itself—it can be easily shared four ways—the chicken enchiladas are stuffed with juicy meat, and the hamburgers, humanely slim, are nonetheless cooked medium rare if that's how you order them. This is a big everyday favorite with local residents. ♦ New Mexican ♦ M-Sa lunch and dinner; Su lunch. De Vargas Center Mall (N Guadalupe St, at Paseo de Peralta). 983.5101

24 **Santa Fe National Cemetery** One of the most moving sights in Santa Fe occurs every evening when the sun, setting low in the west, shines on the slopes of this veterans' cemetery, and nearly 18,000 identical white grave markers glow against the green hills in brilliant ranks. In the early days of World War II, New Mexico had more casualties per capita than any other state—mostly at Bataan in the Philippines—and these hills resemble a small Arlington. Just to the south is **Rosario Cemetery,** where most of the city's nonmilitary funerals have been held for more than a century. ♦ 501 N Guadalupe St (off Paseo de Peralta, across from the De Vargas Center Mall). 988.6400

Most public and municipal buildings in Santa Fe are constructed primarily in Territorial style, though some are of adobe design. This basic, earth-tone construction uses adobe bricks (mud cast blocks bonded by straw and dried) and is generally one story, with recessed doorways and small windows.

Bests

Richard Mahler
Writer/Radio Journalist, Santa Fe

My favorite place to write is at **Nambe Lake,** in the high peaks of the **Sangre de Cristo Mountains.** You'd think you were somewhere in the Canadian Rockies or the Swiss Alps, but you're less than a two-hour hike—through quaking aspens and stately firs—from the **Santa Fe Ski Basin.** The lake itself is a rare jewel, hemmed on three sides by steep cliffs and set beneath a vast, cobalt sky.

What I like to do with out-of-town visitors is take them to nearby Indian pueblos. Feast days and ceremonies are always memorable, but on "ordinary" days we visit studios and galleries, buying direct from the artists themselves. Quality and prices are excellent, as well as the warm hospitality.

My never-fail favorites in Santa Fe include **Pranzo Italian Grill** for wonderful pasta (ask for a booth), the **Pink Adobe**'s **Dragon Room** for drinks and conviviality (try the chile and chicken stew), **Cross of the Martyrs** (the best view in town), and the **Alla** bookstore for the best in Latin American books, music, and art.

Tinkertown Museum is my top choice for eclectic, personal, funny, obsessive museum. It represents one man's unique vision of the world and includes thousands of wonderful treasures ranging from miniature wood-carved villages to a real ocean-going sailboat—all tucked away in the middle of a forest east of Albuquerque. It's a fantastic place for kids of all ages.

Additional Highlights of Santa Fe

Some of Santa Fe's premier attractions are situated just off the beaten path or a short drive away—including several must-sees. The *Girard Collection* of toys, dolls, and masks from around the world set up in hilarious dioramas is the best permanent exhibit in town. It's housed in the **Museum of International Folk Art,** which is about two miles from the Plaza. Children will also enjoy the first-rate, hands-on **Santa Fe Children's Museum.** In summer hit both ends of the economic scale in a single day by browsing through **Trader Jack's Flea Market** in the afternoon, then heading next door to the world-famous outdoor **Santa Fe Opera** at night (buy opera tickets in advance—and take along a warm sweater). In late September or early October, the most memorable experience is a drive into the **Santa Fe National Forest,** where whole mountainsides of aspen trees have turned bright gold. And in winter, outdoor types will want to head up the same road to the **Santa Fe Ski Basin.**

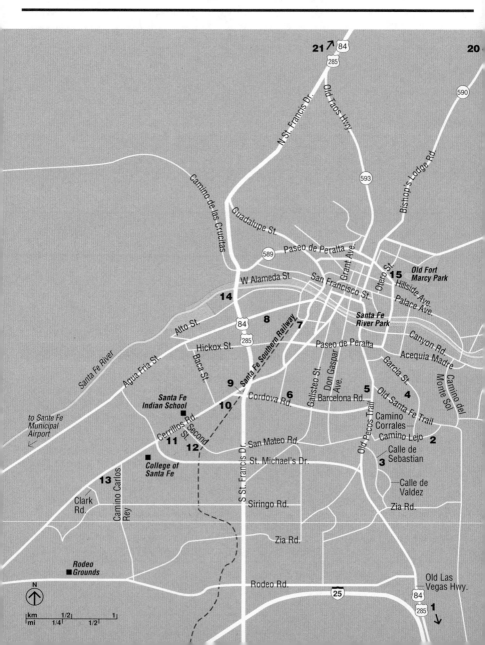

1 Harry's Roadhouse ★★$$ Located on the southeastern outskirts of town, this old adobe house has been converted into the kind of restaurant where Santa Feans go to enjoy hefty portions of creative variations on familiar New Mexican dishes—without paying tourist prices. Typical menu items include meat loaf and a vegetarian burrito packed with black beans, eggplant, and tempeh (a soy product similar to tofu). Dine in one of several rooms in the cozy, old-fashioned interior or alfresco on the patio, which is set in a lovely, landscaped yard complete with an artificial stream cascading through a succession of pools in the shade of tall trees. ♦ Southwestern/American ♦ Daily breakfast, lunch, and dinner. Old Las Vegas Hwy (take Old Pecos Trail south to Old Las Vegas Hwy; continue south on Old Las Vegas Hwy about 1.5 miles). 989.4629

1 Bobcat Bite ★★$ Huge, sizzling, green-chile cheeseburgers keep Santa Feans coming back for more at this long-established, rustic little eatery southeast of town on the old highway that parallels I-25. Known for its generous portions, "The Bite" also serves thick, juicy steaks for dinner. ♦ American/New Mexican ♦ Tu-Sa lunch and early dinner. Old Las Vegas Hwy (take Old Pecos Trail south to Old Las Vegas Hwy; continue south on Old Las Vegas Hwy about 2.5 miles). 983.5319

2 Wheelwright Museum of the American Indian A traditional Navajo hogan (a dwelling made of logs and mud) was the inspiration for the design of the eight-sided building housing this museum. Exhibits in the main gallery change three times a year and include contemporary and traditional American Indian art, with an emphasis on the Southwest. A second gallery presents modern one-person exhibits. On the **Pollen Path** outdoors are sculptures by Allan Houser and others, along with superb mountain views. Mary Cabot Wheelwright, a Bostonian, founded the museum in 1937. Hastiin Klah, a highly respected Navajo medicine man, collaborated with Wheelwright to establish the core collection, which was based on Navajo ceremonies that were in danger of being lost. The museum changed its name from the **Museum of Navajo Ceremonial Art** in 1977 when it broadened its scope. Recent exhibits have included contemporary Navajo pictorial textiles, older Great Plains and Great Lakes pieces from the *Masco* collection, and the works of Navajo painter Clifford Beck and Santa Clara artist Pablita Velarde. Access to the research library is available by appointment. Special activities include storyteller Joe Hayes on Saturday and Sunday at 7PM in July and August; an autumn children's powwow; and others. ♦ Free. M-Sa; Su 1-5PM. 704 Camino Lejo (off Old Santa Fe Trail, near Camino del Monte Sol, behind the Museum of International Folk Art). 982.4636, 800/607.4636

2 Museum of International Folk Art Founded in 1953 to show the work of craftspeople from around the world—just plain folks, as opposed to an artistic elite—this museum has undergone a number of significant expansions in recent years. The first was through the beneficence of the late **Alexander Girard,** the renowned architect and fabric designer who moved to Santa Fe shortly after World War II. **Girard** roamed the world seeking inspiration for his work, and while doing so he became an inveterate collector of

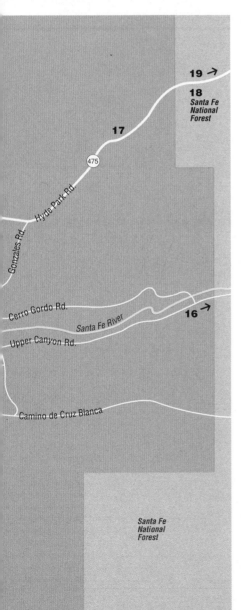

MUSEUM OF INTERNATIONAL FOLK ART

folk art, including handmade toys. By the time he quit globe-trotting, he had amassed more than 100,000 objects, which he donated to the museum. In 1982 he personally oversaw the construction of the **Girard Wing** (see floor plan above), in which about 10,000 pieces from his collection are on permanent display—not on sterile shelves, but in intricate and colorful dioramas that he designed to show village life in the colonial US and in countries around the world. Holes are cut in the dioramas at the level of children's eyes so they, too, can enjoy all the wonders and delicate humor.

In 1989 the museum opened the **Hispanic Heritage Wing,** which displays about 5,000 pieces of folk art dating from the 1600s to the present. Religious art, tinwork, jewelry, and textiles from Northern New Mexico and throughout the Spanish Colonial empire are emphasized. In 1995, Lloyd E. Cotsen, the former CEO for Neutrogena Corporation, gave the museum a $4.4-million collection of 3,000 textiles, ceramics, and folk art objects. A new wing to house the collection will open in 1998. Until then, selections can be seen at the **Governor's Gallery** at the capitol building. ◆ Admission. Tu-Su. 706 Camino Lejo (off Old Santa Fe Trail near Camino del Monte Sol). 827.6350

On 16 March 1949, the piñon was officially adopted as New Mexico's state tree. When the trees' cones open in the fall, hundreds of New Mexicans go piñon picking for the tasty nuts (known as pignoli in Italian). When cold weather sets in, the distinctive incense of the burning piñon logs perfumes the air of villages and towns throughout the state.

Restaurants/Clubs: Red   **Hotels:** Blue

Shops/ Outdoors: Green   **Sights/Culture:** Black

2 **Museum of Indian Arts and Culture** In 1931 the **Laboratory of Anthropology** was established in Santa Fe to preserve artifacts unearthed in New Mexico. Before land can be developed, the laboratory must certify that the site is not of historical significance. The state opened this museum in 1987 to display much of the collection of the adjacent laboratory, which numbers more than 50,000 artifacts. Rotating exhibits deal with every aspect of the Indian culture of the region from pre-Columbian days to the present. Artists in residence are often on the premises demonstrating the techniques of pottery, basketry, and other Indian arts. ◆ Admission. Tu-Su. 710 Camino Lejo (off Old Santa Fe Trail near Camino del Monte Sol). 827.6344

3 **Scheinbaum & Russek Ltd.** Recently relocated from Guadalupe Street, this gallery minutes from downtown features vintage and contemporary works of renowned photographers, including Ansel Adams, Henri-Cartier Bresson, and Sebastião Salgado; in addition, both David Scheinbaum and Janet Russek are the exclusive representatives for the estates of Eliot Porter (Russek was his assistant for many years), Nancy Newhall, and Beaumont Newhall. The owners will pick you up from any location. ◆ By appointment only. 612 Calle de Leon (off Calle de Sebastian, between Old Santa Fe and Old Pecos Trails). 988.5116

4 **School of American Research** This nonprofit institution for archaeological research has been prying into the secrets of the old Southwest since 1907. The school sponsors scholarly research and publications. A large collection of Indian art and textiles is housed inside. ◆ Fee. Tours F 2PM. Reservations required. 660 Garcia St (between Camino Corrales and Acequia Madre). 982.3584

SANTA FE 𝕏𝕏𝕏𝕏𝕏𝕏𝕏 CHILDREN'S MUSEUM

5 **Santa Fe Children's Museum** Big smiles and engrossed looks on the faces of happy children are the biggest attractions here. Hands-on exhibits let kids draw pictures, create their own cartoon movies, make magnetic constructions, divert water streams, and do many other things that are both fun and educational. They can even see live giant cockroaches—definitely not a hands-on display. Founded in 1987 by codirectors Ellen Biderman, Ellyn Feldman, and Londi Carbajal, this is a private, not-for-profit institution that children from roughly ages two to nine and

their parents have a hard time leaving.
♦ Admission. Th-Su. 1050 Old Pecos Trail (at E Barcelona Rd). 989.8359 &

6 Alfalfa's Market An almost-clone of **Wild Oats Community Market** (see below), this store offers a wide range of health and gourmet food including a good selection of low-fat cheese. The take-out department features a variety of delectables to eat here or at the destination of your choice. Seniors get a 10 percent discount on all purchases. A licensed massage therapist gives 15- or 30-minute massages from 11AM to 3PM and 4 to 8PM. ♦ Daily 8AM-11PM. 333 W Cordova Rd (between Galisteo St and Don Diego Ave). 986.8667

7 Santa Fe Southern Railway The re-creation of an old-time railroad trip through the Southwest is available on this small privately owned railway. The line hauls freight from Santa Fe and meets with the main line at the village of Lamy, 20 miles to the south. Passengers ride in an old **Santa Fe Railroad** caboose that holds 16 people as the train winds its way through the hilly landscape for 1.5 hours. Bring a picnic. ♦ Fee. Departs Tu, Th, Sa 10:30AM; returns 4PM. Reservations recommended. 410 S Guadalupe St (just south of Montezuma Ave). 989.8600

8 Ark Books Santa Fe is known for its large New Age population, from serious astrologers and psychics to crystal healers, UFOlogists, and assorted flaky characters. This bookstore is the town's New Age information clearinghouse. Besides a full range of the latest books on everything from holistic health to shamanism, the occult and Eastern religions, there is a good selection of hard-to-find CDs, audio tapes, incense, and offbeat gift items. A bulletin board outside contains fliers pinned up by many local teachers, healers, and psychics, peddling their services and announcing their upcoming workshops. ♦ Daily. 133 Romero St (between W Manhattan Ave and Agua Fria St). 988.3709

9 Wild Oats Community Market One of the most popular grocery stores in town and the perfect place to pick up an extraordinary picnic lunch, this market stocks an amazing array of health and gourmet food items, locally made food products, exotic vegetables, grains in bulk, dietary supplements, natural personal care products, Chinese herbs, and gift items from cookware and incense to "Save the Rainforest" T-shirts. There's also a full deli featuring sandwiches, a salad bar, and such ready-made dishes as tabbouleh and guacamole and an outstanding selection of bread. The indoor dining counter and outdoor tables make this a popular local gathering place. Seniors get a 10 percent discount on all purchases. A licensed massage therapist is on duty daily from 10AM to 8PM, offering refreshing, low-cost 15-minute massages

right in the middle of the busy store. ♦ Daily 8AM-11PM. 1090 S St. Francis Dr (at W Cordova Rd). 983.5333. Also at: St. Michael's Village (1708 Llano St, at St. Michael's Dr). 473.4943

10 Tecolote Cafe ★★$ This plain and simple little coffee shop is where locals go for great breakfasts. Menu choices range from the perennial New Mexican favorite, *huevos rancheros* (fried eggs served on a corn tortilla and smothered in chile salsa), to more familiar fare including overstuffed omelettes, flapjacks with maple syrup, and biscuits and gravy. Lunch features the best chicken-fried steak in town, as well as a standard selection of New Mexican dishes; the green-chile stew is exceptionally good. ♦ American/New Mexican ♦ Tu-Su breakfast and lunch. 1203 Cerrillos Rd (at Alta Vista St). 988.1362

11 Natural Cafe ★★★$$ A wide range of internationally inspired dishes are served at this restaurant that lives up to its name. Most of the food is organic, and there's a heavy emphasis on vegetarian and Asian offerings—the vegetable *gai tua* (grilled tofu and stir-fried vegetables in an Indonesian peanut sauce and served over basmati rice) is a good choice. Farm-raised fish (try the grilled salmon with wasabi-lime sauce) and free-range chicken are also offered. The casual decor is enlivened by works from local artists on the walls; a patio with umbrellas on the tables to protect against the summer's fierce sun is a pleasant place to enjoy alfresco dining. Wine and beer are served. ♦ Tu-F lunch and dinner; Sa-Su dinner. 1494 Cerrillos Rd (at Navajo Dr). 983.1411

12 Taos Furniture Santa Fe is home base for Andy Peterson's worldwide business, despite its name. The heavy wooden furniture—characteristic of Santa Fe—is rugged and simple, yet includes more than 80 styles of beds, chairs, tables, and cabinets. The woodworkers start with local ponderosa pine and kiln-dry it to increase stability. The wood is planed by hand, then burnished with river rocks. Joints are hand-fitted using mortise, tenon, and dowels, and the drawers are dovetailed. The business has outlets in New York, Aspen, Geneva, Milan, Paris, and Tokyo. ♦ M-Sa. 1807 Second St (between the railroad tracks and Cerrillos Rd). 988.1229

13 Jackalope Pottery This huge, sprawling Mexican market created in 1975 by Darby McQuade showcases every kind of craft known to Mexico, where McQuade has his own crew of buyers. Vast amounts of folk art arrive by the tractor-trailer load, including animal pottery and weavings. Other Latin American countries are represented as well. More than just a place to shop, the market also offers a prairie dog village, an aviary, demonstrations by artisans from Mexico, strolling musicians, and a pleasant and inexpensive outdoor cafe. ♦ Daily. 2820 Cerrillos Rd (between Camino Carlos Rey and Clark Rd). 471.8539. Also at: Highway 44, at Rio Grande Bridge, Bernalillo. 867.9813

14 Seckler Studio/Monteverde Gallery
Orange sparks fly and grinding wheels whine indoors and out as four goggled workers translate into steel the sculptural designs of Frank H. Seckler—wonderful Indian mythic figures based on petroglyphs. They are crafted into unusual tables, chairs, screens, light fixtures, wall hangings, and freestanding steel figures. Seckler spent most of his life in the cattle and meat-packing business in Colorado and sculpted as an avocation for 20 years. He moved to New Mexico and started working full time in 1990, opening a studio in Taos late in 1991 and one in Santa Fe a year later. Today galleries throughout the country show his work. His son, Frank B. Seckler (don't call him junior), runs the Taos studio. Adjacent to the working area is the **Monteverde Gallery**—which sells the pieces—run by the artist's wife, Magdalena Monteverde, who hails from the Canary Islands and Spain. She also shows paintings by local artists. Visitors are welcome. ♦ Daily. 150 S St. Francis Dr (at Alto St). 989.4371

15 Cross of the Martyrs During the 1680 Pueblo Revolt against Spanish domination, more than 20 Franciscan priests were killed. A large cross atop a hill above the city is dedicated to their memory. Plaques telling the history of Santa Fe are posted along a brick walkway that leads up the hill. At the top is a bird's-eye view of the city and a vista of the broad sweep of three mountain ranges that rim the plateau: the Sangre de Cristos immediately to the northeast, the Jemez 40 miles to the west, and the Sandias, near Albuquerque, 60 miles to the south.
♦ Walkway begins at Paseo de Peralta (between Hillside Ave and Otero St)

16 Randall Davey Audubon Center
In 1848, when New Mexico became a US territory, a sawmill was built on what is now Upper Canyon Road to provide planks for an army establishment at nearby Fort Marcy. Water diverted from the Santa Fe River powered the mill. After the mill closed in 1856, the

property went through several owners and occupants until it was purchased in 1920 by painter Randall Davey, who had just moved to Santa Fe from the East. Davey used the original mill building, which had 16-inch-thick stone walls, as his home and a former mill storeroom as his painting studio. He lived here until he was killed in an automobile accident in 1964. The Davey home and studio remain intact amid the greenery, and many of his paintings are on display.

The property is now owned by the National Audubon Society and is maintained as a 135-acre wildlife refuge and environmental education center. More than one hundred bird species have been observed at the refuge in Santa Fe Canyon, including, most typically, nuthatches, goldfinches, warblers, stellar jays, brown creepers, and yellow-bellied sapsuckers. Raccoons, coyotes, black bears, mule deer, bobcats, and mountain lions sometimes visit. The visitors' center bookstore specializes in natural history.
♦ Donation requested. Daily May-Sept; M-Sa Mar-Apr, Oct-Dec; M-F Jan-Feb; call ahead for schedules of tours of the Davey home.1800 Upper Canyon Rd (beyond the pavement's end). 983.4609

17 Ten Thousand Waves Japanese Health Spa When Duke Klauck came to this city in 1978, he brought with him a dream of building a traditional Japanese *onsen* (outdoor hot springs resort) in the high desert setting of Santa Fe. A hot springs connoisseur and avid fan of Japanese culture, Klauck had spent years traveling to more than 250 hot springs around the US as well as to the famous Japanese *onsens* of places like Kyoto and Beppu.

Combining the best of Japan and New Mexico, Klauck began building his business according to Japanese design, substituting native New Mexican materials such as adobe and aspen wood for hard-to-get Japanese mud-wattle and bamboo. Today East meets West here in a simple Japanese-style building that sits quietly at 8,000 feet in the piñon-shrouded hills above Santa Fe. Ten exotically designed outdoor teak hot tubs dot the hillsides. Steamy saunas and icy cold plunges also await adventurous bathers who flock to the bathhouse in all kinds of weather to don kimonos and follow wilderness footpaths to tubs that overlook Santa Fe's fabled mountains. But "The Waves," as locals know it, boasts more than bathing. With some 60 massage therapists on hand, visitors choose from everything from soothing Swedish to *watsu* (underwater) massage, as well as facials, herbal wraps, and more. A small retail area features healthy snacks, kimonos, T-shirts, and skin-care products.

Located on the road to the Santa Fe ski area, this is a favorite with the après-ski set, who like to warm up here after a hard day on the slopes. Nature-lovers may even spy a jackrabbit or two prancing about the mountain property. ♦ Daily; hours vary. Reservations recommended. Hyde Park Rd (off Washington Ave), 3.5 miles from Santa Fe. 982.9304 &

18 Santa Fe National Forest/Hyde Memorial State Park For one of the most beautiful sights in the world, visit Santa Fe in late September and early October when the aspen trees that cover the mountain slopes turn a bright burnished gold. Many visitors come just to drive the winding mountain road and walk amid this stunning natural beauty. The largest pull-over spot is known, appropriately, as Aspen Vista. Park here and walk among the golden coinlike leaves. Twelve miles northeast of Santa Fe on Ski Basin Road, the state park offers picnic tables, camping grounds, clear mountain streams, and 350 acres of mountain slopes crisscrossed with hiking trails. It is set in the national forest, which contains thousands of acres of slopes covered with pine and aspen trees and dotted with hiking trails. **Windsor Trail** is the main path. Detailed maps of the hiking trails are available from the **Santa Fe National Forest Headquarters** (1474 Rodeo Rd, Santa Fe, 438.7840). ♦ Take Hyde Park Rd north from Santa Fe and follow the signs

19 Santa Fe Ski Basin Thousands of skiers descend on Santa Fe in the winter months, creating a second visitor season for the city. This basin, at 12,000 feet, is one of the highest ski slopes in the country. From the peak is a vista of 8,000 square miles of mountain ranges and high desert. Most of the runs at the ski basin are for intermediates and beginners, but several, including **Wizard, Big Rocks,** and **Tequila Sunrise,** will challenge even the most advanced skiers. (**Taos Ski Valley,** with its more difficult runs, draws a greater number of experienced skiers.) The ski basin originated in the 1930s when a Denver designer, Graeme McGowen, suggested that runs could be built along Indian trails and sheep trails. The Civilian Conservation Corps built a road to **Hyde Park** and a stone lodge that now houses the **Evergreen Restaurant** (Hyde Park Rd,

984.8190). The first chairlift was built at the present site in the 1950s, using surplus seats from a B-24 bomber.

Today there are four modern lifts and 38 downhill trails—20 percent for beginners, 40 percent for intermediates, and 40 percent for advanced skiers. The runs are protected from the winds by tree cover and the angle of the mountain and offer fine family skiing. The average annual snowfall on the slopes is 225 inches. Snowmaking equipment can supply about 25 percent of the slopes. Skis are available for rent at the base of the mountain as well as in town. Cross-country skiing is also plentiful in the area. Sledding and riding inner tubes—which is great fun for the kids—are permitted in **Hyde Park,** below the ski basin. In summer the ski lifts run to show people the scenic views. ♦ Snow permitting, Thanksgiving to Easter. Ski Basin Rd (NM 475, 15 miles northeast of Santa Fe). 982.4429, snow report 983.9155

20 Bishop's Lodge $$$$ In the 19th century Archbishop Lamy had a private retreat, complete with a personal chapel, in the hills a few miles north of town. Years later Joseph Pulitzer bought the rolling parcel of land as a summer home for the family. In 1917 James R. Thorpe of Denver purchased it and laid the foundation for what was to become this thousand-acre full-service resort that offers four tennis courts, horseback riding (more than 60 steeds), swimming, and skeet-shooting amid rolling green hills. Archbishop Lamy's chapel still stands on the property. The lodge, still owned by the Thorpe family, offers 88 Southwestern-style guest rooms and suites, some with fireplaces and terraces. The serene restaurant (open to the public) serves fine food, such as lamb chops with goat cheese and grilled tiger prawns. ♦ Bishop's Lodge Rd (NM 590, about 3.5 miles north of Santa Fe). 983.6377, 800/732.2240; fax 989.8739 &

Most of Northcentral New Mexico above 6,500 feet is home to oak, juniper, spruce, Douglas fir, and ponderosa pines. Higher precipitation levels and cooler temperatures permit a diverse range of wildlife, including squirrels, chipmunks, and porcupines. Larger mammals like the whitetail deer, black bear, elk, and mountain lion are occasionally sighted, particularly in less populated regions, along with quail and wild turkey. Rattlesnakes can also be found.

M. BLUM

20 Shidoni Foundry

For people who appreciate sculpture, a visit here is a must on any trip to Santa Fe. Large and small works in a variety of media are on display year-round in an outdoor sculpture garden set on green lawns against the backdrop of the Sangre de Cristo Mountains. A newer 5,000-square-foot indoor gallery features sleek contemporary works. Tommy Hicks, a sculptor, founded the place in 1971, on an eight-acre apple orchard in Tesuque, an upscale adobe suburb. It was begun as a foundry and still functions in that capacity. The pouring of molten bronze at a temperature of 2,000 degrees into ceramic shell molds can be viewed by visitors every Saturday, as sculptors transform miniature studies into larger bronze works. Mold making, sand casting, and lost-wax casting are also practiced on the premises. In 1995, Tommy Hicks was given the Governor's Award for his contribution to the arts. ♦ M-Sa. Bishop's Lodge Rd, Tesuque (5 miles north of Santa Fe). 988.8001

20 Rancho Encantado $$$$

In 1968 Betty Egan left her home in Ohio, moved to New Mexico, and purchased an old lodge in Tesuque. She turned her new home into a dude ranch and named it "Enchanted Ranch." The secluded ranch is still flourishing and growing bigger. The main lodge was built in 1932 and contains Southwestern-style bedrooms. An assortment of cottages and casitas (bungalows) with bedrooms, living rooms, fireplaces, and kitchens have been added to the property over the years, making a total of 88 guest accommodations. The 168-acre, year-round resort offers swimming, tennis, and horseback riding, and the restaurant serves breakfast, lunch, and dinner. Notables who've stayed here include Princess Caroline, Robert Redford, and the Dalai Lama. Betty Egan died in 1992, and the hotel is now under the direction of Mike Cerletti, former New Mexico Director of Tourism and a longtime Santa Fe hotelier. ♦ NM 592, Tesuque (about 8 miles north of Santa Fe). 982.3537, 800/722.9339; fax 983.8269 &

21 Santa Fe Opera

The **Santa Fe Opera (SFO)** is one of the best-known and most well-respected opera festivals in the world. Founded in 1957 by general director John Crosby, the company has featured many top stars from New York's **Metropolitan Opera** and elsewhere. Its apprentice programs for singers and technicians give young people just starting out in the opera world a chance to work with professionals and learn more about their trade.

Five works are performed in repertory each summer—two classics, a lesser-known work by a famous composer, a Richard Strauss offering, and an American or world premiere piece. Both the sight lines and the acoustics are excellent. The stage and some of the seats are beneath a curving roof; other seats are open to the elements, which are sometimes cold and wet. A heavy jacket or a blanket is always recommended, even for those seated in the covered sections, because the temperature drops quickly after dark. Although it's best to get tickets ahead, some are available on the same day for some performances. At press time, a bold renovation project was underway and expected to be completed by June 1998. Plans call for a new stage roof to be connected to a new mezzanine roof by a clerestory so that all seats will be covered, new orchestra and mezzanine seating, rebuilding public support facilities, and the installation of an elevator to all levels. **Polshek & Partners** of New York, the architects that handled the refurbishment of New York City's Carnegie Hall, are in charge of the renovations. ♦ Late June-late Aug. Hwy 84-285 (7 miles north of Santa Fe). Information 986.5955, tickets 986.5900

21 Trader Jack's Flea Market

This huge outdoor garage sale operated since the 1970s by Jack Daniels (his real name) features upwards of 500 vendors who cram the dusty acreage every weekend. Hawked here is everything from used paperback books and old magazines for a dime or a quarter to handmade furniture and antiques going for several hundred dollars. Old tools, cheap jewelry, and used boots and clothing abound in every direction while thousands of bargain hunters prowl and haggle. Situated on Tesuque Indian land across from the soaring Sangre de Cristos and just north of the **Santa Fe Opera**, this is a fun place to spend an hour or two. ♦ Weather permitting F-Su Easter-Thanksgiving. Hwy 84-285 (8 miles north of Santa Fe)

Bests

Felicia Ferguson
Director/Owner, Lumina of New Mexico Fine Art & Photography

Sante Fe

Eats: **The Shed** (lunch only), **Cafe Escalera, Santacafe, Pasqual's** (breakfast)

Hotels: **Inn of the Anasazi, La Posada, Hotel St. Francis**

Taos

Bed-and-Breakfast: **Casa Benavides**

Hotel: **La Fonda de Taos**

Restaurant: **Lambert's** (great lunches)

Old Taos

Fechin Institute, Martinez Hacienda, Blumenschein House, Harwood Foundation, Millicent Rogers Museum

Albuquerque

Old Town, San Felipe de Neri Catholic Church, Artichoke Cafe, Sandia Crest

Jay Rosenbaum
Owner/Art Dealer, Hirsch Fine Art

People watching in the lobby of the **Taos Inn.**

Wandering through the **Blumenschein House** and museum of early Taos artists.

Going out to the **Rio Grande Gorge Bridge.**

Walking around the **San Francisco de Asis Church** made famous by Georgia O'Keeffe paintings.

Eating a green-chile cheeseburger at the **Apple Tree** restaurant.

Going to a rehearsal concert given by the **American String Quartet** in the **Taos Ski Valley.**

Driving the **High Road from Taos to Santa Fe** through small, old mountain Northern New Mexican towns.

Martin Berkowitz
Artist/Painter, Santa Fe

The very best deal in town for lunch, if you enjoy Indian food—**India Palace.** Can you imagine salad, eight delicious entrées, and dessert for $6.95—in a charming atmosphere with pink table linens and fresh flower—addictive.

The **Bishop's Lodge,** five miles outside of Santa Fe. Lush green grounds, beautiful. Heated outdoor pool, enchanted dining on the terrace with outdoor kiva fireplace for that special occasion.

The most magical time in Santa Fe—Christmas Eve, the entire city is lighted up with *farolitos* and bonfires, such a feeling of good cheer.

Susan Curtis
Owner/Director, Santa Fe School of Cooking

Santa Fe is a place with great diversity and intensity—in terrain and environment, light, culture, cuisine, politics, outdoor activities, lifestyles, music, and much, much more. I love Santa Fe for it has maintained its uniqueness. Some of my favorite places and activities:

Early in the morning the streets around the Plaza are frequented primarily by delivery trucks and a few merchants scurrying to work. At 8AM, under the portal of the **Palace of the Governors,** individuals from the surrounding pueblos are drawing for their places to sell their wares.

Breakfast at **Tia Sophia's,** a down-home New Mexican breakfast and lunch place, provides a wonderful opportunity to mingle with the local politicians, Native Americans, builders, scientists, writers, artists, and city wackos.

Spectacular trails surrounding Santa Fe are great for hiking, jogging, cross country skiing, and mountain biking (favorite trails are best kept to yourself).

The bar at **Pranzo Italian Grill,** one of the few places where food is available until midnight, makes for great late-night dining.

The best bar in town is the **Dragon Room** of the **Pink Adobe.** You can have the best apple pie in town with your brandy here.

Beautiful flowers, a fountain surrounded by an architecturally interesting historical compound, and a lively menu combine to make the courtyard of **La Casa Sena** restaurant the best patio dining in the summer.

A walk or jog, coffee at **Downtown Subscription,** and a browse through **Garcia Street Books** is a great way to start a Santa Fe day.

A visit to the **Farmer's Market** is a must during the months of July, August, and September. On Tuesday, Saturday, and sometimes Sunday mornings, the market emerges from the parking lot of **Sanbusco Center** off of Montezuma Street. Harvest is in full season during these months and the variety of locally grown food is mouth watering.

The smell of roasting chile at most grocery store parking lots during the peak chile season of August and September embodies the Santa Fe experience.

The local community loves to gather monthly in the summer for free band concerts in **Federal Park,** two blocks north of the Plaza.

Sunset over the **Jemez Mountains** on a warm summer evening is best viewed from the **Bell Tower** of **La Fonda Hotel** or from the **Santa Fe Opera.**

Santa Fe Day Trips

No visit to Santa Fe is complete without at least one drive into the countryside. Only there can you get the feel of what the ancient Indians, the Spanish conquistadores, and eventually the Anglo artists saw in this region. Within easy reach of Santa Fe are small Hispanic towns, the landscape near **Abiquiu** that Georgia O'Keeffe loved so much, **The Downs at Santa Fe** racetrack, and six of the **Eight Northern Pueblos** (the other two are featured in the "Additional Highlights of Taos and Day Trips" chapter). Choose any of these destinations and see piñon-studded hills, soaring peaks, and pine-covered mountains. If possible, make the return trip in the late afternoon or early evening, as the sun is sinking in the west—that's when the landscape takes on a dramatic glow.

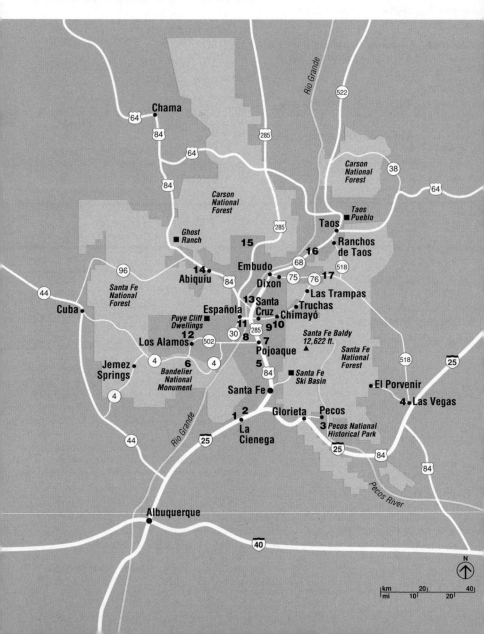

1 El Rancho de Las Golondrinas A 200-acre spread in La Cienega, about 17 miles south of Santa Fe, "Ranch of the Swallows" is a time capsule of the region's Hispanic past. At this way station on El Camino Real, about 70 buildings, some original, some restored, indicate what life was like in the 18th and 19th centuries. The hacienda was the first stop for wagons heading south from Santa Fe and the last one for those coming into town from Mexico. Several weekends during the year—at the spring, summer, and harvest festivals—volunteers dress up in traditional costumes and demonstrate to visitors the old ways of baking bread, making soap, drying chile, milling flour—in general re-creating a lifestyle long gone. This "living museum" is open from June through August for self-guided tours and in April, May, September, and October for guided tours. The place really springs to life on the festival weekends (call for schedules). The biggest of them, the Harvest Festival, coincides with the Albuquerque Balloon Fiesta in early October.
♦ Admission. W-Su Apr-Oct. Take I-25 south from Santa Fe to the Racetrack exit and follow the signs. 471.2261 &

2 The Downs at Santa Fe Not since 1980, when a big, gray two-year-old colt named Pass the Tab was the premier horse at Santa Fe's grade III racetrack, has a horse run as well here. Since pari-mutuel betting has been approved in several neighboring states, including Oklahoma and Texas, the quality of local racehorses has declined. Yet this is still an attractive small-town track, with the Sangre de Cristo Mountains forming a lovely backdrop for the mix of thoroughbred and quarterhorse races. It's very much a family track—not the least bit sleazy—with kids running around and carnival rides sometimes offered on the grassy infield. Ten or eleven races a day are held four days a week from mid-June through Labor Day. (From January through May, the track offers off-track betting and simulcasting of racing in Albuquerque.) Seating is divided among general admission, the **Turf Club** (with a concession stand and cocktail service), and the **Jockey Club** (a full restaurant near the finish line). Fee. Th-F 2-6PM; Sa-Su 1-4:30PM. Frontage Rd (take I-25 south to exit 599, about a 20-minute drive from the Plaza). 471.3311

3 Pecos National Historical Park In a valley set among rolling green hills about 25 miles southeast of Santa Fe are the ruins of a once-flourishing Indian pueblo. The Pecos Indians traded with the pueblos along the Rio Grande—Santa Fe's Canyon Road was part of an Indian trail that led here—as well as with the Plains Indians farther east. Spanish explorer Coronado's men visited **Pecos Pueblo** in 1541. In the 1620s the Franciscans came and built a mission church to convert the Indians. The last residents abandoned the pueblo in 1838, for reasons not entirely clear; historians suspect that disease may have wiped out much of the population. Today the ruins, partly restored and partly in their original condition, are a national historical park. A separate, smaller unit of the park—between the villages of Pecos and Glorieta—preserves part of the Glorieta Battlefield, site of the westernmost military action of the Civil War, where the Confederacy was defeated.
♦ Admission. Daily. Take I-25 to exit 299 or 307, 25 miles southeast of Santa Fe. 757.6414

J. Schuman 79

4 Las Vegas If the chic development of Santa Fe begins to wear thin, the perfect antidote is an hour's drive to Las Vegas, New Mexico. This historic town dates back to 1882, when the city's plaza was an important stop for merchants and traders along the Santa Fe Trail. Doc Holliday, Jesse James, and Billy the Kid also dropped in to make trouble; Wyatt Earp did what he could to promote peace when he passed through. Today the town has over 900 buildings listed on the National Register of Historic Places. The Plaza and Bridge Street district are pleasant for walking past Italianate and Territorial-style buildings, some of which have been renovated into shops selling antiques, funky clothing, and gifts. Las Vegas's 15,000 inhabitants enjoy small-town living and are determined to preserve their beautifully designed homes, offices, and storefronts.

Among the attractions on the town plaza are the **Plaza Hotel** (425.3591, 800/328.1882), built in 1882 and renovated in 1982 to preserve its historic look. The 36 guest rooms are charming, with 14-foot stenciled ceilings, antique armoires, and floral prints. The hotel's **Landmark Grill** serves salmon au poivre, filet mignon, and scallops over linguine. Servers will share hotel ghost stories if prompted. Bridge Street boasts a dozen shops, including **Rough Rider Trading Co.** (No. 158, 425.0246), specializing in Western art, jewelry, weavings, and handmade furniture; **New Moon Fashions** (No. 132, 454.0669), featuring contemporary women's clothing; and **Espresso de Arts** (No. 166, 425.0531), offering fine works by local artists and coffee and homemade pastries.

About five miles north in Montezuma is **Armand Hammer United World College** (I-25 north, 454.4248), where 200 students from around the world study international relations. Another five miles north in Sapello is the **Star Hill Inn** (Rte 518, 425.5605), a study retreat for amateur astronomers, birders, and wildflower lovers. Guests stay in seven cozy cottages on 195 forested acres. State-of-the-art telescopes on outdoor decks are perfect for nighttime star gazing. No meals are served here, but the cottages have kitchens. ◆ Take I-25 north to Las Vegas exit, 60 miles east of Santa Fe

5 Tesuque Pueblo This was one of the first pueblos to have contact with the Spanish settlers, and its members played a major role in the 1680 Pueblo Revolt: Two of its leaders who secretly notified other pueblos of the plan were betrayed and arrested by the Spanish. Originally located elsewhere, the pueblo was established at its present site in 1694. While less picturesque than some, Tesuque does have a central plaza dominated by a Catholic church. The Tewa-speaking tribe operates a bingo parlor that is frequented by Indians and non-Indians alike, as well as a campground and RV park at **Camel Rock,** a local landmark located beside Highway 84-285, where the pueblo also operates a full-scale casino. The Feast of San Diego is celebrated here on 12 November. ◆ Fees for photography, sketching, and painting. Daily. Hwy 84-285, 9 miles north of Santa Fe (the main village is 1 mile west of the highway). 983.2667

6 Bandelier National Monument The remains of a large Anasazi civilization (ancestors of the Pueblo Indians)—one of the most wondrous sites of the Southwest—can be viewed, photographed, and hiked here. Named after scientist Adolph Bandelier, the first anthropologist to explore the site, the monument contains more than 3,000 arch-aeological treasures, most of which are still unexcavated. Why the community was abandoned, whether because of worn-out resources, drought, famine, or disease, is not known. The ruins—caves built from volcanic rock—are located on mesas and in canyons throughout the Pajarito Plateau, originally home to perhaps 400-500 Indians between AD 1100 and 1550. Crops of beans, corn, and squash may have been irrigated with water from Frijoles Creek. A fairly easy hiking trail that winds among the main ruins of Frijoles Canyon takes about an hour. Ladders can be climbed—much as the Indians used to do—to enter cliff dwellings.

There are 70 miles of more strenuous, more remote trails that go to distant ruins among the area's 50 square miles. Free permits, obtainable at the **Visitors' Center,** are required for overnight hikes. During New Mexico's extremely dry 1996 spring, a poorly extinguished campfire burst into flames and burned about 17,000 acres throughout Northern New Mexico. Some 4,700 acres within **Bandelier** were destroyed; at press time the park's back-country areas were closed, and tourists were warned not to hike among the thousands of dead trees. Fortunately the monument itself was not affected. Check with the **Visitors' Center** (see below) about current hiking and camping conditions. Rangers predict one positive result from the fire—an increase in the park's plant and animal life, especially in creating new elk habitat.

◆ Admission. Daily. Take Hwy 84-285 north to Pojoaque, then west on NM 502 and south on NM 4, 45 miles northwest of Santa Fe. Visitors' Center 672.3861 ext 517, 24-hour recording 672.0343

San Diego, Tesuque Pueblo

JOHN DEL GAIZO

Food for Thought

When people talk about eating Mexican food in this region of the country, they are not referring to the cuisine of Mexico, with its chicken mole and shrimp brochettes. The phrase is short for New Mexican food—and that is a very different kettle of chile.

New Mexican food is based on three ingredients: tortillas—either corn or flour, pinto beans, and chile pods. Toss in a little cheese, and these staples can be transformed into a surprising variety of delicious, hearty, and nourishing dishes. Chile pods are grown throughout the state and are typically processed into chopped green chile or red chile powder. (In New Mexico chile is always spelled with an e—the original Spanish spelling—not chili, which is Anglicized to reflect the pronunciation.) New Mexican chile has no resemblance to the mix of beef, beans, onions, and tomato sauce known as Texas chili. Many locals eat a bowl of plain green chile or with beans added in. More often the chile is served as a sauce over enchiladas, burritos, *rellenos,* and other local dishes. Chile is an acquired taste, but once acquired it tends to become a lifetime predilection.

The style of New Mexican cuisine began to evolve centuries ago with the Pueblo Indians, who pounded corn into meal to make tortillas, which were a daily staple. Their diet was later blended with Navajo tastes, then spiced up by Spanish conquistadores and newcomers from Mexico. The resulting recipes are now served in the poorest New Mexican homes as well as a great many excellent restaurants.

Here's a glossary of common New Mexican foods:

Burrito A flour tortilla that is wrapped around meat, beans, or vegetables, and baked.

Chile relleno A chile pod that is stuffed with jack cheese, breaded, and fried.

Chimichanga Just like a burrito, except it is deep-fried and covered with sour cream or salsa.

Enchilada A corn tortilla (sometimes made from blue corn) that is filled with meat, chicken, seafood, beans, or cheese, and baked.

Flauta Cheese- or meat-filled tortilla rolled into a reedlike shape (*flauta* means flute in Spanish) and fried.

Frijoles refritos Refried beans.

Guacamole Mashed avocado, blended with tomatoes, garlic, onions, lemon juice, and chiles.

Huevos rancheros Fried eggs served on a corn tortilla and smothered with cheese and salsa.

Posole A hearty stew made from pork, hominy, chiles, garlic, and spices.

Quesadilla A warm, folded tortilla filled with melted cheese.

Sopaipillas Delicate, deep-fried puffy breads that are often served as an alternative to tortillas. Break one open and add a few drops of honey—the sweet taste complements the chile and reduces the burning sensation.

Taco A corn or flour tortilla, fried and made into a shell, then stuffed with meat, chicken, or beans, and topped with lettuce, tomatoes, onions, and grated cheese.

Tamale Cornmeal paste formed around a filling of seasoned meat or vegetables, then wrapped in corn husks and steamed.

Tortilla Thin crepe made from corn or flour, eaten plain as an accompaniment to New Mexican dishes, or made into a burrito, enchilada, flauta, or quesadilla.

7 Pojoaque Pueblo In the late 1880s the population of this pueblo was almost wiped out by an epidemic of smallpox, and today only small mounds of earth from the original pueblo remain. In 1932 a new pueblo was founded. The **Poeh Center and Museum** (455.2489) exhibits pottery and jewelry, as well as vintage photographs, from the eight Northern Pueblos (**Pojoaque, Tesuque, Nambe, San Ildefonso, Santa Clara, San** Juan, Pucuris,** and **Taos**). Although the pueblo lacks a central village (it is primarily a cluster of stores along the highway on pueblo land), it has an information center and a large tribally owned gift shop (455.3334). The pueblo recently opened the **Cities of Gold** casino (Rte 284, 455.3313). Its feast day is 12 December. ◆ Fees for sketching and filming at the pueblo. Daily. On Hwy 84-285, 15 miles north of Santa Fe. 455.2278

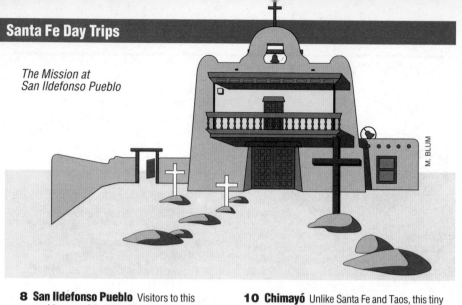

*The Mission at
San Ildefonso Pueblo*

M. BLUM

8 San Ildefonso Pueblo Visitors to this pueblo, one of the friendliest of all those in New Mexico, are welcomed into the large, picturesque plaza. This spot is famous for the black pottery technique developed in the 1920s by Maria Martinez and her husband, Julian. Maria was one of the first potters to sign her work and is the most well known of all pueblo potters. The pueblo operates a museum and gift shop (check at the visitors' center for hours). ♦ Photography fee. Daily. Take Hwy 84-285 15 miles north of Santa Fe, turn left toward Los Alamos at NM 502, and go 6 miles; the entrance is on the right. 455.2273

9 Nambe Pueblo Set in a valley of piñon and juniper, Nambe Falls, one of New Mexico's few waterfalls, is the site of this small pueblo in the Sangre de Cristo Mountains. Visitors come here for fishing, boating, and camping in and around Nambe Lake. On the Fourth of July the pueblo celebrates with dances at the falls. ♦ Fees for sketching, photography, and filming. Daily. Take Hwy 84-285 15 miles north of Santa Fe, then head 3 miles east on NM 503 to the sign for Nambe Falls; the pueblo entrance is 2 miles farther along. 455.2036

10 Chimayó Unlike Santa Fe and Taos, this tiny Hispanic village has for the most part withstood the ravages of commercialism. Screen out the automobiles parked in the plaza, and the scene will resemble the New Mexican villages of centuries long gone. And an unforgettable site awaits here: Situated off the plaza is the **Santuario de Chimayó** (no phone), an old adobe church that has sometimes been called the American Lourdes, after the Catholic shrine in France. In a small back room, there's a hole in the floor beside which visitors can kneel, scoop out dirt, and rub it on parts of their bodies that are ailing. According to legend, the dirt has healing powers. In a narrow room leading to the healing earth, crutches, wheelchairs, canes, and all sorts of other medical aids are hung on the walls, along with written testimonials from people who claim they were healed by the Chimayó dirt. The sanctuary is open daily.

This region is known as a weaving center. The Ortega family has been producing weavers for seven generations, going back to Gabriel Ortega in the 18th century. Their wool blankets, rugs, and apparel are for sale at **Ortega's Weaving Shop** (NM 76, across from the Santuario, 351.4215). The Trujillo family, which also claims seven generations of weavers and is now led by Irvin Trujillo, sells its products at **Centinela Traditional Arts** (NM 76, 1 mile east of Ortega's Weaving Shop, 351.2180). It's a fruitless debate over which family does better work, especially since there has been plenty of intermarrying.

JOHN DEL GAIZO

El Santuario, Chimayó

Many people drive to Chimayó just to eat (lunch and dinner daily and breakfast on weekends) at **Rancho de Chimayó** (351.4444). Set back from the road about a quarter-mile from the plaza, this atmospheric restaurant in a converted ranch house is run by the Jaramillo family. Quality classic New Mexican food is offered here on lovely outdoor terraces in warm weather and indoors year-round. The drive at sunset through New Mexico's back country, amid rolling high-desert hills, is memorable. For those who choose to spend the night, the village has two comfortable bed-and-breakfasts: **Casa Escondida** (County Rd 0100, near the Plaza, 351.4805), an adobe hacienda set on six acres with six rooms furnished with antiques; and **Posada de Chimayó** (Rte. 502, 30 miles north of Santa Fe, 351.4605), with four rooms with fireplaces. ♦ On NM 76, about 25 miles northeast of Santa Fe

11 Santa Clara Pueblo With 2,600 tribal members, this is one of the area's larger pueblos. All are descendants of Indians who lived at the nearby **Puye Cliff Dwellings**, located west of the pueblo. The cliff dwellings are a national landmark, and walking tours—either self-guided or with escorts—can be made through the abodes. The original dwellings were carved out of the cliffs; structures were later built on the mesas and below the cliffs. The site was abandoned as a dwelling circa 1500. Atop the cliff dwellings are the ruins of a 740-room pueblo, which offer a stunning view of the surrounding mountain ranges.

The Santa Clara artisans are known for their intricately carved pottery, including miniature etched pots. Tours of the pueblo are available on weekdays, during which potters can be seen at work. The tribe runs the **Santa Clara Canyon Recreation Area,** where camping, picnicking, and fishing are available. ♦ Admission to Puye Cliff Dwellings includes fee for photography; additional fee for videography. Free admission to Pueblo; fee for photography and escorted tours. Daily. Take Hwy 84-285 north about 15 miles to Española, then NM 30 south; the entrance is on the left. 753.7326

12 Los Alamos In the early 1940s, physicist J. Robert Oppenheimer, who came to know the isolation of Northern New Mexico during boyhood vacations, chose the **Los Alamos Ranch School** as the site for the Manhattan Project, which would bring together scientists from all over the country to create the atom bomb. **Los Alamos National Laboratory** is still on the cutting edge of scientific research—some military, some (strange as this may seem) environmental. The once-closed community known locally as "The Hill" is now a modern, friendly city with much to see and do, especially outdoors. The lab itself is not open to visitors, but the free **Bradbury Science Museum** (15th St and Central Ave, 667.4444) contains displays on how atomic energy works, as well as interactive exhibits on current environmental projects. The **Los Alamos County Historical Museum** (2132 Central Ave, at Fuller Lodge, 662.6272) traces a million years of history in the region and reveals "Life in the Secret City" during the period the bomb was being built. Also on display is historic correspondence between President Franklin D. Roosevelt and the scientists, particularly Oppenheimer and Albert Einstein. Both museums are open daily; a donation is requested at the historical museum.

Overnight visitors can stay at the charming, eight-room **Orange Street Inn** (3496 Orange St, off Diamond Rd, 662.2651). Located on a forested canyon, it's close to the area's attractions.

With over 30 trails and a 1,200-foot vertical rise, the beautiful **Pajarito Mountain Ski Area** (eight miles west of Los Alamos on Rte 502, 662.SNOW, 662.5725) is popular with local families who ski from December until 1 May. The **Mountain Air Cafe** (on the slopes, 662.1969) serves excellent hamburgers, Mexican dishes, and delicious cinnamon rolls. The 18-hole **Los Alamos Golf Course** (Diamond Dr, between Canyon Rd and San Ildefonso Rd, 662.8139), with spectacular mountain and canyon views, is open mid-March to mid-November. ♦ Take Hwy 84-285 north about 16 miles, then head west on NM 502 about 20 miles.

San Juan Bautista, San Juan Pueblo

JOHN DEL GAIZO

13 San Juan Pueblo In 1598 conquistador Juan de Oñate declared this pueblo the first capital of New Mexico; 11 years later the capital was moved to Santa Fe. It was a San Juan native called Popé who organized the

1680 Pueblo Revolt. Today this, the largest and northernmost of the Tewa-speaking pueblos, serves as the administrative headquarters of the Eight Northern Indian Pueblos Council, which was created in the 1960s to help the pueblos speak with a common voice in their own interests. The pueblo has two central plazas where Catholic churches and ceremonial kivas stand beside one another. At the **O'ke Oweenge Arts and Crafts Cooperative,** (852.2372) visitors can see and buy the red pottery that is a San Juan trademark, as well as crafts from many pueblos; it is open Monday through Saturday. Across from the cooperative the **Tewa Indian Restaurant** (no phone) serves fry bread (a puffy bread similar to sopaipillas), chile stews, and other dishes. The tribe runs bingo games, and tribal lakes are open in spring and summer for fishing (permits are available at the pueblo). The tribal Vespers and Evening Dances and Feast Day are held on 23 and 24 June. The Turtle Dance is held on 26 December. ♦ Fee for photography. Daily. Take Hwy 84-285 north about 15 miles to Española, drive a mile north on NM 68, then turn left onto NM 74 at the sign to San Juan Pueblo; the entrance is a mile farther. 852.4400

14 Abiquiu About an hour north of Santa Fe is a wonderland near the village of Abiquiu where the stony hills beside the road are

striated in shades of pink and yellow. The countryside may look familiar—this is Georgia O'Keeffe territory. When she visited Mabel Dodge Luhan in Taos in 1929, O'Keeffe wandered far and wide and discovered the hills here. She later stayed at the nearby **Ghost Ranch** (see below), then similar to a dude ranch. O'Keeffe began spending summers painting in the area and later bought two places of her own. Her home in the hilltop village of Abiquiu (685.4539), looking much the same as it did when she lived here, is now open for tours to groups of six people on Tuesday, Thursday, and Friday on the hour from 10AM to 3PM. An exterior tour is given Thursday at 4PM to groups of 15. There's an admission charge, and reservations are required.

The **Ghost Ranch Study and Conference Center** (Hwy 84, 685.4333), whose name is derived from the tale of the female spirits who allegedly haunted the place, crying over a man who was murdered there, hosts year-round workshops in dozens of subjects from the arts to paleontology (see "Ghost Ranch" on page 76). The center is open daily to the public; no admission charge.

In the old days, the skull of a steer marked the turnoff to the dirt road to **Ghost Ranch.** Nowadays there's a sign bearing the outline of a steer's skull. Turn onto this bumpy dirt road and be patient for several hundred yards. Suddenly it will open onto a broad meadow surrounded by stunning mesa walls in purples and ochers and golden stripes. The sight is magnificent, and there are several hiking trails from which to choose.

Lourdes Chapel, San Juan Pueblo

JOHN DEL GAIZO

Nearby is the **Ghost Ranch Living Museum** (Hwy 84, no phone), a small zoo that presents indigenous animals in their natural settings. Most of the animals were saved after being wounded by bullets or automobiles, and many are later returned to the wild. The museum is open daily and a donation is requested.

♦ Take Hwy 84-285 to Española, then take Hwy 84 (the road to Chama) for about 20 miles

15 Ojo Caliente While many people flock to the **Santuario de Chimayó** (see page 72) to try the holy dirt, others prefer to be healed at **Ojo Caliente Mineral Springs** (off Hwy 285, 583.2233), which is billed as North America's oldest health resort. In the 1500s Cabeza de Vaca, a Spanish explorer, wrote: "The greatest treasure that I found these strange people to possess are some hot springs which burst out at the foot of a mountain that gives evidence of being an active volcano. So powerful are the chemicals contained in this water that the inhabitants have a belief that they were given to them by their Gods. These springs I have named Ojo Caliente." Five bubbling mineral springs contain iron, soda, lithium, sodium, and arsenic. A health resort at the springs offers mineral baths in the waters, as well as massages and herbal wraps. The village of Ojo Caliente (Spanish for "hot eye") has an adobe mission, general store, and three cafes surrounded by desert slopes. Once a mecca for the sick, this region is now more of a place to go and relax. The proprietors claim the mineral waters offer the best results if you drink them as well as bathe in them in order to eliminate excess acids from the body. ♦ Off Hwy 285, about 35 minutes north of Española

16 Taos via New Mexico Highway 68 The most direct route to Taos from Santa Fe follows NM 84-285 to Española—where low-rider vehicles abound—and continues north on NM 68. The trip takes roughly 1.5 hours. About 40 miles into the drive, just past Velarde, the highway enters the twisting canyon of the Rio Grande and becomes a scenic drive that climaxes when it rises out of the canyon and Taos Mountain suddenly becomes visible on the plateau above. In late summer, fresh fruit stands along the way offer peaches, chile, and corn; in autumn they sell locally grown apples and pumpkins. The return drive is beautiful late in the day when the sun turns the river to molten gold.

Along the way, stop for something to eat at the inexpensive **Embudo Station** (NM 68, 852.4707)—watch for the short bridge across the river. Open 15 April through 15 November, this place offers first-rate American and imaginative New Mexican

food outdoors under tall cottonwood trees beside the river. Lunch or dinner here makes a relaxing getaway from the Santa Fe scene.

Off NM 68 in Dixon is **La Chirapada Winery** (751.1311), one of New Mexico's leading wineries. The tasting room is open to visitors Monday through Saturday from 10AM to 5:30PM, Sunday from noon to 5PM.

17 High Road to Taos Consider using this roadway to Taos. It takes approximately two hours to cover the same distance as the direct route because the second half is spent on looping switchbacks in the mountains. On the plus side, it passes through some old-fashioned mountain villages that have a rugged appeal of their own. At Española, take NM 76 (there's a flashing light at the intersection), which leads to Chimayó (for more on this famous weaving center, see page 72), then northward to the village of Truchas, across from the beautiful Truchas Peaks, which are covered with snow much of the year. In winter, if the roads are clear but snow is still on the ground, Truchas, with its snowy fields, wooden fences, and grazing horses in the foreground and the peaks behind, is a photographer's dream (but beware of unfriendly dogs). Farther north in Las Trampas is a Spanish Colonial church built in 1763. At the village of Peñasco, take NM 75 east for a few miles, then go north on NM 518. This section passes through Carson National Forest, whose pristine woods will soothe the spirit. The road joins up with NM 68, the main road into Taos, just south of town. An alternate beginning to the high road out of Santa Fe is to take NM 503 east from Pojoaque and connect with NM 76 at Chimayó. Many people prefer to take the high road up to Taos and use the more direct Rio Grande route on the way back to Santa Fe.

An expedition of paleontologists led by Dr. Edwin Colbert in 1947 discovered a remarkable example of the Coelophysis dinosaur in the Triassic Chinle Formation near Ghost Ranch.

Ojo Caliente Mineral Springs is the only natural hot springs center in the world boasting five different geothermal waters.

Chalchihuitl is the Indian word for turquoise. Chemically the stone is a phosphate of aluminum that carries small quantities of copper and iron, from which its color comes, and a green mineral—variscite.

Restaurants/Clubs: Red   **Hotels:** Blue

Shops/♥ Outdoors: Green   **Sights/Culture:** Black

Ghost Ranch

"I wish you could see what I see out the window," Georgia O'Keeffe wrote her New York friend Arthur Dove from her home at **Ghost Ranch,** "the earth pink, and yellow cliffs to the north—the full pale moon about to go down in an early morning lavender sky behind a very long beautiful tree-covered mesa. A feeling of much space, I wish you could see it."

The breathtaking landscape around this 20,000-acre educational center remains just as O'Keeffe described it: gargantuan mesa-topped canyons in shades of red, purple, and ocher—shaped like chimneys, space ships, and dinosaur toes. Reigning supreme in the distance is flat-topped **Pedernal Mountain,** immortalized by O'Keeffe in her paintings. At night the ranch glows under an ebony blanket of stars and a rising yellow moon.

Diverse programs are offered: Artists can take workshops in painting, pottery, weaving, silversmithing, folk art, crystalline glazing, still photography, and creative techniques with a camcorder. Literary types can delve into travel writing, journal writing, poetry, storytelling, and playwriting. Nature lovers explore the wilderness on backpacking, hiking, horseback-riding, and camping day- and weeklong trips led by guides and naturalists. For those who want to enjoy the landscape on their own, Pedernal is a challenging hike, but there are easier treks right on **Ranch-Chimney Rock** and **Kitchen Mesa.** Both curve slowly

upward to spectacular views. Wandering among cacti and desert wildflowers, inhaling the sweet sagebrush, and marveling at a big blue dome overhead is a perfect activity unto itself.

And there are also unusual intellectual opportunities, such as working with environmental designers to build a solar home, studying Spanish roots of New Mexican culture, or playing Bach as part of a chamber orchestra. Another special aspect of the center is its seminars on spirituality: Although it is the **National Adult Study Center** of the Presbyterian Church, **Ghost Ranch** is nevertheless committed to offering perspectives from all religions and beliefs.

Another aspect of the center is its involvement in local and national organizations. Children from neighboring towns and villages are given swimming lessons, some of the land is leased out to local farmers for livestock grazing, and paleontology sites have been designated National Historic Landmarks for the scientific importance of the fossils that have been excavated—notably the Coelophysis dinosaur. The center's museums—**Florence Hawley Ellis Museum of Anthropology** and **Ruth Hall Museum of Paleontology**—showcase important artifacts unearthed at the ranch.

For more information, contact **Ghost Ranch Conference Center** (HC 77, Box 11, Abiquiu, New Mexico 87510-9601, 685.4333; fax 685.4519. The center is wheelchair accessible.

MICHAEL STORRINGS

Bests

Pat Harbour

Owner/Innkeeper, Adobe Abode Bed & Breakfast Inn, Santa Fe

From March to the end of November, the outdoor **Trader Jack's Flea Market** right under the **Santa Fe Opera** (also a BEST). Go early for the best buys. . . then go later in case you missed something. Ranks right up there with the best flea markets in the country.

Watching the golden glow of sunset from the **Rooftop Cantina**—be sure to get a table on the outside edge to look west down **Water Street;** or sunset from the very top of **La Fonda** in the bell tower.

An obvious choice: dinner at 8PM Saturday at **Santacafe** for the best dining experience in town. I also like **Geronimo** on a weeknight (their kitchen is not as good when overtaxed with too many people).

A nighttime stroll to the Plaza to get ice cream at **Häagen-Dazs.** The spectacle of hordes of Santa Fe teenagers just hanging out on the corner on Friday and Saturday nights is not to be missed.

Biking the "ridge" from way out **Tano Road** to **Highway 285,** continuing east the length of **Circle Drive** to **Bishops Lodge Road.** Turn north and bike the curvy length of Bishops Lodge to **Tesuque.**

At least a half-day at **Bandelier National Monument**—such a glorious spot filled with history (home to the Anasazi cliff dwellings from years ago), fabulous hiking (go to the waterfall and climb the 210 feet of ladders to the **Ceremonial Cave**), and a sense of spirituality that's like nowhere else in Santa Fe. When the wind blows down the ancient rock crevasses, you can actually *feel* the Anasazi Indians all around you.

A leisurely drive to **Chimayó**—of course to see the **Santuario** which is very special—but also to drop by **Centinela Traditional Arts** on the road to Las Truchas. The Trujillo family, now in its tenth generation, has the very best rugs in the area, and it's always a treat to talk to them about weaving.

Several hours at the **Museum of International Folk Art,** with a briefer stop at the **Museum of Indian Arts and Culture** to see their incredible pot collection.

Drinks and a game of pool at **Evangelo's.**

If you only see one gallery, let it be **Nedra Matteucci's Fenn Galleries** on Paseo de Peralta. Do not miss the sculpture garden in the back. Another tasty gallery, when you're tired of Native American art, is **Dreamtime Gallery** on **Canyon Road** (Australian aboriginal art), particularly when they're having an open house on Friday night with live didgeridoo playing.

Friday night after dinner at **El Farol**—try to sit at a table of locals (it shouldn't be hard, the place is always packed) as most people here are very friendly and will fill you in on Santa Fe gossip. The music is fun, too.

A Sunday afternoon in **Madrid** shopping.

Drinks and popcorn at the **Pink Adobe** bar. Don't get too full before going across the alley for steak dunigan, BY FAR the best dish on the menu.

Shopping your heart out in the **Plaza** area for about two days and just before the credit cards explode, heading up Canyon Road for some *real* shopping.

The International **Albuquerque Balloon Fiesta** the first two weeks of October. Take it from one who collects "events," this is superb, spectacular, and definitely a once-in-a-lifetime experience. Do not get there any later than 6AM to have an easier time parking, to eat Indian fry bread smothered with honey in the darkness and cold, and to watch the sun come over the **Sandia Mountains** and illuminate the balloons. You'll be awestruck!

A coffee and sweet at **Downtown Subscriptions**—not downtown at all, it's at the corner of Garcia and Acequia Madre. You could hang out here all day (many locals and movie stars do) and be satisfied.

Elizabeth Kay

Author, *Chimayo Valley Traditions*/Artist, Pythea Productions

Pink Adobe Dragon Room Bar—Casual and cozy atmosphere for an early evening drink, especially tempting on chilly evenings when the fireplace is lit.

Ten Thousand Waves—A spa of outdoor public and private hot tubs with multiple massage facilities. It doesn't get any more elegant and indulgent than this.

Stroll through **Shidoni Sculpture Gardens** or the seasonal **Trader Jack's Flea Market** off of Highway 285.

Bandelier National Park—Take your pick of trails: prehistoric Indian cliff dwellings, three miles and two waterfalls to the **Rio Grande,** a knee-buckling ladder climb to the kiva, a long day's there-and-back hike to the stone lions.

Ojo Caliente Mineral Springs—Hot and healthy lithia, soda, iron, and arsenic waters for soaking and drinking. Public and private pools and tubs. Massage facilities. Lovely old hotel with plumpy sofas and solid food. Located in the peaceful middle of nowhere.

Ghost Ranch Study and Conference Center—Not only Georgia O'Keeffe's spirit haunts these multihued cliffs. Indians gave the place its name long before her arrival and departure. Very beautiful, very intense. Wear a hat.

El Santuario de Chimayó—Very early in the morning before tourists arrive and shops open. The spiritual heart and soul of Northern New Mexico.

High Road to Taos—There is an unwritten rule that everyone who gets to Santa Fe must go on to Taos. The High Road to Taos follows the pilgrimage route to **Chimayó,** then climbs to the mountain villages of **Truchas, Las Trampas, Peñasco,** and on to Taos.

D.H. Lawrence Ranch—Frieda had D.H. buried here under mounds of cement topped with a stone eagle so that Mable Dodge wouldn't steal the ashes.

Rio Grande Gorge Bridge—Acrophobics may want to avoid the cliff-edged road along the steep north end of the gorge.

Taos

Beautiful as the setting of Santa Fe is, the natural location of Taos may surpass it. Upon arriving in Taos in the 1920s, D.H. Lawrence wrote: "I think the skyline of Taos the most beautiful of all I have ever seen in my travels round the world." The British writer made an isolated cabin in the region his home for several years, and his ashes are part of a shrine that's open to the public.

The drive to Taos almost equals the destination. Forty miles north of Santa Fe, at the apple-growing village of Velarde, the highway winds into the canyon of the **Rio Grande**. For 20 miles it twists and turns beside the river, climbing at last onto a broad plateau, with the majestic hulk of **Taos Mountain** looming in the distance. At the base of this brooding peak ancient Indians built the spectacular **Taos Pueblo** around 1450, more than 150 years before the Spanish settled Santa Fe. The pueblo, two large adobe apartment buildings five stories high, is a stunning creation of rooms, ladders, doorways, and primitive beauty. Spanish settlers led by Fray Pedro de Miranda established a colony about two miles from the pueblo in 1617, which evolved into the modern Taos. The 1680 Pueblo Revolt against Spanish occupation led to the flight or death of most of the Spanish settlers, but others returned to the area when an uneasy peace was restored in the early 18th century.

Like Santa Fe, Taos was discovered by Anglo artists from the east in the late 19th and early 20th centuries, and such painters as Irving Couse, Oscar Berninghaus, Robert Henri, and Ernest Blumenschein, among others, formed the basis of an art colony devoted to renderings of the landscape and the Indians. After New York socialite Mabel Dodge Sterne moved to Taos in 1918, divorced her painter husband, and married a Taos Indian, Tony Lujan, she played host in an adobe mansion (now a bed-and-breakfast), which she built into a cultural salon that attracted D.H. Lawrence, Georgia O'Keeffe, Ansel Adams, and others.

Taos today is a tidy little town of about 4,500 residents that easily could be tucked into one of Santa Fe's side pockets. It, too, looks like a Mexican town, all brown and beige adobes that are one and two stories high and filled with galleries and shops. And like Santa Fe, Taos is fighting the battle of controversial modernization.

Because of its size, Taos can be explored casually in a single day or more extensively in two. The central **Plaza** has been taken over by T-shirt shops, but it's still a nice place to sit and watch the world go by. Taos has only two main streets. On **Kit Carson Road**, which runs east from the Plaza, is the **Total Arts Gallery**, the town's first-rate representational gallery, and the **Kit Carson Home**, former residence of the Indian fighter, now an Old West museum. On the north-south artery, **Paseo del Pueblo**, is the **Stables Gallery**, housed in an old adobe in which the most puzzling unsolved murder mystery in Taos—the beheading of a wealthy rogue named **Arthur Manby**—took place in 1929; the **Fenix Gallery**, which shows the best in abstract art; and **Trading Post Cafe**, a four-star restaurant serving continental and American dishes with exquisite taste in all respects. For lunch try the **Bent Street Deli and Café**; for the tastiest New Mexican fast food anywhere, stop at **Mantes' Chow Cart**. And be sure to walk over to **Ledoux Street**, a center of the original art colony, and browse the **Harwood Foundation**, which has the finest collection of the early Taos painters.

1 Plaza Like most Hispanic towns, Taos grew out from a central plaza, which makes it the natural starting point for any tour. Once a meeting place for Indian, Spanish, and Anglo traders, this is now the modern equivalent—T-shirt, souvenir, and moccasin heaven. A few quality shops and galleries are located on its perimeter. The center of the plaza is paved in brick. A large cross is dedicated to the men of Taos County in Battery H of the 200th Coast Artillery Regiment who died in the battle of Bataan and its aftermath. A bandshell shaped like a gazebo is off to one side, and tree-shaded benches allow for people watching.
♦ Between Paseo del Pueblo Sur and Camino de la Placita

2 La Fonda de Taos $ This late-1930s hotel dominates the south side of the Plaza. The lobby decor exudes tradition: Elaborately costumed *muñecas* (fancy Spanish dolls, often ceramic, for display only), toreador "suits of lights," a bullfighter's cape emblazoned with an image of *Nuestra Señora de Guadalupe* (Our Lady of Guadalupe), and old Navajo blankets. The walls are absolutely packed with dozens of paintings representing the Taos art community from the early days to the present. Most of the 24 rooms are small and charming, yet despite the vibrant Southwest decor, show signs of the passing years. For a fee nonguests can see a locked side room that contains erotic paintings by

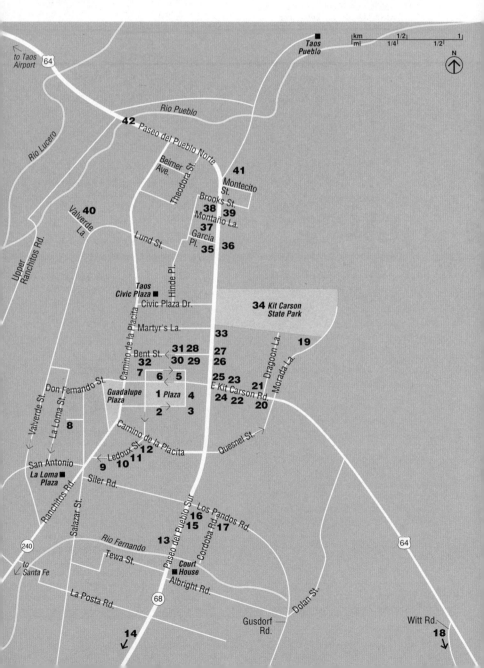

D.H. Lawrence, which were banned in England in 1929. There's no restaurant. ◆ 108 South Plaza (between East Plaza and West Plaza). 758.2211

3 Maison Faurie Antiquités Looking to buy a dentist's drill from 1900, an instruction booklet from a turn-of-the-century embalming school, or a stethoscope used by a doctor who's long dead? Then this is definitely the place to shop. Owner Robert R. Faurie, who hails from France, has been in business here since 1980, collecting and selling anything that strikes his fancy—and just about everything does. In addition to cases filled with old medical objects are antique letter openers, inkwells, candlesticks, Art Deco lamps, straight razors, and a collection of US military wings from World Wars I and II large enough to supply a small air force. ◆ Daily. Cantu Plaza N (southeast of the Plaza). 758.8545

4 Ogelvie's Bar & Grille ★$$ The main attraction of this restaurant and piano bar is its second-floor location overlooking the Plaza. On sunny afternoons, people sometimes wait hours for a table on the large, open balcony. The menu is eclectic and is big on appetizers and finger foods, making it a good place to eat light (the quesadillas are the best in town). Entrées include stir-fry, charbroiled rib-eye steak, and shrimp Hawaiian (stir-fried with pineapple), as well as more local fare such as fajitas and *carne adovada* (barbecued beef marinated in chile sauce) chimichangas. ◆ American/New Mexican ◆ Daily lunch and dinner. 103/I East Plaza. 758.8866

The artists' colony in Taos got its start in 1898 with American artists Bert Phillips and Ernest Blumenschein, who were on their way to Mexico on a painting expedition when their wagon broke a wheel outside of town. Stranded long enough to discover the charm of Taos, they decided to stay, and their paintings lured other artists from the East Coast and Europe.

Restaurants/Clubs: Red   **Hotels:** Blue
Shops/ ❦ Outdoors: Green   **Sights/Culture:** Black

5 New Directions Gallery This modern gallery is owned by Cecelia Torres and often presided over by Ann Emory, a Taos native who remembers when Indian buckboards lined the Plaza, their horses tied to hitching posts. The Plaza's new direction is T-shirts, but this gallery stands out for its distinctive artwork. Displayed here is the abstract work of Taos artists such as Larry Bell, whose work has been acclaimed worldwide; Ted Egri, who makes modern sculpture; and Gloria Corbett, whose childlike paintings are inspired by such classic books as *The Magic Mountain* and classical music, including *Pictures at an Exhibition*. ◆ Daily. 107/B North Plaza (at Juar Largo La). 758.2771

6 Garden Restaurant ★$ Doors gaping wide right on the Plaza, this restaurant is under the same ownership as **El Patio de Taos** (see below) but has an ersatz feel aimed at the passing tourist parade. It calls itself a cheerful hometown place, and the decor, including fake greenery, could come from Anywhere, USA. So could most of the food. You can slake your hunger here, but the sandwiches, salads, and New Mexican and Italian dishes are unmemorable. ◆ American ◆ Daily breakfast, lunch, and dinner. 115 North Plaza (at Teresina La). 758.9483

7 El Patio de Taos ★★$$$ It is said that one wall of this building dates back to before the Spanish discovered Taos Valley. Today it houses a popular restaurant and bar with a stone fountain in the main dining room, located down a walkway at the northwest corner of the Plaza. In the 17th century the building held a **Taos Pueblo** trading post, and for 200 years the Spanish government used it for administrative offices. The ambitious menu has separate pages for New Mexican, Italian, and French cuisines, and the portions are large. The duck chimichanga is quite good, as are most of the more traditional New Mexican dishes. The continental fare is more erratic. ♦ New Mexican/Continental ♦ Daily lunch and dinner. 125 North Plaza (at Teresina La). 758.2121

8 La Posada de Taos $$ Tucked away on a quiet street of private adobe homes, yet just a few blocks from the Plaza, this charming bed-and-breakfast offers six guest rooms beautifully appointed with country antiques and sumptuous private baths. Nancy Brooks Swan, who formerly worked for the White House, decorated each room with a sense of humor, visible in everything from rawhide chairs to handmade quilts. Queen-sized beds, fireplaces, private entrances, and skylights add to the comfort. Husband Bill, a former Air Force fighter pilot, customizes activities for each guest, providing suggestions and maps on Taos's best nearby hiking, fishing, and ski trails. Both have their breakfast with guests, making for some wonderful conversation. Outdoor patios and gardens make this a most enchanting and relaxing haven. ♦ 309 Juanita La (off Manzanares). 758.8164 &

9 Harwood Foundation About 550 paintings, drawings, and sculptures by the early Taos artists are in the collection of this museum, often overlooked in favor of the better-known **Millicent Rogers Museum** (see page 92). Dating to 1923, this is the second-oldest museum in the state. It's located at the end of Ledoux Street—a center of the artistic community in the early days—next to the **Blumenschein House.** The first two-story building in Taos outside of **Taos Pueblo,** and the first to have electricity, it was a frequent gathering place for local artists when it was the home of Burt Harwood and Lucy Case Harwood. When Burt Harwood died in 1921, Lucy officially set up the foundation as a communal arts center. It has been operated by the **University of New Mexico** since 1935. A wide staircase leads to galleries on the second floor, where a major attraction is the 1932 oil *Winter Funeral* by Victor Higgins, which depicts a funeral in the village of Arroyo Hondo with Taos Mountain rising in the distance. Other works in the collection range from paintings by Ernest Blumenschein and Andrew Dasburg to such contemporary artists as Fritz Scholder and Larry Bell. ♦ Donation. M-Sa. 238 Ledoux St (at Ranchitos Rd). 758.3063

10 Blumenschein House Among the founders of the Taos art colony early in this century were Ernest and Mary Greene Blumenschein. They lived in this stunning Taos adobe built in 1797. The house (pictured at top right) is now a museum, which displays paintings by both Blumenscheins and their daughter, Helen, as well as those of other prominent Taos artists. The house has been kept much the way it was when the artists lived here; the furnishings are

COURTESY OF KIT CARSON HISTORICAL MUSEUM

a mix of rustic Taos furniture and European antiques, and the walls have been restored to the original adobe plaster. ♦ Donation. Daily. 222 Ledoux St (between Camino de la Placita and Ranchitos Rd). 758.0505

11 Navajo Gallery This is Taos painter R.C. Gorman's personal gallery. All those outlines of Indian women make their first home here. Name the medium, Gorman works in it: drawings, lithographs, silkscreens, bronzes, ceramics, paper casts. Gorman books and videos are also sold here. ♦ Daily. 210 Ledoux St (between Camino de la Placita and Ranchitos Rd). 758.3250

12 Collins-Pettit Gallery Among the highlights in Karen Pettit's fine gallery are sensual figure studies by Ron Barsano; lovely small albumen prints by Zoe Zimmerman that have an extraordinarily peaceful quality; colorful landscape and flower oil paintings by Robert Daughters; and monoprints of figures in landscapes by Joyce Stolaroff. ♦ Daily. 1 Ledoux St (at Camino de la Placita). 758.8068

13 Mantes' Chow Cart ★★★$ In the early 1970s Mantes Chacon started a food wagon on the Plaza (where **Ogelvie's Bar & Grille** now stands) from which he served tamales, *chalupas* (open-face tacos), and such. He later wheeled the cart around, found a permanent place, and in 1995, tore that down and completely rebuilt the restaurant. Today the simple indoor space sports light-blond wood walls, pale green formica tables, and a counter. Some of the concoctions are named after friends of Chacon: The Susie is a *chile relleno* (a whole green chile pod stuffed with cheese, breaded, and fried) rolled in a tortilla with beans and sour cream. The Lucero is even better—the same ingredients with meat added; it's a taste sensation. If the weather is nice, eat outdoors under shade trees on round stone tables, and in late summer and early fall you'll see, and smell, the fresh chiles being roasted a few feet away. Call ahead for orders to go or order from your car and drive around to the pick-up window. ♦ New Mexican ♦ M-Sa breakfast, lunch, and dinner. 402 Paseo del Pueblo Sur (between Tewa St and Siler Rd). 758.3632

14 Sagebrush Inn $$ This Pueblo Revival-style motel was one of the few tourist accommodations in Taos when it was built in 1929. Georgia O'Keeffe lived here for six months when she first arrived in New Mexico. Today the inn's shady interiors evoke the Taos of a bygone era. The 81 guest rooms are dimly lighted, cool, and romantic, and some have fireplaces. All are individually decorated with antiques that include original art by early-day Taos painters and authentic American Indian pottery and rugs. Guest facilities include a restaurant, tennis courts, a swimming pool, and hot tubs. ♦ 1508 Paseo del Pueblo Sur (2.5 miles south of the Plaza). 758.2254 ᴅ

15 Shougun Restaurant ★★$$ Hidden in a nondescript shopping strip across the road from **Mantes' Chow Cart,** this new restaurant with dark wood walls and stained-glass windows is a testimony to the sophisticated eating tastes of Taoseños. The sushi bar offers an excellent variety of Japanese favorites, from *maguro* (tuna) to *unagi* (broiled eel) to monkfish liver, all flown in fresh three times a week from Los Angeles. Other Japanese fare includes vegetables with *udon* noodles; chicken, beef, and salmon teriyaki; and beef sukiyaki. There's also an extensive Chinese menu: fried and stewed prawns, sesame beef, hot spicy chicken, crispy duck, and bean curd in brown sauce. ♦ Japanese/Chinese ♦ M-Sa lunch and dinner. 321/C Paseo del Pueblo Sur (between Albright and Los Pandos Rds). 758.7645

Lamberts

16 Lambert's ★★★★$$$ This popular restaurant run by two generations of the Lambert family is set in a remodeled Victorian house with no frills—just plain white walls in several dining rooms. Some tables have a view of Taos Mountain. The food is excellent—the menu changes according to what's available fresh from the market—and in an unusually

thoughtful arrangement, can be ordered in full or petite sizes. Prices of the petites are quite reasonable, and, combined with a shared appetizer, the portions are likely to satisfy. An appetizer of grilled shrimp with mango salsa is a treat to treasure and quite sizable. The pepper-crusted lamb with garlic pasta is also good, as is the shepherd's pie. The service is casually impeccable and never intrusive. Good California wines are available, and some are surprisingly inexpensive. ♦ Continental ♦ M-F, Su lunch and dinner; Sa dinner. Reservations recommended. 309 Paseo del Pueblo Sur (at Los Pandos Rd). 758.1009

17 Casa de las Chimeneas $$ On a shady lane within walking distance of the Plaza, this bed-and-breakfast has four units with private baths; the largest is a suite with a separate living room, two fireplaces, and a study containing a library of local-interest books and magazines. The guest rooms are filled with antique furniture and little extra touches—like sheepskin mattress pads—and open onto a terrace and tastefully landscaped gardens. There's also a hot tub on the property. ♦ 405 Cordoba Rd (at Los Pandos Rd). 758.4777

Old Taos Guesthouse

18 Old Taos Guesthouse $$ After years as world travelers, skiers, and bartenders, owners Tim and Leslie Reeves decided to renovate a 150-year-old adobe hacienda into a lovely inn set on 7.5 acres. Tim's talent as a furniture maker is evident in each of the eight cozy rooms (all with private baths) adorned with handwrought wooden beds, whimsical dressers, and oversized chairs. Leslie's decorating flair is obvious in the hand-carved doors and bed frames, stained-glass windows, lighted *nichos* (small alcoves), and skylights over beds for stargazing. Less than two miles from Taos Plaza, the property has spectacular views of Taos Valley, gardens, and an inviting outdoor hot tub. Healthy breakfasts consist of oatmeal, granola, homemade breads, and muffins. 1028 Witt Rd (a half-mile from Kit Carson Rd). 758.5448, 800/758.5448

19 Mabel Dodge Luhan House $$ Back in 1918, when artist Maurice Sterne, who was painting Indians in Taos, urged his wife Mabel to join him, he could hardly know what he was setting in motion. Mabel was a prominent socialite in New York who liked to keep a salon of creative types around her. When she moved to Taos, she quickly became the center of its artistic world. Mabel stayed in the **Arthur Manby House** (see **Stables Gallery** on page 87) while renovating and adding onto a 200-year-old adobe for her own use. She courted, and was courted by, a tall Taos Indian named Tony Lujan. Sterne returned to the East and Mabel, divorced, married Lujan, despite the fact that he already had a wife at the **Taos Pueblo.** (Mabel's friends back East could never get the hang of pronouncing a *j* like an *h,* so Mabel spelled her new name Luhan.) When she moved into her renovated house—a three-story, 22-room hacienda—in 1922, she made it a gathering point for celebrities the world over. She induced D.H. Lawrence to move to Taos and supplied the Lawrences with a ranch out in the mountains. Lawrence painted the windows of the second-story bathroom in the "Big House," as it was called, which are still visible. Mabel invited Georgia O'Keeffe to visit from New York in 1929. After two summers, O'Keeffe could no longer abide Mabel's company, but she fell in love with New Mexico and never willingly spent another summer anywhere else, eventually making it her permanent home after husband Alfred Stieglitz died. Willa Cather and Aldous Huxley also came to visit at Mabel's house, and the outdoor patio was once the scene of a lecture by Carl Jung.

The huge house has adobe archways, vigas, *latillas* (wooden ceiling slats), flagstone patios, and pigeon roosts. The gates in the surrounding adobe wall were part of the original **San Francisco de Asis Church** in Ranchos de Taos. After Mabel died in 1962, the hacienda was purchased by actor Dennis Hopper, who lived here while filming *Easy Rider.* The house is now a bed-and-breakfast and retreat/conference center. Visitors can stay in **Mabel's Suite,** which still contains her bed, or in **Tony's Bedroom.** There's also the **O'Keeffe Room,** where Georgia stayed for a time; the **Cather Room,** where the novelist visited; and **Spud's Room,** where Spud Johnson, Mabel's secretary, worked. You also can visit a glass room where Mabel sunbathed in the nude. Some guest rooms have shared bathrooms. A guest house nearby has private baths and fireplaces in each room. ♦ 242 Morada La (off E Kit Carson Rd). 758.9456, 800/846.2235; fax 751.0431

19 Lumina Gallery Right next to Mabel's house is a beautiful, tree-shaded, multitiered adobe with mullioned windows that was the home of Victor Higgins, one of the most experimental of the early Taos painters. He also once ran for mayor of Taos. Felicia Ferguson, descendant of an old Taos family, and photographer Chuck Henningsen bought the Higgins house in 1981 and turned it into the most gorgeous gallery in town. Art is displayed on the walls and tables as it would be in someone's home. Henningsen's technically intriguing photographs—many of them symbolic, ghostlike montages—are also on display, as are photographs by Ansel Adams and André Kertész. Most of the artists represented have been working at their craft for the last 25 years in New Mexico. A sculpture garden displays work from around the world. ♦ Daily. 239 Morada La (off E Kit Carson Rd). 758.7282

20 Hirsch Fine Art Here's a gallery that looks like a museum, owing to its serene ambience in a historic adobe home. Once owned by Irving Couse, who came to Taos in 1902 to paint the Taos Pueblo Indians, the home has been beautifully restored and decorated with antiques by gallery owner Jay Rosenbaum. It is the only gallery that exclusively shows historic Southwest art by artists found in major national museums: Joseph Henry Sharp, E. Martin Hennings, Gustave Baumann, and Gene Kloss are among his favorites. Watercolors, etchings, lithographs, and drawings are available. ♦ Daily noon-5PM. 146/B E Kit Carson Rd (between Quesnel St and Paseo del Pueblo Sur). 758.2478

20 Mission Gallery In 1962 Ivan and Rena Rosequist moved from New York to Taos and opened this gallery in a building that was once home to painter Joseph Sharp. (His fellow painter, Irving Couse, lived next door.) The Rosequists represented Andrew Dasburg from the time he was 75 until his death at 92, and Howard Cook, who was 60 at the time, until his death many years later. The gallery, still run by Rena, now shows aquatints by Doel Reed, watercolors by Mary Hoeksema, and photographs by Van Deren Coke and Eliot Porter, among others. ♦ M-Tu, Th-Su. 138 E Kit Carson Rd (between Quesnel St and Paseo del Pueblo Sur). 758.2861

"No man who has seen the women, heard the bells, or smelled the piñon smoke of Taos will ever be able to leave."

—Kit Carson,
Indian fighter and Taos resident for 42 years

It has been said that the combined areas of Taos and Santa Fe contain more art galleries than Paris, France.

21 Casa Benavides Bed and Breakfast Inn
$$ Many people consider this place, just a block from the Plaza, the finest bed-and-breakfast in Taos. Most of the 30 rooms are spacious; all have private baths, are furnished in Southwestern motifs with a different emphasis in each room, and feature antique and handmade furnishings, kivas, and down comforters. The accommodations are in a sprawling compound of restored historic buildings, and two rooms in the house down the block where the owners grew up. There is a hot tub on the premises. The staff is friendly, and owners Barbara and Tom McCarthy make sure that their guests are well fed. Breakfast includes homemade granola, yogurt, fruit, muffins, eggs, tortillas, salsa, pancakes or waffles, and coffee. In the afternoon, tea and home-baked cake or pastries are served. ♦ 137 E Kit Carson Rd (between Dragoon La and Paseo del Pueblo Norte). 758.1772 &

22 Total Arts Gallery Six rooms strung out in railroad-car style and separated by adobe archways make up the most agreeable representational gallery in town. Owner Harold Geller, who hails from Toronto, began the gallery in 1969 off a grassy courtyard and added more rooms as people left the adjoining spaces. His humanistic sensibility permeates the works shown. The variety of human personality shines through every painting, whether they are figure studies, still lifes, or landscapes. Each small room has its own feel, yet they are all linked by a unifying taste, from the serene oil figures by Milt Kobayshi, to the more "hip" oil figures of Kim English, to the strong still lifes of Joan T. Potter, to the semiabstract landscapes of Teruko T. Wilde, Gay Patterson, and Ovanes Berberian, to the nudes of Sherrie McGraw, the rich oil portraits by David A. Leffel, and the Mexican pastels of Albert Handell. ♦ Daily. 122/A E Kit Carson Rd (between Quesnel St and Paseo del Pueblo Sur). 758.4667

The name Taos is believed to be an adaptation of the Tiwa Indian word, *towih,* meaning "red willow." It was first recorded in history by Juan Belarde, Secretary to the Governor, Juan de Oñate, in 1598.

Restaurants/Clubs: Red   Hotels: Blue
Shops/♥ Outdoors: Green   Sights/Culture: Black

22 Taos Book Shop The oldest bookshop in New Mexico (it was founded in the 1940s), this store has the feel of an extended home library, complete with a few chairs. Under the current owner, Taos native Deborah Sherman, it specializes in Southwestern books and out-of-print titles, and Spanish and Indian music tapes. There's a separate room full of children's books. ♦ Daily. 122/D E Kit Carson Rd (between Quesnel St and Paseo del Pueblo Sur). 758.3733

22 Caffe Tazza ★★$ Bob Dylan or Joni Mitchell is likely to be playing on the tape deck when you enter this place, the best feature of which is an outdoor patio beside a grassy courtyard. The menu offers homemade soups and locally made tamales as well as assorted coffee drinks and desserts. Live entertainment is provided on weekend evenings. ♦ M-Th breakfast and lunch; F-Su breakfast, lunch, and dinner. 122 E Kit Carson Rd (between Quesnel St and Paseo del Pueblo Sur). 758.8706

22 El Rincón Trading Post Also known as "The Original Trading Post" (there's one in every city in New Mexico), this place is filled with fine Indian crafts and jewelry, some of it Old Pawn, and all sorts of Old West memorabilia. It really is original, dating back to 1909, when it was founded by Ralph Meyers, who came from Germany to become one of the first traders in the area. Meyers was a painter, furniture maker, weaver, Indian trader, and jack-of-all-trades who also taught jewelry making and pottery making to the Indians under WPA (Works Progress Administration). In his trading days he collected early Indian artifacts; many are on display, but not for sale, in a museum within the trading post. Meyers's wife still runs the well-stocked shop. ♦ Daily. 114/A E Kit Carson Rd (between Quesnel St and Paseo del Pueblo Sur). 758.9188

22 El Rincón $$ A 12-room bed-and-breakfast right beside the trading post goes by the same name and is run by Meyers's daughter, Nina, and Paul Castillo. Each guest room is furnished differently: the **Pioneer Room** has a Franklin stove and is decorated with a Winchester rifle and buffalo hides; the **Yellow Bird Deer Room** is brightened by Indian pottery and beadwork; the **Paisley Room** has Oriental rugs, teak woodwork, and a Balinese goddess of fertility giving her blessing over the queen-sized bed. All have private baths;

ten have fireplaces, and five have whirlpools. You can't get more into the heart of Taos—or its ancient spirit—than this place. ♦ 114/B E Kit Carson Rd (between Quesnel St and Paseo del Pueblo Sur). 758.4874 &

COURTESY OF KIT CARSON HISTORICAL MUSEUM

23 Kit Carson Home No name blankets the region more than that of this renowned frontiersman, scout, hunter, soldier, and Indian fighter. The old home in which he lived during his years in Taos is now a museum, and the street it sits on—the second largest in Taos—bears his name; the park in which he is buried is also named after him, and tens of thousands of acres of surrounding greenery are known as the Carson National Forest.

A native of Kentucky, Carson ran off when he was 17 with a group of fur traders headed for Santa Fe. Adopting Taos as his spiritual home in 1826, he bought this 1825 12-room adobe (pictured above) in 1843 as a wedding present for his bride, Josefa Jaramillo. Carson and his family lived here for 25 years, though he was often away months at a time fighting battles and blazing trails from New Mexico to California. In 1868 Carson and his wife died within a month of each other. Three of the rooms in the museum are furnished much the way they would have been back then. Other rooms include gun exhibits and mountain-man lore. ♦ Admission. Daily. 113 E Kit Carson Rd (between Dragoon La and Paseo del Pueblo Norte). 758.0505

24 Brooks Indian Shop In Margery Hanisee's modern Indian shop, almost all the work is signed by the artists. Fine pieces by Julian Lovato of **Santo Domingo Pueblo** are the standout in the jewelry case. Black pottery made by the grandchildren of Maria Martinez is another highlight. Also featured are intricate black-and-white Acoma pots by Geraldine Sandia and **Jemez Pueblo** pots by Lucy Lewis and her daughters, Emma and Delores. Drums and kachinas are also on display. ♦ Daily Memorial Day-Labor Day; M-Sa the rest of the year. 108/G E Kit Carson Rd (at Paseo del Pueblo Sur). 758.9073

25 Horse Feathers Almost everything that has do with the Old West can be found here, including hats (the store's specialty), old spurs, boots, books, playing cards, a Lone Ranger board game, Western movie memorabilia, and assorted junk. Owner Lindsey Enderby presides in a cowboy hat and a friendly Western smile, beneath a sign that says "Where the West Lives On." ♦ M-Sa. 109 E Kit Carson Rd (at Paseo del Pueblo). 758.7457

26 Taos Inn $$ A National Historic Landmark, parts of the building date to the 1600s, though it was renovated in the 1980s while retaining its historic charm. The lobby is a rustic orchestration of wood furniture, adobe archways, and walls adorned with rugs and artwork. The 40 guest rooms have the same Southwestern motif, with Indian-style wood-burning fireplaces; cable television brings guests into the late 20th century. Off the lobby is the **Adobe Bar,** a popular hangout for local artists, writers, and anyone else who wants to come. ♦ 125 Paseo del Pueblo Norte (between E Kit Carson Rd and Kit Carson State Park). 758.2233, 800/826.7466 &

Within the Taos Inn:

Doc Martin's ★★★★$$$ The home of Dr. Paul T. Martin from the 1890s to the early 1940s, today this is one of the city's best-known and best-loved restaurants. Repeatedly honored for its extensive wine list by *The Wine Spectator* (the wines are also available for purchase in the inn's wine shop), this dining spot also offers friendly service and a selection of excellent New Mexican food and continental specialties, including seafood and game dishes. Chef Patrick Lambert composes his original, interesting dishes by juxtaposing tastes against one another. He works magic with Yucatán lime soup (seasoned chicken broth with chicken timbale and fried tortilla strips), the popular grilled venison medaillons with red-wine and cherry sauce, and chocolate mousse with roasted banana sauce and crème anglaise. ♦ New Mexican/Continental ♦ Daily breakfast, lunch, and dinner. Reservations recommended. 758.1977

27 Michael McCormick Gallery When the Japanese-born artist Michio Takayama was 60 years old, he came to Taos on a sketching trip from his home in California. He and his wife fell in love with the place and moved here. The internationally renowned Takayama continued painting his delicate personalized landscapes through his late eighties. His work is one of the two anchors of this gallery; the other is Taos painter Miguel Martinez, whose family has lived here for generations and whose stylized oils and oil pastels of women are rapidly gaining favor with collectors. His women—a blend of Hispanic, Indian, and occasionally Asian—are strong, colorful, and evocative, proffering a mysterious silence that is an agreeable challenge to live with. New to the gallery is J.D. Challenger, an artist internationally acclaimed for his sensitive renderings of the Native American Ghost Dance period. ◆ Daily. 106/C Paseo del Pueblo Norte (between E Kit Carson Rd and Kit Carson Park). 758.1372, 800/279.0879

28 Governor Bent House Charles Bent was a prominent 19th-century trader who ran wagon trains along the Santa Fe Trail. When the US moved into New Mexico in 1846, Bent was named its first governor. But many local Indians and Hispanics did not care for the idea of US rule, and on 19 January 1847, they surrounded Bent's house and began to pound down the doors. When Bent asked what they wanted, he was told, "We want your head, gringo!" And they got it. Bent's family was permitted to leave, but the governor was killed and scalped in his own home. Today the house is a museum displaying frontier memorabilia. It also contains a gift shop and a gallery of Western art. ◆ Donation. Daily. 117 Bent St (between Paseo del Pueblo Norte and Camino de la Placita). 758.2376

28 Brazos Fine Art Specializing in impressionist oils, watercolors, and bronze and alabaster sculptures that reflect the color, wildlife, and landscape of New Mexico, this gallery offers the works of a number of renowned artists. Ray Vinella for example, is considered one of the "Taos Six"—a group of artists given credit for the creation of the colorist style in Northern New Mexico. Isa Barnett has been painting the New Mexico landscape for over 50 years, and Mitch Caster is an Emmy–award-winning TV graphics designer who now does lovely oils of ballerinas. ◆ Daily. 119 Bent St (between Paseo del Pueblo Norte and Camino de la Placita). 758.0767

29 Bent Street Deli and Café ★★★$ This centrally located deli serves first-rate food indoors and on heated patios. The menu is relatively small but is original and tempting. The Reuben, filled with lean corned beef, may be the best this side of New York City. The Taos (sliced turkey, fresh green chile, bacon, and guacamole rolled in a flour tortilla) is excellent. The kitchen will also create a sandwich mixing any of 14 ingredients. Breakfast is served until 11AM, and hot dishes are also offered at dinnertime. A glass counter at the front features meats, cheeses, and desserts to go. The service is faultless. This is one of those places that clearly aims to please—and does. ◆ Deli ◆ M-Sa breakfast, lunch, and dinner. 120 Bent St (between Paseo del Pueblo Norte and Camino de la Placita). 758.5787

30 Moby Dickens A clever name has helped put this bookstore on the Taos map. Founded in 1984 by Art and Susan Bachrach, it's a good, complete shop that rambles on down a series of narrow rooms on two floors, while two cats sleeping in a basket seem bored with the notion of literature. Found here are Southwestern out-of-print titles, books on tape, and local Native American music. ◆ Daily. 124/A Bent St (between Paseo del Pueblo Norte and Camino de la Placita). 758.3050

30 G. Robinson, Old Prints and Maps The cartographer's art depicting every segment of the globe as it was recorded from the 16th to the 19th centuries hangs on the walls or is stacked for perusal at a nearby shop. Old-fashioned prints and engravings offer variety. Perhaps to mix it up with the real world, George Robinson also serves as manager of the **Dunn House** (no phone), the two-story complex that houses Robinson's store, **Moby Dickens, La Tierra Mineral Gallery,** and about 20 other shops and galleries. ◆ M-Sa. 124/D Bent St (between Paseo del Pueblo Norte and Camino de la Placita). 758.2278

30 La Tierra Mineral Gallery Wonderful fossils in which whole schools of fish have been captured in a single rock are among the many natural wonders in this small gem of a shop run by Ellen Ross. "Made in the U.S.A. 75,000,000 Years Ago," says a sign, and Mother Nature was doing good work even back then. Fossilized dinosaurs, sea scorpions, and mammoths' teeth are on display behind glass cases along with crystal formations and other natural treasures. This is a quiet, thoughtful resting place amid the myriad art galleries that surround it. ◆ M-Sa. 124/G Bent St (between Paseo del Pueblo Norte and Camino de la Placita). 758.0101

31 Apple Tree Restaurant ★★$$$ Located in a historic two-story house that's painted yellow with white trim like a country cottage, this restaurant is one of Taos's most reliable dining spots. The outdoor patio is dominated by an enormous apple tree, and the white-cheddar and green-chile hamburger is good, as is the chicken mole. The menu also features several vegetarian entrées. At lunchtime there's usually a guitar player on the patio. ◆ New Mexican ◆ Daily lunch and dinner. 123 Bent St (between Paseo del Pueblo Norte and Camino de la Placita). 758.1900

32 Tapas de Taos Café ★★$ Día de los Muertos (the Mexican Day of the Dead) is the decorative theme of this offbeat restaurant, with a collection of carved wooden skulls set row after row on the walls of one room in a 300-year-old adobe. There are also pleasant outdoor patios in front and back. The choice of tapas on the menu is limited, but very good. One dish is satisfactory for a light lunch, and two should do nicely at dinner, when, happily, the prices remain the same. The shrimp and vermicelli pancake is superb, and the fried calamari tasty. More robust Mexican dishes are also served. ◆ Tapas/Mexican ◆ Daily lunch and dinner; often closed 13 November-15 December, call ahead. 136 Bent St (between Paseo del Pueblo Norte and Camino de la Placita). 758.9670

33 Stables Gallery Once the grandest home in Taos, this lovely adobe building was the site of the city's most enduring murder mystery. In 1883 Englishman **Arthur Rochford Manby** came to New Mexico to get rich by speculating in ranching, mining, and other schemes in the newly opened American West. In 1898 he bought seven parcels of land just north of Kit Carson's home, and—trained as an architect—he designed and built a 19-room Spanish hacienda set in a square with three wings and stables in the rear. He laid out gardens in the English style, with sunken pools, trees, lawns bordered by roses, holly-hocks, and poppies. Within a few years it was filled with English furniture. In 1917, when New York socialite Mabel Dodge Sterne arrived in Taos, she rented the **Manby** house. When she built her own home two years later, **Manby** moved back in. On 3 July 1929, his body was found in one room of the house, decapitated—his head was found in an adjoining room. The head was so mutilated that some said it was not **Manby**, that he had procured a body and faked his own death to escape people who were after him. To this day the murder has not been solved. According to some, his ghost still appears from time to time in the middle patio.

The house is now home to the **Stables Art Gallery**, a gallery run by the Taos Art Association. The group was founded in 1952 by Emil Bisttram and other local artists to promote art and help the artists show their work. They purchased the house, turned it into a museum, and converted the stables into a gallery. The museum project soon became unmanageable and was discontinued, and the art center moved to the front of the house (the **Twining Weavers** shop is housed in the former stables; see below). In its early years the cooperative gallery existed to show the work of artists on the cutting edge who were denied space in the more conservative galleries in town. Today it hosts 10 shows annually and is open to any artist. Be sure to spend a few quiet moments in the lovely courtyard out back. ◆ Daily. 133 Paseo del Pueblo Norte (opposite Martyr's La, adjoining Kit Carson State Park). 758.2036

33 Twining Weavers The long, low adobe stables behind the **Manby** house that used to house the gallery are now home to a large shop that features weaving and contemporary crafts. The old adobe bricks peek through the outer walls in spots. Huge skeins of wool in many colors are visible from the courtyard as you approach. Inside, owner Sally Bachman plies her craft and shows her handwoven rugs, tapestries, and pillows, as well as work by other gallery artists in fiber, basketry, and clay. ◆ Daily. 135 Paseo del Pueblo Norte (behind the Stables Art Center). 758.9000

34 Kit Carson Memorial State Park A few steps north of the stables that house **Twining Weavers** is the entryway to this welcome green space in the middle of town. As you move into the park away from the road a sense of solitude overtakes you, and with the rims of the mountains visible in the distance, you can see why a settlement arose here. This land was once part of the grounds of the **Arthur Manby House.** Toward the rear is a cemetery where Kit Carson is buried next to his wife. An iron fence surrounds the simple grave of the Indian fighter, who died on 23 May 1868 at the age of 59. A number of his descendants who were also named Kit are buried nearby. In a far corner of the cemetery, almost unnoticeable, is the grave of Mabel Dodge Luhan, Taos's famous hostess, who died in 1962. Also here is the grave of Padre Antonio José Martinez, who was defrocked and excommunicated by Bishop Lamy in 1856 over religious differences. The padre, who reportedly helped spur the 1848 Taos Indian revolt, founded his own church and had his own followers until his death in 1867. Just outside the cemetery fence, for some reason, is the grave of **Arthur Manby,** where his body and head are reunited. ◆ Paseo del Pueblo Norte (between E Kit Carson Rd and Montaño La)

35 Brodsky Bookshop Taos abounds with visitors who come here to go skiing, hiking, hunting, and fishing. The best place for them to get their bearings is in this shop, which specializes in all sorts of three-dimensional and topographical maps of the region, as well as outdoor guides. It is also a solid all-purpose bookshop. ♦ Daily. 218 Paseo del Pueblo Norte (between Civic Plaza Dr and Garcia Pl). 758.9468

35 Patrick Dunbar A long rectangular enclave of grass divided by an unpainted boardwalk leads from the street to one of New Mexico's veteran antiques merchants. Old wagons, an adobe camel, and a gorgeous ornate garden swing fit only for the courting of a princess preside over the lawns. Stacked against the outside walls are antique Oriental rugs, old wooden cabinets, and architectural relics. Inside is a busy bazaar of rugs and antique treasures. ♦ Daily. 222 Paseo del Pueblo Norte (between Civic Plaza Dr and Garcia Pl). 758.2511

36 Fechin Institute Renowned painter **Nikolai Fechin** emigrated from Russia to Taos and became one of the leading lights of the village's art colony. Also an architect, **Fechin** designed and built this two-story house in 1928, long considered one of the marvels of adobe architecture. It contains hand-carved woodwork that combines Russian and Spanish traditions. The building, which contains **Fechin**'s own work and his art collection, is now used as a cultural and educational center. Tours are available. A new gift shop sells Russian lacquer boxes, amber necklaces and earrings, Marushka dolls, and Fechin posters and notecards. ♦ Admission. Tu-Su. 227 Paseo del Pueblo Norte (near Montaño La). 758.1710

Behind the Fechin Institute:

Fechin Inn $$ Located on the grounds of the **Fechin Institute**, this is the first new hotel to open in Taos in over a decade. **Nikolai Fechin**'s bold ornamental designs were echoed by the Morrelli Corporation to create many of the hand-carved doors and interior furnishings. The 85 spacious rooms, including 14 suites, offer armoires, Morrelli chairs, stone slab tables, and muted colors. Most have balconies or private patios, and some have gas fireplaces. Rocking chairs on the front porch, an outdoor hot tub that's excellent for star gazing, and a full-time massage therapist are just some of the other relaxing features of the hostelry. There's no

restaurant, but continental breakfast is served in the serene lobby. ♦ 758.1000, 800/811.2939; fax 982.6638 &

37 Fenix Gallery Named to conjure associations with the myth of the phoenix, this gallery represents 18 contemporary artists, all of whom live in Taos at least part of the year. The space is simple and bright, a no-nonsense place to show art; it's a must-see for serious collectors visiting the area. Gallery owner Judith Kendall says, "Anything original and new, particularly when it comes from the archetypal—that's what I respond to." Among the things she has responded to recently are the bold mixed-media creations of Ginger Mongiello, the abstract oils and ceramics of Lee Mullican, one of her best-known artists, and the expressionist oils of Alyce Frank, as well as the paintings of Earl Stroh, among the last of the old-time Taos "Modernists." ♦ Daily. 228/B Paseo del Pueblo Norte (at Montaño La). 758.9120

38 Michael's Kitchen $ Owned by the Ninneman family, this casual place is one of the more popular low-priced restaurants in Taos. The food, especially at dinnertime, is somewhat pedestrian—the hamburger with green chile is a bit greasy, and their version of a Reuben sandwich is made with ham, not corned beef. Still, there is usually a waiting line, and the breakfast items—eggs, pancakes, and waffles—are served all day. ♦ American/New Mexican ♦ Daily breakfast, lunch, and dinner. 304/C Paseo del Pueblo Norte (between Montaño La and Brooks St). 758.4178

39 Spirit Runner Gallery This gallery of Indian images, which is only open in the summer season (in the winter it becomes **Adventure Ski Rental and Ski Wear**) is owned by Ouray Meyers, who must be the only offspring of a German immigrant named after a Ute Indian chief. Ouray is the son of the late Ralph Meyers, who founded the **El Rincón Trading Post** (see page 84) back in 1909. A photo taken by Ralph of Walter Ufer and Tony Lujan picnicking with Mabel Dodge Luhan hangs on the wall. The most evocative work in this uneven gallery is by Ouray himself, who paints airbrushed watercolors of spirit runners, both human and equine. His most moving piece in the gallery is an all-white paper cast of an Indian woman gazing longingly at **Taos Pueblo** in the distance. You can't tell if she is leaving for good or coming home after a long absence; it makes you want to know. Ross Lampshire fashions evocative pottery with three-dimensional pueblo ruins set into the sides. ◆ Daily Apr-Oct. 303 Paseo del Pueblo Norte (between Montaño La and Brooks St). 758.1132

40 Orinda Bed & Breakfast $ This updated and enlarged adobe residence in a valley just outside of town, surrounded by pastures and woodlands, provides country-style peace and privacy within a 15-minute walk of the Plaza. The three guest accommodations, ranging from a single room with a queen-size bed to a large suite that can sleep up to six people, have private baths, kiva fireplaces, beamed ceilings, and plenty of Southwestern charm. A gourmet continental breakfast is served in a dining room decorated with Navajo rugs and paintings by local artists. Guests also have use of a living room with a library, fireplace, and media center. ◆ 461 Valverde La (off Valverde St, near Camino de la Placita). 758.8581

41 Van Vechten-Lineberry Taos Art Museum Edwin C. Lineberry long dreamed of building a museum in honor of his first wife, artist Duane Van Vechten. In 1994, this lifelong resident of Taos realized his goal by opening the doors of Taos's newest and most modern museum. Works in the permanent exhibit feature paintings by early Taos founders. Also here are paintings and drawings by Van Vechten, who studied at the Chicago Art Institute before moving to New Mexico in 1928 when she began her studies at the **New Mexico Museum of Art** at the **University of New Mexico** and with Taos artist Emil J. Bisttram. She lived and worked in Taos until her death in 1977. The 150 works of art are displayed in a beautiful mansion within a 10-acre walled park, now maintained by Lineberry and his wife, Novella.

◆ Admission. ◆ Tu-F 11AM-4PM; Sa-Su 1:30-4PM. 501 Paseo del Pueblo Norte (take the right fork at Camino del Pueblo intersection). 758.2690 ୧

42 Laughing Horse Inn $$ This 1887 adobe hacienda became the home of Spud Johnson when he arrived in Taos in 1924. A writer and satirist, Johnson worked as secretary to Mabel Dodge Luhan while publishing from this adobe, on a handset press, *The Laughing Horse Press,* a sheet of satirical and literary works of the time. When D.H. Lawrence came to town, Spud gave him a bed, and that was the start of his open-door policy. Georgia O'Keeffe, Gertrude Stein, and Alice B. Toklas came to visit; frequently on the premises was Santa Fe poet Witter Bynner, who was Johnson's partner in life. Today, this colorful, ramshackle inn offers four small rooms that have loft beds, six rooms with regular beds, two suites, and a penthouse. Only the penthouse and suites have private baths; the other guests share three bathrooms in the inn, although each room has a VCR and color TV set. There's a central hot tub and music and video libraries, and the whole place snuggles like a shaggy dog under shade trees on the banks of the Rio Pueblo. Across the road is an adobe double guest house (each with its own bathroom and fireplace) with redwood decks; one section sleeps four, the other six, and the door between them can be opened to accommodate a household of ten. Mountain bikes are available free for guests. There is no restaurant, but a full breakfast is served daily. ◆ 729 Paseo del Pueblo Norte (near Upper Ranchitos Rd). 758.8350, 800/776.0161; fax 751.1123

Bests

Bill Hemp
Author/Illustrator, *Taos Landmarks & Legends*

La Posada de Taos—A delightful bed-and-breakfast where hosts Bill and Nancy Swan make you feel really at home.

Hacienda de Martinez—Takes you back into the early history of Taos with a blacksmith shop, oxcarts, and rooms where a real family lived.

Millicent Rogers Museum—A wonderfully eclectic collection of jewelry, pottery, and artifacts beautifully displayed.

Taos off the beaten track—I love snowshoeing up the **Bull-of-the-Woods Trail** in **Taos Ski Valley.**

The best-known artist in Taos, R.C. Gorman, is Navajo. He moved there in 1968. "I came as a tourist and refused to leave," he says. "Taos is the most beautiful place I know."

Additional Highlights of Taos and Day Trips

Some of the best things to see and do on a visit to Taos are on the town's perimeter or farther afield in the surrounding countryside. A visit to **Taos Pueblo** is the prime emotional reason for coming to Taos. The pueblo can be visually breathtaking, illuminating in its historical context, and depressing in its moody mixture of pride and subjugation—all at the same time. **Taos Ski Valley** is 19 miles northeast and offers the most spectacular skiing in New Mexico, a challenge to world-class skiers as well as a safe haven for beginners. The largest ski area in New Mexico, Taos is the only place in the state with more visitors in winter than summer. The **Rio Grande Gorge Bridge**, where nature's handiwork and human ingenuity intersect between two steep cliffs, is sure to induce a moment of vertigo as well as awe at the sight of the gorge itself. A superb collection of Indian art is housed in the **Millicent Rogers Museum**. The church at **Ranchos de Taos**, one of the most painted and photographed in the world, will please any shutterbug.

The town of Taos is surrounded by **Carson National Forest**, a 1.5-million-acre expanse of pine, aspen, and Douglas-fir forest on the slopes of the **Sangre de Cristo Mountains**. Several roadless areas of the forest have been set aside as federally protected wilderness areas, including **Wheeler Peak**, the highest mountain in New Mexico at 13,161 feet, and the northern part of the vast,

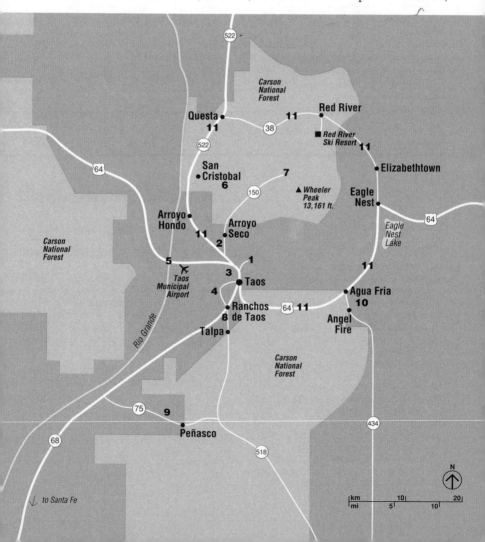

alpine **Pecos Wilderness**, which extends all the way to Santa Fe, Pecos, and Las Vegas. The **Enchanted Circle,** a loop drive of about 100 miles of scenic views in the forest, offers photo opportunities galore. Unpaved roads off the drive suitable for four-wheel-drive travel into the forest expand touring, mountain biking, and hiking possibilities. The area also includes **Picuris Pueblo,** the smallest pueblo in the state, and **Angel Fire Resort,** a ski area with less advanced slopes than those at the Taos ski basin.

Taos Pueblo

JOHN DEL GAIZO

Additional Highlights

1 Taos Pueblo One of the most intriguing creations in the American West, this pueblo (illustrated above) is just a few miles north of town. Two huge multistoried brown structures (the tallest section is five stories high) built out of mud and straw rise from the plain on either side of the Rio Pueblo, which divides the plaza. Wooden ladders lead from one level to the next, and doorways are visible on every level. Men and women wrapped in blankets move about, some baking bread in outdoor ovens. This is the oldest continuously occupied apartment dwelling in the US. It existed in much the same form as far back as 1540, when members of the expedition led by Spanish explorer Francisco Vásquez de Coronado came upon it during their search for the Seven Cities of Cibola—the legendary seven cities of gold. If they happened to arrive at sunset, they must have thought this was one of them. (Some historians believe it was the Indian pueblos that gave rise to the legend.)

An Indian community existed at Taos more than 500 years before Columbus came to the New World. The pueblo, with its soft mud curves, was the forerunner of the architecture that is now symbolic of the entire region. And the people, though primarily peaceful, were the most rebellious of all the pueblos in their resentment against foreign intrusion. It was this pueblo that led the revolt that drove the Spanish from the region in 1680. Even when the southern pueblos were subjugated by Don Diego De Vargas in 1692, **Taos Pueblo** continued to rebel for another five years. A century later, when the Taos Valley was under repeated attacks by Plains Indians, many of the Spanish settlers took refuge in the pueblo's massive buildings. About 1,500 Taos Indians (who speak the native Tiwa language) now reside here.

A visit to the pueblo can be both inspirational and depressing. A certain exhilaration is sparked by the age and primitive beauty of the structures themselves. Yet the reality is that the pueblo derives much of its income from tourism. Visitors are charged for parking and charged again if they want to photograph, sketch, or paint the pueblo; if you want to photograph individuals, you are expected to ask permission and to tip them as well. Some ground-floor apartments contain small shops where the residents sell jewelry and other crafts to visitors. They are a proud, independent people, as their rebellious history demonstrates, and pueblo residents understandably do not wholly welcome the intrusion of tourism.

The pueblo feast-day celebration is held on 29 and 30 September. Other special days are the Turtle Dance, 1 January; Deer or Buffalo Dance, 6 January; Foot Races, 3 May; Corn Dances, 13 June and 24 June; the Powwow, second weekend in July; Santiago's Day, 25 July; and Deer Dance or *Matachines* on Christmas Day. Dances are open to the public, but (except for the Powwow) cannot be photographed. ◆ Admission. Daily. Paseo del Pueblo Norte (2 miles north of Taos). 758.9593

2 Quail Ridge Inn $$ This sleek, sprawling Neo-Pueblo-style resort four miles north of Taos on the way to the ski valley was designed with tennis buffs in mind. The central attraction is the six indoor and two outdoor tennis courts that are open year-round—in winter the outdoor courts are covered with a huge inflatable dome. The 110 guest rooms range from standard hotel rooms to individual 1,600-square-foot casitas. All have large fireplaces, and many have kitchenettes and patios or balconies. ◆ Taos Ski Valley Rd (off NM 522). 776.2211 &

Within the Quail Ridge Inn:

Renegade Cafe ★★$$$ A comfortable place to carboload before a day of double diamond skiing, this place features Florentine omelettes, buttermilk pancakes, and stuffed French toast to get you going in the morning. Lunchtime offerings include peppered tuna salad, grilled eggplant sandwich, or fried calamari. Dinner entrées run the gamut from a grilled 12-oz. New York strip steak to medaillons of chicken breast in cranberry sauce to shrimp on a stick. ◆ Continental ◆ Daily breakfast, lunch, and dinner. Reservations recommended. 776.2211

3 Millicent Rogers Museum Millicent Rogers was an art patron, designer, and oil heiress who moved to Taos in 1947 and died here in 1953. In that short time, she assembled one of the Southwest's premiere collections of Native American jewelry and textiles. After her death, the family founded a museum in her honor and to preserve her finds. The family and other donors added major selections of Hispanic art, ceramics, metalwork, baskets, and other decorative arts. Today, the museum exhibits a unique collection of pottery by the famous Maria Martinez of **San Ildefonso Pueblo,** some jewelry designed by Millicent Rogers, and changing exhibits of historic and contemporary works by artists and designers from the region. The museum celebrated its

40th anniversary in 1996 with a special exhibition of treasures acquired over four decades. Other programs include lectures by leading artists and historians, classes, seminars, children's events, and musical performances. ◆ Admission. Daily Apr-Oct; Tu-Su Nov-Mar. Off NM 522, 4 miles north of Taos Plaza. Turn left (west) just before the blinking light and follow the museum signs. 758.2462 &

COURTESY OF KIT CARSON HISTORICAL MUSEUM

4 Hacienda de Martinez Dating to 1780, this classic Spanish Colonial hacienda (pictured above) looks like an adobe fortress from the outside. It was built without windows in the exterior walls as protection against raids by the Apache or Comanche. Twenty-one rooms face out onto two courtyards. Now a museum, the hacienda features rooms illustrating lifestyles of the colonial period and exhibits depicting the history of trade on El Camino Real. The place is named after Severino Martinez, scion of a prominent family that built the hacienda two centuries ago. His son, Padre José Martinez, was a popular clergyman who allegedly participated in the 1847 revolt against American occupation and who was later excommunicated by Bishop Lamy. ◆ Admission. Daily. NM 240 (Ranchitos Rd), 2 miles south of Taos. 758.1000

5 Rio Grande Gorge Bridge For millions of years the Rio Grande—which in truth does not appear very grand in this region—has been cutting its own canyon into the ancient lava flows that formed this area. In 1965 a steel bridge spanning the gorge was completed. Park beside the bridge and walk out to its center, and you are almost certain to experience a moment of vertigo as you look down the steep canyon to the river, which flows like a tiny ribbon far below. The bridge, 650 feet above the river, is the third-highest in the US, after the Royal Gorge Bridge in Colorado (1,053 ft.) and the New River Gorge Bridge in West Virginia (876 ft.). The reality is awesome, but photos cannot capture it. ◆ On Hwy 64, about 12 miles northwest of Taos

6 D.H. Lawrence Memorial Driving north on State Road 522 there is a well-maintained dirt road on the right that wends into the mountains for another 4.5 miles until it reaches the ranch that Mabel Dodge Luhan tried to give to D.H. Lawrence in the 1920s. Lawrence did not want to be beholden to Mabel and declined the ranch, but his wife, Frieda, accepted it in exchange for the original manuscript of *Sons and Lovers*. In one of the wooden cabins clustered together here, Lawrence wrote parts of *The Plumed Serpent*. The Lawrences lived here for several years before returning to Europe, where the writer died in France in 1930. Some years later Frieda had his body exhumed and cremated, and she returned to Taos to bury his ashes in the mountains he loved. Fearful that the covetous Mabel would steal the ashes, Frieda had them mixed into the cement of a small shrine, which looks like a miniature white cabin, built on the ranch. (Frieda is buried just outside the shrine.) Visitors from all over the world now come to pay homage to the author and sign the guest book. The shrine is located up a zigzagged walkway from the ranch buildings. The ranch is now owned by the **University of New Mexico** and is maintained as a scholarly retreat. ♦ Free. Daily. Call ahead in winter for road conditions. NM 522, about 11 miles north of Taos. 776.2245

7 Taos Ski Valley Serious skiers from all over the country come to the Taos ski basin. Its stunning alpine setting—the peak elevation is 11,819 feet, base elevation is 9,207 feet—gets more than 26 feet of snow annually. There are 72 ski runs: 36 are classified expert, 19 intermediate, and 17 beginner.

New Mexico ski pioneer Ernie Blake, who took up residence in Santa Fe after World War II, founded the resort. While he was manager of the Santa Fe ski basin in 1949, he began to implement his dream of creating his own ski resort. A native of Switzerland, Blake made repeated flights over the Sangre de Cristo Mountains looking for a spot in which to re-create the Alpine retreats of his youth. He chose a valley north of Taos with stunning views of the **Carson National Forest,** and the resort has been attracting skiers from all over the world ever since. The **Ernie Blake Ski School** has been ranked number one by *Snow Country* magazine for its group and private instruction. Over 25 lodges located at the ski valley, in the alpine village, and on the road to the valley provide rooms for more than one thousand skiers. Many offer ski package rates exclusively. At others you can book rooms alone. ♦ Thanksgiving weekend–early Apr. 18 miles northeast of Taos via Hwy 64 and NM 150. 776.1111, snow report 776.2916

At Taos Ski Valley:

Georgia on My Mind

In popular American iconography, two legendary figures have become the most prominent symbols of New Mexico. The southern, cattle-raising half of the state is the gunslinging, murderous province of William H. Bonney, aka Billy the Kid. But Northern New Mexico belongs, perhaps for all eternity, to a solitary woman who dressed all in black, her hair pulled back in a bun as severe as her personality. Like one of the ghosts of local lore, the image of Georgia O'Keeffe still stalks the land.

Born in Wisconsin in 1887, O'Keeffe became famous in New York City through the efforts of her husband and chief promoter, photographer Alfred Stieglitz, who featured her work in his 291 Gallery. She was 41 years old and a fixture in the New York art scene before she fell in love with New Mexico.

Accepting an invitation from Mabel Dodge Luhan to visit Taos in 1929, O'Keeffe came west by train with her friend Rebecca Strand. She was immediately taken with the fierce desert beauty. She spent that summer, and the next, painting the landscape near Taos, the church at **Ranchos de Taos,** and huge crosses that she could see from Mabel's house. Roaming far afield, she discovered

Abiquiu, a village 60 miles north of Santa Fe (for more on Abiquiu, see page 74). She decided at once that this was her spiritual home. Beginning in the mid-1930s she spent every summer at Abiquiu, apart from her husband, who refused to travel to the primitive, wild West. When Stieglitz died in 1946, O'Keeffe moved to Abiquiu permanently and lived there until her death at age 98.

To drive through that region today is to see the work of O'Keeffe come to life. The red hills she captured on canvas are there, along with the hills striped horizontally in pink, white, and yellow, and the hills tinted dark gray, where she often found solace and where she walked alone in later life. She also painted the cow skulls she found in the desert, the dry bones, the wildflowers, the bright blue sky—everything except the people. For in the world of O'Keeffe, the land was the only star; there was little room for humanity. She never learned to speak Spanish, the language of the villagers all around her. She remained as aloof, tough, forbidding, and hostile as the landscape itself. But had she diluted her artistic energy with socializing, she might not have become as enduring as the stunning hills she chose to call home.

Ranchos de Taos Church

M. BLUM

Inn at Snakedance $$$$ If the idea of sliding out of bed and onto the ski lift sounds appealing, then this hotel is ideal. You can even watch skiers schuss down **Al's Run** from the breakfast table. Sixty comfortable rooms all feature mini-refrigerators, bar sinks, and reading chairs, and some also have wood-burning fireplaces. The spa has a super whirlpool in a colorful muraled room, and there's a mini-grocery store on site. The **Hondo Restaurant & Bar** serves delicious grilled fare, and its outdoor deck has one of the best views in town. ♦ 776.2277, 800/322.9815

Edelweiss $$$$ Another good choice for a slopeside hotel, this place offers 21 newly redecorated guest rooms, some with vaulted ceilings and two-story bedrooms. Other amenities include down comforters and plush robes to wear to the indoor sauna or outdoor hot tub. In the restaurant, chef Timothy Wooldridge whips up gourmet meals extraordinaire, featuring wild rice and shiitake mushroom soup, blackened scallops, and smoked-peppered filet mignon. Locals say this is the ski valley's best restaurant. ♦ 776.2301

"The moment I saw the brilliant, proud morning shine high up over the desert of Santa Fe, something stood still in my soul, and I started to attend. There was a certain magnificence in the high-up day, a certain eagle-like royalty..., Ah, yes, in New Mexico the heart is sacrificed to the sun and the human being is left stark, heartless, but undauntedly religious."

—D.H. Lawrence

Andrew Dasburg, a prominent American cubist, moved first to Santa Fe and then to Taos early in this century. "I felt as though I had come upon the Garden of Eden," he said.

8 Ranchos de Taos Church Although the proper name of this church is **San Francisco de Asis Church,** it is more widely known as "Ranchos de Taos Church" because Georgia O'Keeffe named it thus in numerous paintings. In 1929 and 1930 O'Keeffe painted the rear of the church, with its sweeping mud walls that look like natural creations, omitting the crosses in the front and any other sign of the human touch. The church (illustrated above) has been open since 1815 and is still used for masses, weddings, and funerals. The curving rear supports face west, and the changing light and shadows have made this one of the most painted and photographed churches in the country. A slide show depicting the history of the church is given several times a day at the church office across the street. ♦ St. Francis Plaza, on Hwy 68 just south of NM 240, Ranchos de Taos, 4 miles south of Taos. 758.2754

8 Trading Post Cafe ★★★★$$ Award-winning chef Rene Mettler, who hails from Switzerland, England, the Caribbean, Florida, and Hawaii, and his wife Kimberly opened this extraordinary restaurant in Ranchos de Taos. Kimberly ably manages the dining room where the pink-beige stucco walls are adorned with paintings by resident artists and photographs of local actors and artists. Rene talks with guests from his open kitchen counter while preparing gourmet dishes that span Mediterranean and Asian cuisines. Appetizers might be gravlax with Japanese noodles, country pâté served on a sheet of marble, or escargots with fried angel-hair pancakes. Entrées change weekly, but might include *fettuccine alla carbonara* (with pancetta, eggs, and cheese), grilled lamb chops, or fresh grilled Norwegian salmon. Desserts are worth every calorie, especially the raspberry tart and crème caramel. ♦ Mediterranean/Asian ♦ Daily lunch and dinner. Hwys 68 and 518, 4 miles south of Taos. 758.5089

Restaurants/Clubs: Red   **Hotels:** Blue
Shops/ ❦ Outdoors: Green   **Sights/Culture:** Black

The Unknown American Revolution

Before the arrival of the first Spaniards in 1536 in Northern New Mexico, Pueblo Indian society was remarkably peaceful, though often subject to marauding nomadic bands of neighboring Navajo, Apache, and Athabascan seeking food and horses. The pueblos cultivated crops, hunted, and traded with each other, and celebrated a culture of unity and balance with nature.

At about the same time as the Spanish (starting with Francisco Vásquez de Coronado's expedition in 1540) were looking for wealth beyond what is today Mexico, the Franciscan order was hoping to expand its missionary efforts among the Native American population. These two interests coincided: the Franciscans needed the military clout the conquerors could provide, and the profiteers required the guise of saving souls under the auspices of the Church in order to proceed with their commercial ventures.

Under the command of Juan de Oñate, a Spanish expedition crossed the **Rio Grande** above El Paso in April 1598 and claimed the territory for Spain. Oñate secured the allegiances to the Spanish crown of the last pueblos—Zuni, Hopi, and Acoma—by October.

As in other parts of Spain's empire in the New World, the Spanish expansion completely uprooted the lives of the pueblo population. The pueblos' grain and other food supplies were taken by force and deposited into the Franciscan missions. To avoid starvation, the people had no choice but to embrace the Church. Slavery, theft of land and possessions, mutilation, torture, and murder were other aspects of the new system. Despite aggressive proselytizing by the Franciscans, accompanied by their contempt for and horror of traditional pueblo ways, there was resolute resistance to the Christian religion, and the Native Americans clung to their culture, often secretly.

Drought, famine, and continued misrule by successive governors fractured the Spanish control over the pueblos and the neighboring Navajo, Apache, and Athabascan nomads. Tensions steadily increased, and Popé—a Tewa medicine man from the **San Juan Pueblo** in exile in Taos— began to coordinate plans for a general uprising of all the pueblos in the area. On 9 August 1680 Popé led a revolt against the Spanish. After five weeks the united pueblo nations had rolled back the entire Spanish population across the Rio Grande. The Native Americans held their ground for 12 years until Spanish forces retook the colony in 1693.

Although the pueblo people's freedom was fleeting, the 1680 Pueblo Revolt was unique in the history of the Western Hemisphire—at no other time before or since have Native Americans succeeded in eliminating foreign control over their homelands.

Day Trips

9 Picuris Pueblo The smallest pueblo in New Mexico is tucked into Hidden Valley, about 20 miles south of Taos. It was first settled around AD 1200 and over the next two centuries grew into a multistory adobe structure. The pueblo was abandoned after the 1680 Pueblo Revolt but was reestablished in the 1700s. Ruins of the original pueblo are still visible and can be toured. If hunger strikes, stop in at the pueblo's **Hidden Valley Restaurant** (587.2957), which serves traditional pueblo food as well as American fare. The tribe also runs a gift shop/museum and offers fishing in two stocked lakes. Business ventures have expanded to the capital—the pueblo is 51 percent owner of the **Hotel Santa Fe.** The tribal feast day is 10 August. ◆ Fees for photography, sketching, and filming. Daily. Off NM 75, about 28 miles southwest of Taos. 587.2957

So numerous were Indian pueblos and cliff dwellings on the Pajarito Plateau around Los Alamos and Bandelier National Monument that the plateau's population was larger in AD 1300 than it is today. Of the 7,000 known archaeological sites on the plateau, many are still used for secret ceremonies today by Pueblo Indians.

10 Angel Fire Resort Founded in 1967 by Texan Roy Leubus, this ski resort offers families affordable lodging and ski programs for kids. The slopes are mostly for beginning and intermediate skiers, though there are a few runs that challenge the experts. Offbeat events, such as the world shovel race championships, in which contestants shoot down the mountain at high speeds on scoop shovels, are also available to guests. And when there's no snow, fishing, hiking, bicycling, golfing, and camping are among the activities. ♦ Take Hwy 64 to NM 434, 24 miles east of Taos. 377.6661, 800/446.8117, snow report 377.6401

11 Enchanted Circle North of Taos, this one hundred-mile loop of highways offers spectacular views. If you have the time, do not miss it, and be sure to take your camera. You can drive in either of two directions, pass beyond New Mexico's highest mountain, Wheeler Peak, which tops off at 13,161 feet, and not have to return to your starting point along the same route. The drive alone takes less than two hours, but chances are you'll want to take in some side sights along the way.

If you head east out of Taos on Highway 64—out Kit Carson Road—you'll switchback through forestland and come to a turnoff to **Angel Fire.** For the Enchanted Circle, however, proceed on Highway 64. You'll quickly arrive at the **Disabled American Veterans Memorial Chapel** (377.6900). Built in the shape of wings, it peers down from a hill overlooking the Moreno Valley. The chapel was built by Dr. Victor Westphall in memory of his son David, a marine who was killed in action during the Vietnam War. An emotional video is shown in the chapel daily at 9AM.

The next stop along the way is **Eagle Nest,** nestled in a valley beside a lake of the same name. Stop and fish here along 15 miles of shoreline, or rent a boat. At Eagle Nest, the Enchanted Circle continues on NM 38, to **Elizabethtown,** an Old West ghost town with a long-deserted mining camp. Look for a cattle guard on the left to find it. Continuing north on 38, you start a long ascent over Bobcat Pass (check the road conditions in winter). Behind you is an incredible view.

As you bottom out of the pass, you'll be in the town of **Red River.** In the 19th century gold was discovered in the hills, and Red River became one of the wildest towns in the West. By 1905 there were 3,000 people in the village. There were four hotels, 15 saloons, and a red-light district. But by 1925 the mines had played out. Today the population is down to 350, and the hell-raising is mostly a memory. The wild life offered now is mostly hiking and fishing, though country music swings in the nightspots.

Whether you stay overnight or keep going, the next stop on NM 38 is **Questa.** High on a hill, this village offers stirring views of the valley below. Hiking, fishing, and camping are available at the nearby **Wild and Scenic Rivers Recreation Area** (758.8851), where the Red River and the Rio Grande come together just southhwest of town.

Heading south on NM 522, you'll pass the turnoff to the **D.H. Lawrence Memorial** (see page 92) on your left. Then it's past the village of **Arroyo Hondo,** where famed Native American artist R.C. Gorman lives in the big house on the left, and back into Taos.

Paul Fischer
Owner, Partridge Company

The brightly lit tree in the 2.5-story lobby of the historic **Taos Inn** proclaims yuletide in Taos. Settle in next to the kiva fireplace and enjoy a margarita while you listen to some foot-stomping flamenco music.

A large apple tree, heavy with fruit, shades diners in the summertime in the secluded adobe-walled courtyard of the **Apple Tree Restaurant.**

Highway 285 winds through the **Sangre de Cristo Mountains** with the **Rio Grande** guiding your drive from Santa Fe to Taos. The road travels through orchard valleys with fruit stands along the way, mesas and cliffs dotted with piñon trees until a steep horseshoe turn in the road. The first views of Taos are the breathtaking, 600-foot-deep **Rio Grande Gorge** and the majestic **Taos Mountain.**

Dr. Alan Reed
Director, University of New Mexico at Santa Fe

Living and working in Northern New Mexico is a constant adventure. Some of my favorite spots are:

The **Trading Post Cafe**—the new favorite with Taoseños, haute cuisine melded with a cowboy roadhouse.

A perfect day in Santa Fe (and there are many) includes shopping at **Sanbusco Center** where you can find home-grown produce and have a chair massage.

A weekend in Albuquerque means lunch or dinner at **Sakura** in **Nob Hill** where sushi is delivered on a mini-boat. All the shops on **Central Avenue** between **Carlisle** and **Girard** offer upscale, arty purchases. When downtown, don't miss the **Rio Bravo** microbrewery. Take in any production at the Pueblo Deco **KiMo Theatre.**

Albuquerque

On 23 April 1706 New Mexico Governor Francisco Cuervo y Valdes composed a formal letter to his sovereign, the Duke of Alburquerque, viceroy of New Spain, from the capital of Santa Fe. He wrote: "I certify. . . to the most excellent señor viceroy that I founded a villa on the banks and in the valley of the Rio del Norte in a good place as regards land, water, pasture, and firewood. . . and named it the *Villa de Alburquerque*." He continued to boast, "I do not doubt. . . that in a short time this will be the most prosperous villa. . . ."

This remote, arid valley stretching along a broad bend of the **Rio Grande** had an ideal location: the river was a good irrigation source and the *bosque* (wooded area) and nearby mountains produced ample wood. By naming the new settlement "Alburquerque" (the first "r" was dropped later on) in the Duke's honor, the governor felt assured of his superior's approval. He won it, and in the midst of his political maneuvering, the tiny Villa de Alburquerque was born.

Nearly three centuries later, Cuervo y Valdes's assertion has proved no less than visionary. Indeed, with a population of 645,000, Albuquerque today is the biggest city in New Mexico and home to one-third of the state's residents. A major center of transportation, science, education, and technology, the city is the state's economic and industrial core. Tourism is big business, too, and an estimated six million people visit the city each year. As home to a multicultural mix of Hispanics, Native Americans, Anglos, and more, the city is also a nucleus for centuries of ancient regional culture, history, and lore.

From its humble adobe beginnings beside a plaza on the city's southwest side, Albuquerque has survived several incarnations. In the late 1800s, the arrival

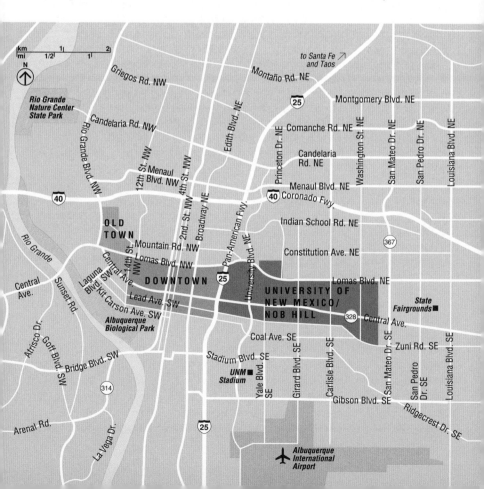

of the railroad two miles east of the original town site brought droves of new people, spurring a shift in population and commerce that resulted in the creation of a vital **New Town** beside the tracks. Later, as the city began to spread out around it, New Town became **Downtown**, the city's central business district. There in 1926, **Route 66**, the historic highway of legend and song, sliced through the downtown area along **Central Avenue**, transforming the provincial "Duke City," as the city is commonly called, into a burgeoning neon strip of hotels, diners, truck stops, and more.

World War II made the city a major national center for military research and production, and a new influx of arrivals wasn't far behind. By the mid-1950s, however, residents old and new began shifting their buying power from Downtown to the new **Northeast Heights**, a modern and rambling residential quarter with strip malls at practically every turn. Downtown fizzled as the city continued to sprawl in all directions. During the next 30 years, as Albuquerque slowly came to terms with its urban identity, the city settled into the vast metropolis that exists today.

Sitting in central New Mexico at the crossroads of **Interstates 25** and **40**, modern Albuquerque stretches 12 miles east from the Rio Grande to the towering **Sandia Mountains**, 3.5 miles west to the rugged remnants of ancient volcanoes, and 14 miles north and south through the lush agricultural **Rio Grande Valley.**

Commanding the view on the city's eastern edge are the Sandia (Spanish for watermelon) Mountains, massive granite outcroppings that blush shades of watermelon at sunset. **Sandia Crest,** the cool 10,678-foot-high mountain summit, is reached via an 18-minute aerial tramway ride, the world's longest single span tram. Climbing almost three miles from the northeastern outskirts of the city to the rocky crest, the tram passes above craggy cathedral cliffs and forests of aspen and pine, providing a stunning view of the entire city. To the far west are the lava-crested mesas that serve as reminders of the city's volcanic past. There, along miles of volcanic escarpment, you can glimpse the world of early Indian inhabitants, who as long ago as AD 1300 etched some 15,000 petroglyph drawings into the dark basalt. The city's rural north and south valleys provide a meandering mix of farms, orchards, chile fields, and fruit and vegetable stands.

Albuquerque hosts the state's two largest annual events: the New Mexico State Fair, a down-home celebration of exhibits, entertainment, and regional cuisine held in September, and the October Kodak Albuquerque International Balloon Fiesta, the largest gathering of balloonists in the world. It's home to the **Albuquerque Dukes,** the Triple-A Pacific Coast League farm team of the **Los Angeles Dodgers;** to **Kirtland Air Force Base** and Sandia National Laboratories, major centers for defense, high technology, and science; and to the **University of New Mexico,** the state's largest educational institution. It's surrounded by the homes of ancient Pueblo Indian tribes—**Acoma, Cochiti, Isleta, Jemez, Laguna, Sandia, San Felipe, Santa Ana, Santo Domingo, Zia,** and **Zuni**—who continue to practice their traditional ways of life. Albuquerque's wide open spaces, stunning vistas, and magical natural light also provide an inspirational home to scores of artists, photographers, writers, nature lovers, and more.

Divided into north and south by Central Avenue and east and west by the Downtown railroad tracks, the city is composed of four quadrants—NE, NW, SE, and SW. Due to its size, Albuquerque is best toured by automobile, with walking tours in the most historic sections of town. **Old Town,** the site of the city's original settlement, retains the architectural charm and cultural spirit of its Spanish founders. Today, as the city's top tourist draw, Old Town enjoys the most foot traffic. Other popular walking spots include Downtown, the **University of New Mexico,** and the **Nob Hill** district, all of which feature a mix of the historic and the contemporary and lend a more modern appeal to ancient Albuquerque.

Miles of Mountains

The richly colored granite and red-gold volcanic rock formations of Northern New Mexico's mountains—all part of the **Rocky Mountains**—are set off by tall, silent forests of ponderosa pine and shimmering stands of aspen (at elevations above 9,000 feet). Atop the majestic crags of the highest peaks, steep slopes covered with Douglas fir give way to alpine meadows. Hundreds of unpaved roads (some suitable for passenger cars and others only for high-clearance and four-wheel-drive vehicles) wind into these vast stretches of wilderness; where these rugged roads end, narrow trails continue, taking hikers, horseback riders, mountain bikers, fishers, and skiers (downhill and cross-country) into this region's remote interior, home to eagles, bears, and elk.

The greatest and highest of New Mexico's mountain ranges is the **Sangre de Cristo Mountains,** named for the rich red clay which covers many of its slopes. These tremendous peaks (the highest is **Wheeler Peak** northeast of Taos at 13,161 feet) rise abruptly from the eastern city limits of both **Santa Fe** and **Taos** and extend northward in a solid wall of forbidding rock for more than 200 miles to central Colorado. The New Mexico segment of the mountain range spans two national parks, the **Carson National Forest** (headquarters 758.6200) and **Santa Fe National Forest** (headquarters 438.7840). Together, they contain more than 400 miles of trails, numerous trout streams, high-country fishing lakes, dozens of campgrounds with a total of 899 tent and RV sites, and seven downhill ski areas.

A half-dozen crests in the Sangre de Cristos are high enough to be covered with snow for almost nine months of the year. Temperatures average 25 to 30 degrees cooler than in Santa Fe and Taos year-round, causing clouds to condense around the summits and drop about 40 inches of precipitation a year—almost four times as much as in Santa Fe. Snow and rain in these mountains provide almost all of the drinking and irrigation water for Santa Fe, Taos, and **Albuquerque.**

At the heart of the Sangre de Cristos, the 223,667-acre **Pecos Wilderness** encompasses some of the most spectacularly varied high-mountain scenery in the state. Hugging its summits are enormous thickets of spruce and fir, flower-filled meadows, high-altitude lakes, and two spectacular peaks, **Santa Fe Baldy** (elevation 12,622 feet) and **Truchas Peak** (13,102 feet), with its ancient forest and remote fishing lakes. Motorized and wheeled vehicles are prohibited in the wilderness area; it is only open to hikers, cross-country skiers, horseback riders, and llama trekkers (the llamas carry your gear as you walk with them).

Beyond Santa Fe, smaller mountain ranges rise from the desert. Between Santa Fe and Albuquerque, **Sandia Crest,** a single massive mountain with a ridgeline that runs 30 miles north and south, offers panoramic views of Albuquerque (and approximately half the state of New Mexico) from a wilderness vantage point a mile above the city. North of Albuquerque, on the western horizon from Santa Fe, the **Jemez Mountains** around **Bandelier National Monument** and **Los Alamos** were formed by a huge prehistoric volcano; here, visitors will find surreal forest landscapes with hot springs, strange lava and ash formations, ancient Indian pueblos and cliff dwellings, and colorful cliffs that plunge straight down for as much as a thousand feet.

Old Town

Sitting squat and unassuming in a southwest corner of a sprawling city, Old Town, with its ancient adobe architecture and serene village ambience, might appear to be no more than a quaint reminder of days past. Yet **Plaza Vieja**, as the area's Spanish founders called it, remains the heart of Albuquerque's centuries-old Hispanic heritage.

Established in 1706, along the winding banks of the **Rio Grande**, Old Town is the prized site chosen by Provincial Governor Don Francisco Cuervo y Valdes to become the *Villa de Alburquerque,* in honor of the Duke of Alburquerque, viceroy of New Spain. It began as a scattering of small farms and a simple

adobe church, and the new settlement drew nourishment from the waters of the Rio Grande and a deeply rooted Catholic faith.

By about 1780 a traditional Spanish town had taken shape: A central plaza was surrounded by rows of humble earthen homes, shops, and civic buildings, while a newer and larger New Mexican-style church—**San Felipe de Neri**—loomed peacefully overhead. Within a century, the town was firmly established as a burgeoning center of commerce, a community of nearly 2,000 residents where traders traveling the Santa Fe and Chihuahua Trails met to sell and exchange their wares.

The arrival of the railroad in 1880 spurred new opportunities for growth and trade, along with an influx of Anglo-Americans to the region. But the location of the railroad two miles east of the established town caused a dramatic shift in population. The result was the birth of a booming New Town—today's Downtown—alongside the railroad tracks and the demise of Old Town as the area's economic hub.

Now, more than a hundred years later, even as a bustling city of over 645,000 has grown up all around it, Old Town hasn't died. Though the area declined during the initial post-railroad era, it was rediscovered in the 1930s by artists inspired by its timeless architectural beauty and merchants who believed the arts, cuisine, and traditions of the Hispanic residents held tremendous tourist appeal. During the next 20 years, Old Town was transformed as original buildings were restored in the Pueblo Revival style. And by the 1970s, a delightful mix of shops, galleries, and restaurants had sprung up to make Old Town one of Albuquerque's top tourist attractions.

Although it's now geared primarily to tourists, Old Town retains an air of history and charm. Ancestors of many of the original settlers still live in the area, and significant buildings and sites are now listed on state and national registers of historic places. Its secluded patios and winding brick paths harbor hidden gardens and other intriguing finds, while the tree-shaded **Old Town Plaza** (known to locals as the "Plaza") is the perfect place for people watching or enjoying an occasional performance of music or dance. Wild West gunfights are staged on **Romero Street** on Sunday afternoons. And on Christmas Eve, those willing to brave the winter chill bask in the golden glow of some 500,000 *luminarias* (small candles set in sand at the bottom of a small paper bag) that cover Old Town from sidewalk to rooftop, an age-old tradition symbolizing a lighting of the way for the Christ child.

Concentrated within an area of approximately four square blocks, Old Town can be explored easily on foot. In fact, parking opportunities are few and far between, so walking is usually unavoidable. The downside is that with nearly 200 shops, restaurants, and galleries in the area—most of them specializing in Southwest something or other—your chances of encountering one too many wooden howling coyotes and machine-made "ancient" Indian artifacts are pretty high. The suggestions included here will guide you to some of the most authentic and intriguing spots.

1 Sheraton Old Town $$$
Larger-than-life-size *bultos* (traditional Hispanic hand-carved images of saints) flank the lobby of this modern 11-story structure. The giant statues are part of the annual April Founder's Day procession commemorating Albuquerque's establishment in 1706, and they lend an air of Southwest tradition to this otherwise contemporary inn. The 190 large guest rooms are adorned in desert hues with simple hand-wrought furnishings and Southwest-style crafts, and the south-facing rooms, which overlook Old Town, have private balconies. **Old Town Place,** the hotel's gallery/gift shop row, sells Southwestern goods. The hotel is within walking distance of the historic sites

and shops of Old Town, as well as **The Albuquerque Museum** and the **New Mexico Museum of Natural History & Science.** ◆ 800 Rio Grande Blvd NW (between Mountain Rd NW and Bellamah Ave NW). 843.6300, 800/237.2133; fax 842.9863 ♿

Within the Sheraton Old Town:

Rio Grande Customs House ★★$$$ Set in a rustic atmosphere reminiscent of early seafaring days (very non-New Mexican), this restaurant and pub specializes in beef, seafood, and New Mexican cuisine, as well as combinations of the above. Try the red chile-dusted shrimp or the guacamole hamburger (green chile is optional). The prime rib is also a favorite, and Sunday features an excellent Champagne brunch. ◆ New Mexican/American ◆ M-F lunch and dinner; Sa dinner; Su brunch and dinner. Reservations recommended. 843.6300 ♿

Cafe del Sol ★★$ This coffeehouse is a casual breakfast and lunch spot offering everything from snacks to full meals. The menu includes a variety of New Mexican dishes as well as soups, salads, and sandwiches. Liquor service is also available. ◆ New Mexican/American ◆ Daily breakfast and lunch. 843.6300

Albuquerque Children's Museum Shops line the indoor walkway that connects the dignified lobby area of the **Sheraton Old Town** to this children's museum full of hands-on exhibits. There's a bubble zone, giant loom, dress-up area, capture-your-shadow wall, giant camera, and make-it, take-it art activities. ◆ Admission. Tu-Su. 842.5525 ♿

2 Maria Teresa Restaurant & 1840 Bar ★★★$$$ Salvador Armijo, a prominent merchant and politician, built this sprawling adobe hacienda for his family more than a hundred years ago. Constructed with 32-inch-thick adobe bricks and few windows, the structure is a classic example of 19th-century New Mexico architecture—when defense was as big a consideration as aesthetics—and is listed on the National Register of Historic Places.

Today the building houses one of the city's most elegant restaurants. Seven of its twelve rooms are now individual dining areas that bear the names of Armijo family members and are decorated in a mix of Victorian antiques and early Spanish-American furnishings, including a wine press and piano belonging to the original family. The lounge features an

1840 bar that hails from an old-time saloon in the southern part of the state. Outside, a beautiful courtyard and garden is a favorite place for warm-weather diners.

An innovative dinner menu features steak, chicken, seafood, and a host of classic New Mexican specialties. Recommended are raspberry chicken, *carne adovada* enchiladas (cubed pork marinated in a rich red-chile sauce on a blue-corn tortilla), and lamb fajitas. Lunch always includes some excellent fish dishes, and Sunday brunch offers a good mix of New Mexican dishes and traditional breakfast fare. Weekday Happy Hours are a good excuse to try the fresh lime margaritas. ◆ Steak/Seafood/Southwestern ◆ Daily lunch and dinner. Reservations recommended. 618 Rio Grande Blvd NW (between Mountain Rd NW and Bellamah Ave NW). 242.3900 ♿

3 Plaza Don Francisco Cuervo y Valdes Dedicated on 23 April 1988, this site is highlighted by a massive bronze sculpture of Albuquerque's founder, Don Francisco Cuervo y Valdes, created by artist Buck McCain as part of the city's Arts in Public Places program. Looking dashing and noble, like any good Spanish conquistador should, the sculpture depicts a triumphant Cuervo y Valdes, in flowing cloaks and armor, trotting on horseback into the tiny village he founded on the banks of the Rio Grande on 23 April 1706. Native landscaping completes this picturesque point of interest, a popular spot for taking tourist pics. ◆ Bounded by Rio Grande Blvd NW, Main St NW, and Mountain Rd NW

4 Candy Lady Take just one step inside this house of sweets, and you'll be hard put to decide which is more sinful: entering the room to your right marked with a sign that reads "This Room Rated X" or moving straight ahead to counters chockablock with chocolates and other candy treats. After almost two decades in Old Town, owner Debbie Ball knows how to lure visitors of every ilk.

Whatever your pleasure, fudge fans revel in the 15 to 20 varieties offered daily, including a special red-chile recipe mixed with bits of the spicy stuff. The piñon, New Mexico's buttery native nut, is deliciously combined with toffee, chocolate, or caramel and has become a favorite replacement for the peanut in brittle. Jalapeño jelly beans are another fiery favorite, and the chocolate-dipped strawberries are always fresh. The shop also boasts the city's best selection of "diabetic" chocolate sweets, up to 30 types of hard and soft candies made with all-natural sugars.

The X-rated section features such explicit sweets as candy panties, chocolate male members, and protuberant pink mint-candy breasts. Anatomically correct cakes can also be special ordered. ◆ Daily. 524 Romero St NW (at Mountain Rd NW). 243.6239

5 Adobe Gallery Once the site of the **Old Town Post Office,** this 1879 Territorial-style home is the perfect setting for a gallery specializing in historic Southwest art. Emphasizing works of the Southwest Indians, the gallery features a high-quality, handpicked selection of pre-1940 Navajo textiles; pueblo pottery dating from 1860 to 1930; pre-1940 Navajo and Zuni jewelry; plus a fascinating array of Hopi kachina dolls and some contemporary pueblo pottery. Shop owners take credit for bringing to popularity the now-famous Storyteller doll—the open-mouthed pottery figurine who spins legendary Indian tales to piles of children on its lap. On display is a select collection of the dolls created by the master Storyteller-makers of **Cochiti Pueblo,** who still use strictly traditional materials and techniques, as well as beadwork and dollhouse-size kachinas, baskets, and pottery. The gallery's east end is a showcase for works by deceased artists, including Carl von Hassler, dean of the early Albuquerque art colony. There's also a fascinating library of more than 500 titles on everything you've ever wanted to know about Southwest Indian art. ◆ Daily. 413 Romero St NW (between North Plaza NW and Mountain Rd NW). 243.8485

6 Tanner Chaney Gallery Weekend Navajo weaving demonstrations are just one of the highlights to be found in the spacious adobe showrooms of this fine gallery of American Indian art. The collection includes one of the city's most impressive displays of quality Indian jewelry as well as historic and contemporary pottery, weaving, sculpture, kachinas, baskets, and fetishes (objects said to have the power to protect their owner)—all handmade by Indian artists from around the country. Equally impressive is the historic gallery space (one of the oldest haciendas in Old Town), which provides some fine examples of early New Mexican architecture and spills out onto an airy outdoor patio awash in hibiscus and bougainvillea. The owners also run **Native Gold** (Native American gold jewelry; 400 Romero St NW, at Church St NW, 247.4529, 800/255.5425) and **Legends** (classic Native American arts; 2047 South Plaza NW, between Romero St NW and Rio Grande Blvd NW, 243.7300, 800/243.7302). ◆ M-Sa; Su noon-6PM. 410 Romero St NW (between Church and Charlevoix Sts NW). 247.2242, 800/444.2242

7 Christmas Shop One of Old Town's old-time merchants, this shop specializes in all things Christmas year-round. Stocking everything for

tree and trim, the store features an international hodgepodge of handmade holiday crafts hailing from as far away as Russia, Poland, and Germany, as well as the Southwest. Check out the red-and-green-chile lights and ornaments, the pueblo pottery nativity scene, and the cactus cookie cutters that come in either saguaro or prickly pear. ◆ Daily. 400 Romero St NW (at Church St NW). 843.6744

8 Sunbird Southwestern Fashions This out-of-the-way women's clothing store, tucked behind the historic **San Felipe de Neri Catholic Church,** features natural fibers in simple, casual styles. The shop emphasizes Out Westwear you can actually wear: hand-embroidered and fine art T-shirts; back-to-basic blouses; denim, cotton, leather, and rayon skirts; and even cowboy boots. There's also a wide assortment of accessories: belts, bags, hats, and jewelry all made by local artisans. ◆ Daily. 2113 Church St NW (between San Felipe and Romero Sts NW). 243.5909

9 Esperanza Fine Furniture Fortunately, woodworker Mark Gonzales didn't lose *esperanza* (hope) when a fire destroyed his furniture factory and showroom (pictured above) just outside of Albuquerque many years back. Instead, the sixth-generation New Mexican relocated to Old Town, where he rebuilt his business into the area's only exclusive collection of fine hand-crafted furnishings. Using Spanish, Indian, and country motifs, Gonzales fashions all of his pieces after the historical designs of the Southwest, combining ponderosa pine and red oak with hand-forged iron hardware. A local staff of master craftspeople then hand-carve his interpretations into finely detailed dining room, living room, and bedroom collections that echo the simple functional furnishings of the past. The collection fits right into the beautiful adobe showroom (ca. 1912). Don't miss the other showroom upstairs. Best of all, there's ample parking in the rear. ◆ M-Sa; Su 12:30-6PM. 303 Rio Grande Blvd NW (at Hollywood Ave NW). 242.6458

10 Santo Domingo Indian Trading Post Though it may look a little dark and dusty, this small shop offers some of the best bargains in Albuquerque on traditional turquoise-and-silver Indian jewelry. ◆ Daily. 2049 S Plaza NW (at Rio Grande Blvd NW). 766.9855. Also at: 401 San Felipe St NW (between Church St NW and Mountain Rd NW). 764.0129

11 Last Straw Art & Gift Gallery An Old Town favorite since 1975, this tiny shop of collectibles is a showcase for more than 40 of New Mexico's Hispanic, Anglo, and Indian artists. Exclusive to the shop are the works of internationally known Robert Rivera, who tailors classic Indian motifs to the natural shape, first painting the gourds, and then often embellishing them with rare stones and other natural touches. Also featured here are the exquisite hand-painted eggs of Ruben Gallegos, the traditional *retablos* of Irene Martinez Yates, watercolors by Noami Slater, **Acoma Pueblo** pottery miniatures, and a sleepy cat that's usually lounging in the window. ◆ Daily. 2039 S Plaza NW (between Romero St NW and Rio Grande Blvd NW). 243.2175

12 Smiroll's International Cuisine ★★★ $$$ This understated dining spot offers a quaint Old World setting and a menu that's quite different from the typical New Mexican cuisine that's so popular in these parts. It bills itself as the House of Veal, and the tender calf is indeed the specialty here: Decide among francese, piccata, cordon bleu, parmigiana, scallopini, and a delightful Wiener schnitzel. The duck and Cornish game hen are tasty, too, and the homemade Italian sausage or prosciutto with melon are super starters. An extensive selection of seafood, pasta, and fine wines rounds out the international repertoire. ◆ International ◆ Daily dinner. Reservations recommended. 108 Rio Grande Blvd NW (at Central Ave). 242.9996 b

13 Turquoise Museum If you're wondering about the authenticity of all the turquoise on display throughout New Mexico, stop by this museum/shop for a real education. On display is J.C. Zachary Jr.'s private collection, perhaps the world's largest, consisting of turquoise from Iran, China, Australia, and the US. Among the prized pieces are a 16-pound nugget from the Bisbee mine in Arizona and the astonishing George Washington stone, weighing 6,880 carats and measuring 10 inches by 11.5 inches. Joe Dan Lowry, Zachary's grandson, is a turquoise aficionado who gives fascinating educational tours at the museum. Lowry also travels throughout the US offering seminars to future turquoise collectors. According to Lowry, only 10 percent of turquoise sold on the market is natural; every piece here is totally pure. ◆ Admission. M-Sa. 2107 Central Ave (in the Old Town Shopping Center, at Rio Grande Blvd NW). 247.8650

14 Casas de Sueños $$ A scant two blocks south of Old Town, these little "houses of dreams" are situated amid 2.5 acres of intricate English gardens abloom with hollyhocks and roses. Built in the 1930s by J.R. Willis, the cluster of 12 adobe casitas was created as a haven for artists and writers who came to work and relax inside its private environs. But since 1990, when Albuquerque native Robert Hanna took over, this charming, 19-room bed-and-breakfast has been the choice of visitors who want privacy plus the convenience of having the pleasures of Old Town nearby.

Dwellings range in size from a single bedroom that comfortably fits two people to a two-bedroom suite with a drawing room that's suitable for four. House interiors also vary from an elegant English and Oriental antique decor to a classic Santa Fe–style motif with brick floors, exposed adobe, and kiva fireplace. Another of the old artist's studios is now a dining room with a fireplace and French doors leading to an outdoor eating area that's enveloped by a lush rose garden. A gourmet breakfast is served daily and includes exquisite dishes such as asparagus cheese soufflé and baked curried fruit as well as home-baked pastries and bread, fresh juice, and gourmet coffee. Afternoons feature a traditional English tea service complete with scones, wine, and real English tea.

A small gallery within the main office frequently offers readings and exhibits by local artists. Even the office itself (unusually built in the shape of a snail) was created by the well-known local architect **Bart Prince,** whose strangely shaped structures have brought him international acclaim. Inside the "snail" is an extensive concierge service to help you plan your stay. ◆ 310 Rio Grande Blvd SW (between Alhambra Ave SW and Central Ave). 247.4560, 800/242.8987; fax 842.8493 b

15 Moccasin Shop More than 200 styles of authentic Native American footwear are sold here. Popular leather and suede slip-ons, ankle-high "squaw boots," and over-the-calf boots by moccasin makers from the historic **Taos Pueblo,** as well as tribes in Minnesota and upstate New York, are available in adult and children's sizes. ◆ Daily. 106 Romero St NW (between Old Town Rd and S Plaza). 243.7438

15 Antiquity Restaurant ★★★★$$$ Originally built as a honeymoon cottage almost a century ago, this ancient adobe still has romance lingering in the air. The secluded restaurant provides two intimate dining areas lined with traditional brick floors and bordered by walls clad in regional art. These rooms look out upon an open kitchen and grill, whence comes an exquisite filet mignon; *crêpes de poulet* (chicken-and-mushroom crepes in béchamel sauce); and the special chateaubriand for two, charcoal-broiled and carved tableside. Other beef, seafood, and pasta entrées and appetizers are equally delicious, and dessert—*polyczenta* (ground walnuts, cream, and rum wrapped in crepes and drizzled with hot chocolate sauce)—doesn't get any better than this. ♦ Continental ♦ Daily dinner. Reservations recommended. 112 Romero St NW (between Old Town Rd NW and S Plaza NW). 247.3545

MARIPOSA GALLERY

16 Mariposa Gallery Providing a wonderful change of pace from the local Indian art galleries, this adobe art space features an extensive (though not necessarily expensive) selection of fine contemporary American crafts. Exhibiting works primarily by New Mexican crafts artists, owners Fay Abrams and Peg Cronin emphasize traditional craft media—wood, glass, clay, metal, fiber, and mixed media. The wire sculpture, ceramic bolo ties, and hand-painted leather purses are just a sampling of the fun, while hand-painted silk scarves, hand-crafted tableware, and spectacular jewelry exhibit the finer side of things. Don't miss the Día de los Muertos (Day of the Dead) pieces—functional ceramics with skeletal images—by Steve Kilborn. The changing gallery exhibits feature works by some of the area's most innovative emerging artists. ♦ M-Sa; Su noon-5PM. 113 Romero St NW (between Central Ave and S Plaza NW). 842.9097

17 John Isaac Antiques A second-story nook overlooking the Plaza is where folk-art fan John Isaac found his niche when he brought his antique pieces here from back East and settled in Old Town in 1985. Isaac's collection has grown considerably since then, evolving into an impressive display of antique folk and Native American art works that would intrigue any serious collector and could convince even the casual admirer to start buying.

Isaac has divided his simple studio into display areas that spotlight various artistic genres and historical periods. One fascinating room is devoted to the devotional materials of the Spanish Empire, and includes *retablos,* ex-votos (offerings of thanks for miracles

performed), and other religious objects from 18th- to early-19th-century Guatemala, Ecuador, Mexico, and the Philippines. Another room houses pre-1930 Pueblo and Hopi pottery, baskets, and textiles, while the Latin American folk art display highlights traditional Mexican works, including an incredible collection of jewelry dating from the 1920s to the 1960s.

His even rarer collection of religious works by renowned early New Mexico *santeros* (traditional Hispanic folk artists) can be viewed by appointment only. And his **Antigua, Arts of the Americas** gallery showcases a specialized selection of Mexican painted furniture, pottery, ironworks, and tin. ♦ M-Sa. 2036 S Plaza NW (between San Felipe and Romero Sts NW). 842.6656

18 Old Town Plaza The hub of activity in traditional Spanish Colonial village life was always a plaza, a town square of sorts where residents could gather to talk, take a break from a hard day's work, or simply sit and enjoy the scenery. Thus this plaza, built in 1780, served for centuries as a social center for scores of local denizens whose families have inhabited the area for generations.

Today, however, the Plaza, with its towering cottonwoods, winding brick paths, wrought-iron benches, and graceful white gazebo, provides a shady haven for visitors who wish to take a respite from their sight-seeing and shopping jaunts. Situated across from the **San Felipe de Neri Catholic Church,** the Plaza is still the core of the original Albuquerque and is surrounded by many of the same adobe structures that the first settlers built, which now house Old Town's popular galleries, shops, and restaurants. At the Plaza's east end stand two reminders of a Civil War skirmish that took place in Albuquerque on 8 and 9 April 1862. The pair of cannons are replicas of those buried behind the **San Felipe de Neri Catholic Church** by retreating Confederate troops. The originals can be seen a few blocks away at **The Albuquerque Museum.** And on Christmas Eve, visitors marvel as Plaza sidewalks are set aglow with some 500,000 traditional *luminarias* that light up the night. ♦ Bounded by San Felipe and Romero Sts NW, and S and N Plazas NW

Cattle and sheep ranching and farming were the basis of Albuquerque's economy during Spanish colonial times. A very pungent native tobacco was grown here, and fine vineyards at Bernalillo and Isleta exported wine back to Spain.

Restaurants/Clubs: Red   **Hotels:** Blue

Shops/♦ Outdoors: Green   **Sights/Culture:** Black

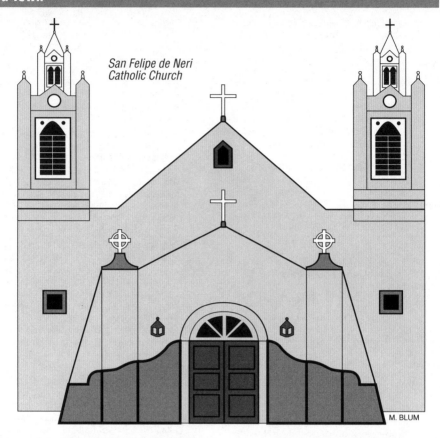

San Felipe de Neri Catholic Church

M. BLUM

19 San Felipe de Neri Catholic Church

The 16th-century Florentine saint Filippo Neri, for whom Albuquerque's oldest church (illustrated above) is named, was known as a fastidious man who avoided religious dispute. But the church that has served as the anchor of village faith and the focal point of the Old Town Plaza for nearly three centuries has certainly seen its share of change—and the controversy that often comes with it.

Beginning as a small adobe structure among a group of farms on the banks of the Rio Grande, the church was established by Franciscan friars at the same time Albuquerque was founded in 1706. By 1793, the village population was burgeoning, but the tiny earthen church collapsed after years of erosion. Following a decree by then-Governor Fernando de la Concha, a new church was erected. That building, dedicated to San Felipe de Neri, was designed in the traditional New Mexican architectural style, with a flat roof, ceiling vigas, and hand-carved wooden corbels. Today it forms the heart of the present church.

Two centuries later, the church has grown into a massive and curious combination of architectural styles, bearing Spanish Colonial, Gothic, Pueblo Revival, and modern motifs

that are far from its simple beginnings. This diversity is the product of the culturally varied group of priests who have overseen the structure through the years, including those of Spanish, Mexican, New Mexican, French, and Italian descent. Each managed to leave his personal mark on the church, but all had to endure the grumblings of their parishioners in the process.

The gradual transformation that eventually would cover up the traditional New Mexican church structure began in the 1850s when it was redecorated under the supervision of the French priest Father Joseph Machebeuf. The major change was the addition of the ornate Victorian bell towers that still loom above the entrance. Then in 1868, Italian Jesuit priests refurbished the interior, covering the vigas and corbels in tin, adding nontraditional woodwork throughout, and applying trompe l'oeil painting to various surfaces to give the appearance of polished marble. Finally, as recently as 1978, a veneer of artificial stone was applied to the facade and other portions of the church, lending it the look of a suburban ranch house. By this time, the church had been listed on both the state and national registers of historic landmarks, and Father George Salazar, the priest who ordered the stonework, was cited for an infraction of a city ordinance protecting such landmarks. Father Salazar went to court, where the judge ruled the ordinance unconstitutional.

Despite the changes, today the church sits regally amid a crush of Old Town tourist shops and restaurants and still serves an estimated 800 local families. Picture taking is allowed, but be considerate of those who may be at prayer. For an extra special taste of local culture, attend the Spanish Mass on Sunday. A museum (open daily; no admission) features a collection of Jesuit vestments from the 1800s and *santero* wood carvings. ◆ 2005 N Plaza NW (between San Felipe and Romero Sts NW). 243.4628

20 Anitra's Old Town Poster Company and Gallery This small family-run poster shop and gallery offers the only complete selection of Southwest posters and limited edition prints in Old Town. Included are posters by Amado Peña, R.C. Gorman, Doug West, and, naturally, Georgia O'Keeffe. Also featured are original artworks by Oklahoma Cherokee artist Bill Rabbit and the official posters of the annual Albuquerque International Balloon Fiesta. ◆ Daily. 201 San Felipe St NW (at Old Town Rd NW). 842.1858

21 Böttger Mansion $ Built in 1912 by a German immigrant, this pale-blue Victorian-style home was obviously a blatant departure from the surrounding adobe earth tones and architectural styles that had long characterized the area. Today run by the Garcia family as the only bed-and-breakfast in Old Town proper, the quaint two-story building is still considered unique to the area and is listed on the National Register of Historic Landmarks.

Situated in a quiet southeast corner of Old Town, the mansion offers a choice of seven guest rooms. All are drenched in Victorian-era decor, with delightful floral motifs bouncing off original tin ceilings and large brass beds. One room features a comfortable sunroom overlooking the patio garden; the second has an elaborate hand-painted mural created by an original Böttger family member; while the third boasts glossy marble floors and a private patio. A smattering of pottery and other regional art adds a tasteful Southwestern touch.

Outside, an enclosed grassy courtyard with marble patios shelters guests from the area's tourist bustle. Breakfast is served in the patio garden during the warmer months, and usually features scrambled eggs smothered in green chile or fabulous apricot French toast. And there is always fresh fruit, coffee, juice, tea, and homemade *bizcochitos* (cookies made from anise, lard, sugar, and flour), New Mexico's official state cookie. The management happily picks up the tab for parking across the street. ◆ 110 San Felipe St NW (between Central Ave and Old Town Rd NW). 243.3639 &

22 American International Rattlesnake Museum There are more than 20 rattlesnake species on display in this specialty "museum" of natural history. The tiny museum (with two aisles of some 28 rattlers enclosed in natural settings) is billed as the largest multispecies exhibit in the country and features snakes from North, Central, and South America. Popular draws include such oddities as the albino Marilyn and the only patternless Western diamondback rattlesnake in known captivity. The display was mounted in 1990 by one-time biology teacher Bob Myers, who wants to dispel the myth of the ferocious rattler. "Rattlesnakes don't attack; they only defend," Myers says, "and they're essential to the ecological balance of the hemisphere." Thus, he strives to educate visitors with a mix of videos and rare artifacts—fangs, skeletons, skins, and the like—dating from as far back as 15 million years. An adjacent display area features unusual and entertaining memorabilia, and a gift shop offers rattlesnake-related souvenirs. No petting, please. ◆ Nominal admission. Daily. 202 San Felipe St NW (at Old Town Rd NW). 242.6569 &

22 Montoya's Patio Cafe ★★$ Veronica Montoya's homey New Mexican cafe is a winner in the warmer months, when diners sit outside on the patio munching on the massive Montoya burger (a half-pound burger heaped with green chile and guacamole) and watching the world go by. The beef or chicken fajitas are famous here, too, and the Mexican combo (enchilada, taco, tamale, beans, rice, chile, and tortillas) should satisfy all your cravings for Southwestern food. Some American fare is served, too, and kids have their own menu. Indoor seating is also available. ♦ New Mexican/American ♦ Daily breakfast, lunch, and dinner. 202½ San Felipe St NW (at Old Town Rd NW). 243.3357 &

LA PLACITA

23 La Placita Dining Rooms ★★$$ Directly facing Old Town Plaza, the rambling hacienda now named for Don Ambrosio Armijo dates back to the city's founding in 1706. Besides housing the prominent Armijo clan, it later served as the family store, where women's lace gloves sold for 10¢ a pair and men's linen underwear went for a buck. During the tumultuous settlement years, the house was also used as a military fort, where soldiers sought refuge behind its three-foot-thick adobe walls. In peacetime, however, the house was alive with music and revelry as Don Ambrosio, known for his love of parties, hosted some of the most lavish balls in town. In 1872, when his daughter, Teresa, married, Don Ambrosio added a second floor to the house and a rich walnut staircase that ran the length of her wedding train. Later, the house fell into disrepair but was restored to its original state in 1930.

Today guests dine in six spacious rooms with fine regional art and furnishings that echo the warm, rustic ambience of early New Mexico. One room, formerly an outdoor patio, has a great tree growing through its roof. Upstairs, **La Placita Gallery** is a showcase for classic Native American and other Southwest art. Strolling Mexican troubadours entertain nightly. Both lunch and dinner feature a selection of traditional New Mexican dishes, such as plump *chiles rellenos* (whole green chiles stuffed with cheese), flat and rolled blue-corn cheese or chicken enchiladas, scrambled eggs with green chile and spicy homemade Mexican sausage, and fluffy sopaipillas drenched in honey. The house favorite is a whopping Mexican dinner that includes a red-chile cheese enchilada, *chile relleno*, beef taco, beans, Spanish rice, salad, and sopaipillas. Other entrées include beef, chicken, and fish, and there's a children's menu, too. ♦ New Mexican ♦ Daily lunch and dinner. Reservations recommended. 208 San Felipe St NW (east side of Old Town Plaza). 247.2204

Outside La Placita Dining Rooms:

La Placita Portal Beneath the wooden portal that runs the length of the hacienda, Native American artists and craftspeople sell jewelry, pottery, and other wares to passersby. This way of doing business continues a longstanding Old Town tradition. ♦ San Felipe St NW (east of Old Town Plaza)

24 Perfumes of the Desert and Candle Shop Follow your nose through the unusual smells of the Southwest in this family-owned house of fragrance. Located in Old Town since 1948, three generations of perfumers from the Mollenkopf family have created an original array of rare desert scents inspired by the aromatic mountainsides, deserts, and canyons of New Mexico, Colorado, and Arizona. The Mollenkopfs' secret formulas are derived from select native plants of the Southwest and are formulated for the region's dry climate by containing more oil than most perfumes. Yucca, purple sage, ginger blossom, desert mistletoe, and cactus flower are just some of the savory scents found here. Women's perfume and cologne are featured, although men may be tempted by an exotic piñon aftershave. Candles, incense, and other fragrant sundries are available, too. ♦ Daily. No. 4 Patio Market (behind La Placita). 242.1745

25 Old Town Card Shop An Old Town staple, this shop specializes in richly colored silk-screened cards of Southwest vistas and themes. Hundreds of other greeting cards, postcards, and note cards from more than 75 independent makers also boast regional motifs from the likes of Ansel Adams and Georgia O'Keeffe. And the rare collection of European paper models of famous castles, cathedrals, and other landmarks might make you dream of a vacation abroad. ♦ M-Sa; Su noon-5PM. 1919 Old Town Rd NW, Plaza Hacienda No. 1 (between 19th and San Felipe Sts NW). 247.9634

26 La Hacienda Restaurant ★★$$ A charming mural on the outer wall depicts the founding of the city of Albuquerque and the building of this traditional adobe home at the turn of the 18th century. Today, the house has been transformed into a casual New Mexican restaurant where a shady front patio looks out onto the activity of the Old Town Plaza. Inside, the atmosphere is cozy and intimate. The most unusual items on the menu are Mexican-style seafood dishes such as *chimichangas de pescado* (fried burritos made with fish) and tacos Monterey (stuffed with shrimp, crabmeat, and whitefish). Other specialties are regional and include *carnitas asadas* (pork marinated in red or green chile), *tostadas compuestas* (deep-fried corn tortillas topped with meat, beans, guacamole, and sour cream), and a savory chile-tortilla soup, as well as such delicious homemade desserts as

---

Restaurants/Clubs: Red   **Hotels:** Blue

Shops/♥ Outdoors: Green   **Sights/Culture:** Black

flan, blueberry piñon ice cream, and tequila lime sherbet. Margaritas here are made for a variety of tastes and include melon, Kahlua, apricot, raspberry, and peach. ♦ New Mexican ♦ Daily lunch and dinner. Reservations recommended for large parties. 302 San Felipe St NW (opposite N Plaza NW). 243.3131

26 Delmonico's Leslie and Bob Delmonico concentrate on casual Southwestwear in denim and suede and the accessories to go with it. Most notable is the selection of traditional Navajo skirts: Crushed velvet styles come in deep, rich shades of earth and sky, while the cotton quarter-inch pleated "broomstick" design is created by tightly pleating the skirt around a broomstick. The 100-percent cotton boots and shoes are another Southwest classic. ♦ Daily. 304 San Felipe St NW (near N Plaza NW). 243.9500

26 Schelu Decorative and functional items for hearth and home are featured in this Southwest interiors gallery. Showcasing the works of more than 65 area artists, the six-room space is crammed with everything from handmade lamps, pillows, and place mats to tableware, canisters, pitchers, and pottery. Traditional territorial New Mexican ponderosa pine furniture is also scattered throughout, as well as textiles, designer sculpture, and scores of Southwest knickknacks. ♦ Daily. 306 San Felipe St NW (near N Plaza NW). 765.5869

27 Nizhoni Moses, Ltd. *Nizhoni*, in Navajo, means "beautiful," and the Moses family has been bringing some of the area's most beautiful Indian fine art to Old Town for years. With pieces from most of the state's 19 Indian pueblos, this small gallery has amassed an incredible collection of Pueblo pottery, including the renowned black pottery of the late Maria Martinez and her great-granddaughters, Barbara Gonzales and Kathy Sanchez. **Acoma, Isleta, Zia,** and **Santa Clara** potters are also represented, as well as Navajo potters Alice Cling and Sue Williams. A few contemporary artists are shown here as well, notably sculptor Dennis Andrew Rodriguez of **Laguna Pueblo.** Pieces of rare Zuni and Navajo jewelry from the famed *Egeland Collection* are featured along with works by Navajo jeweler Thomas Singer. Also from Navajo land: a select display of weavings (from transition rugs circa 1900 to contemporary textiles), plus fun, one-of-a-kind "mud toys," the whimsical play ornaments of Navajo children. ♦ Daily. 326 San Felipe St NW (between Old Town Plaza and Church St NW). 842.1808

28 La Crêpe Michel ★★★$$ Finding a French bistro in the heart of Old Town is kind of like finding green chile in Paris: a happily unexpected surprise. This intimate little cafe offers impeccable French classical cuisine, with an emphasis on an inventive array of chicken, seafood, beef, vegetarian, and dessert crepes. The onion soup, escargots, and fresh-baked bread are also classically French, while the luscious chocolate mousse is just plain classic. Diners have their choice of the indoor cafe, an enclosed patio, or an outdoor patio, all of which are equally romantic. Bring your own liquor: City law dictates that the restaurant's proximity to the **San Felipe de Neri Catholic Church** makes it ineligible for a liquor license. ♦ French ♦ Tu-Su lunch and dinner. Reservations recommended. 400 C-2 San Felipe St NW, in Patio del Norte (between Pueblo Don Gaspar and Patio Escondido). 242.1251

28 V. Whipple's Mexico Shop Old Mexico meets New Mexico here in Virginia Whipple's exotic Mexican market. Once yearly, Whipple travels to southern Mexico to handpick her specialty stock of Mexican folk art, furniture, dinnerware, jewelry, and glass by artists hailing from such places as Oaxaca, Guerrero, Jalisco, Michoacán, and Guanajuato. Highlights include hand-blown glassware in aqua, cobalt, and amber hues; lead-free dinnerware; hand-punched tin; *milagro* charms (traditional offerings for good health); terra-cotta patio furniture; and such traditional Día de los Muertos artifacts as pop-up coffins and sugar skulls. A small selection of Huichol Indian art is also featured, and the bronze door knockers (in the shape of gargoyles, lizards, frogs, and the like) are truly bizarre. ♦ Daily. 400-E San Felipe St NW, in Patio del Norte (between Pueblo Don Gaspar and Patio Escondido). 243.6070

29 Chapel of Our Lady of Guadalupe Though it looks as if it could have been erected by original Old Town settlers, this small secluded chapel was built in 1974 under the direction of Sister Giotto Moots, a colorful and controversial figure who once ran a school of religious art on the site. Dedicated to Our Lady of Guadalupe, the patroness of the indigenous peoples of the Americas, the picturesque adobe chapel boasts traditional

New Mexican woodwork and a brilliant large-scale image of Our Lady of Guadalupe painted in flaming colors on a prominent inside wall. The chapel is a symbol of the deeply entrenched Catholic faith of the area and provides a nice opportunity for a moment of quiet reflection in the midst of Old Town's tourist flurry. ◆ 404 San Felipe St NW, in Patio Escondido (between Patio del Norte and Mountain Rd NW)

29 Stern's Leatherback Turtle New York refugee Steve Stern has been selling leather goods in Old Town for almost a quarter-century. Featuring fine leathers from around the world, his collection is all handmade in New Mexico and caters to tastes that range from the briefcase-toting executive to the Southwest-style aficionado seeking a traditional hand-beaded Native American deerskin dress. Other clothing and accessories include skirts, jackets, wallets, handbags, luggage, and belts, many of which feature such fun Southwest touches as fringe or Western-style hand-tooling. ◆ M-Sa; Su noon-5PM. 404 San Felipe St NW, in Patio Escondido (between Patio del Norte and Mountain Rd NW). 842.8496

30 Good Stuff Richard Hulett offers a large and diverse collection of Southwest antiques and memorabilia at this shop. From the Old West comes his stock of antique cowboy collectibles—bits, spurs, saddles, hats, chaps, and branding irons—dating from the turn of the century to 1940. From Indian country comes vintage pots, baskets, and Navajo rugs plus a prime selection of aged Old Pawn Indian jewelry. From the Hispanic world come antique textiles, Mexican masks, and religious relics from Old and New Mexico. You might also find that ox yoke you've been yearning for in the "primitives" section, next to the old cheese boards and worn wooden doors. ◆ Daily; evenings by appointment. 2108 Charlevoix St NW (at San Felipe St NW). 843.6416

31 High Noon Restaurant & Saloon ★★★ $$$ Located on the corner of a block once full of brothels and saloons, this 1750 former woodworking shop mixes a 19th-century saloon atmosphere with a touch of upscale class. The setting is traditional New Mexican territorial, with ceiling *vigas* (exposed wooden beams), brick floors, and handmade Southwest-style tables and chairs. An interesting blend of Native American and New Mexican art dots walls, ledges, and windowsills, while a skylight in the roof surrounds diners with subtle plays on light and dark, depending on the time of day. Steak is a specialty here, with choices of rib eye, T-bone, fillet, and a hot and hearty pepper steak cooked with cracked black pepper, red peppercorns, and a cream-and-Cognac sauce. The High Noon red trout

(dusted with blue-corn flour, panfried, and served with avocado margarita salsa) is another favorite, as are the rack of lamb (oven-roasted with fresh herbs) and the chicken à l'orange (grilled chicken breast in a zesty sauce of oranges, lemons, glazed leeks, and brandy). Seafood, veal, and a host of New Mexican favorites round out the entrées, and the potent margaritas complement any dish. ◆ New Mexican/Steak ◆ Daily lunch and dinner. Reservations recommended. 425 San Felipe St NW (at Charlevoix St NW). 765.1455

32 The Albuquerque Museum Documenting 400 years of New Mexico's history, this huge museum houses the largest collection of Spanish Colonial artifacts in the US. Anchoring the collection are two life-sized bronze models of Spanish conquistadores (see floor plan below), which symbolize the earliest arrival of the Spanish in New Mexico in 1540. Other artifacts include ancient maps from as early as the 15th century

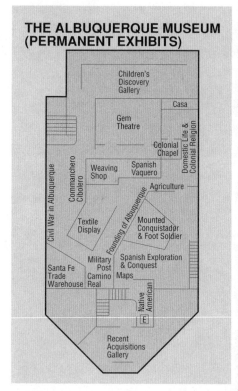

THE ALBUQUERQUE MUSEUM (PERMANENT EXHIBITS)

(when the Rio Grande spilled into the Pacific), arms and armor used during the Hispanic conquest, and coins and domestic items traded from the 16th to the 18th centuries. A permanent exhibit, *Four Centuries: A History of Albuquerque,* charts the city's evolution from the earliest Hispanic presence to its current existence as the state's industrial center, while a multimedia audiovisual presentation chronicles the development of the city since 1875. Other highlights include permanent and changing exhibits of traditional and contemporary works by New Mexican artists, an extensive photo archive, special children's exhibits, and an outdoor sculpture garden. The museum also hosts hourlong walking tours of Old Town. Museum: free; tours: fee. Museum: Tu-Su; tours: M-W 11AM, Sa-Su 1:30PM; call for reservations. 2000 Mountain Rd NW (between 19th and San Felipe Sts NW). 242.4600 &

33 **San Felipe Plaza** Albuquerque's newest indoor/outdoor mall has 18 shops and galleries, water fountains, and a covered parking lot. ♦ Mountain Rd (east of Rio Grande Blvd, across the street from The Albuquerque Museum) &

Within San Felipe Plaza:

Western Warehouse This shop boasts a large selection of Western boots, hats, and apparel, as well as Western-style gifts, pottery, drums, books, and furniture. ♦ M-Sa; Su 11AM-5PM. 244.9515

Palace Design Accessories, lighting, handmade chandeliers, wall sconces, and folk art are featured at this shop. ♦ M-Sa; Su noon-5PM. 248.1088

Maxwell Museum and Museum Shop This branch of the **University of New Mexico**'s **Maxwell Museum of Anthropology** displays some of the Maxwell family's extensive collection of native rugs, pottery, and jewelry. The shop offers art, jewelry, books, and music from Native American and other cultures. ♦ M-Sa; Su noon-4PM. 247.1440

Seasons Rotisserie and Grill ★★★$$ Brushed-copper bar tops, maple wood fixtures, fresh flower arrangements, and an open kitchen create a warm atmosphere at this popular dining spot. The second story patio has a lovely view of Old Town and the Sandia Mountains. Try the roasted garlic and goat cheese bruschetta, follow with the tender spit-roasted chicken, and indulge in the creamy tiramisù for dessert. The wine list offers such favorites as Ferrari-Carano Cabernet (by the glass or bottle); or choose a gold margarita, sangria, or one of the beers on tap. ♦ American ♦ M lunch; Tu-Su lunch and dinner. 766.5100

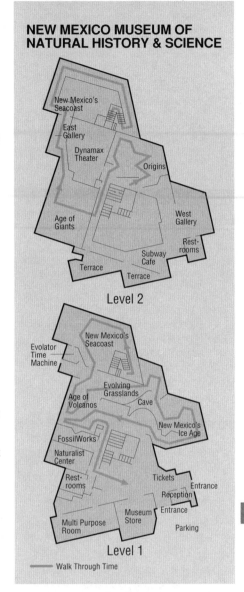

NEW MEXICO MUSEUM OF NATURAL HISTORY & SCIENCE

Level 2

Level 1

——— Walk Through Time

34 **New Mexico Museum of Natural History & Science** Spike the pentaceratops and Alberta the albertosaurus greet visitors at the front door to this state museum, and they are just two of the natural wonders in this treasure-trove of New Mexican natural history. Strikingly modern, the museum entices adults and children alike to bone up on 12 billion years of history with some of the most interesting, innovative, and entertaining educational exhibitions anywhere. Indeed, a good part of this world of wonders was designed by professional Disneyland artists who know the meaning of the word adventure.

The adventures here include the *Evolator* (see floor plan above), an impressive high-tech video ride through 35 million years of New Mexico's geologic history and time; an active volcano that oozes hot lava beneath a see-through glass floor; a cool Ice Age cave; and a 3,000-gallon shark tank that evokes the New Mexico of 75 million years ago, when Albuquerque and most of the state were covered by an inland sea. Today, there's a lot less water in the state, and the museum's 85-footlong replica of the Rio Grande educates visitors about the state's most precious water resource. Another permanent exhibit charts the evolution of the horse.

The museum is also home to the incredible **Dynamax Theater,** whose 2.5-story screen magically transports viewers into the earth's vast natural land- and seascapes. The theater is a favorite for kids, who are also encouraged to participate at the **Naturalist Center,** where they can touch snakes and frogs, buzz about beehives, and make tracks of New Mexico's indigenous animals in the sand. ◆ Admission. Daily. 1801 Mountain Rd NW (between 18th and 20th Sts). 841.2800 ♿

Within the New Mexico Museum of Natural History & Science:

Subway Sandwiches ★★$ Dine in the shadow of a giant pterodactyl and choose from a sandwich menu, a sampling of which includes tuna, seafood, and chicken salads, and Italian meats, all served on a 6" or 12" homemade loaf. There's a lovely view of the Sandia Mountains from the outdoor terrace. ◆ American ◆ Daily lunch. 841.2800 ext 59

35 **Duran Central Pharmacy** Established in 1912 by Pete Duran a few blocks west of its current location, this pharmacy quickly rooted itself in the hearts and stomachs of local residents by featuring some of the finest *remedios* (traditional herbal remedies) and one of the most popular luncheon counters in the city. Two moves and more than 80 years later, its present owner, Albuquerque native Robert Ghattas (he bought the pharmacy in 1964), hasn't messed with Duran's formula for success; good personal service and good local grub are still the standards here.

In addition to its established collection of more than a hundred medicinal herbs, such as *osha* (good for colds and flu) and *yerba buena* (good for upset stomachs), today's spotless, sprawling pharmacy includes a huge selection of sundries ranging from cosmetics to candy, greeting cards to gift wrap, coffeemakers to comic books. Some unexpected finds are imported soaps and colognes as well as a number of discontinued products, like Monkey Shine toothpaste. The pharmacy is still a family-run business—Mona Ghattas oversees the pharmacopoeia—and prescriptions are still delivered to your door,

free of charge. ◆ Daily. 1815 Central Ave (between Laguna Blvd NW and San Pasquale Ave NW). 247.4141

Within the Duran Central Pharmacy:

Duran Central Pharmacy Restaurant
★★★$ From this simple, 48-seat restaurant tucked at the pharmacy's south end, one hears hungry customers say, "I'll have the *huevos rancheros,* please. And make that Christmas." That's New Mexican for two eggs swimming in cheese and both red and green chile. The dish, which comes with beans, potatoes, and a tortilla, has been a breakfast favorite here for years. The Torpedo (potatoes, chile, and cheese wrapped in a flour tortilla) is another popular option. Or just forget all the extras and order a steaming-hot bowl of red or green chile straight up. Take-out orders are available except during the busy lunch hour. No smoking is allowed. ◆ New Mexican ◆ Daily breakfast and lunch. 247.4141

36 **Garcia's Kitchen** ★★$ Move over, Wheaties. The breakfast of champions in this local hot spot is *menudo,* a hearty portion of beef tripe topped with a thick layer of red chile, which New Mexicans-in-the-know swear will cure the most horrendous of hangovers. Andy Garcia (no relation to the actor) and family have been serving the stuff in this kitschy New Mexican kitchen for decades, but if the thought of stomaching stomach is too much to take, the Garcias are famous for lots of other traditional New Mexican dishes, too. Most notable are the *carne adovada,* the green chile stew, and bottomless baskets of hot and fluffy homemade tortillas. Breakfast is served all day. ◆ New Mexican ◆ Daily breakfast, lunch, and dinner. 1736 Central Ave (between Laguna Blvd SW and San Pasquale Ave SW). 842.0273. Also at: Numerous locations throughout the city

Route 66—America's most famous highway—carried people and energy that shaped the Southwest from its opening in 1926. Every May Albuquerque celebrates the thoroughfare with a Giant Route 66 Festival, featuring a classic-car rally, carnival, and musical concerts. Today's I-40 roughly parallels the historic Route 66.

Bests

Larry Barker
Television Investigative Reporter, KOAT-TV

Barbecue wasn't invented in Texas, it was born at **The Quarters** and everyone in Albuquerque knows it! I don't know if it's the sauce, the hickory smoke or the tender, mouth-watering flavor, but those baby back ribs are the best, this side of the Pecos River.

In winter the Texans ski at Taos, the locals ski at **Sandia Peak Ski Area** on the backside of the **Sandia Mountains.** In summer take the ski lift to the top and mountain bike back down after watching the hang gliders leaping off the 10,000-foot cliff edge!

No tourist can resist the lure of Indian arts and crafts. But beware of turquoise fakes that have invaded New Mexico. The **Turquoise Museum** in **Old Town** wrote the book on turquoise. They'll show you what the good stuff looks like, and everything they sell is backed by a written guarantee.

Honorable Bill Richardson
US Congressman

Santa Fe

The Museum of International Folk Art houses one of the finest collections of folk art in the country.

Wheelwright Museum of the American Indian has a good gift shop in the basement.

Walk up **Canyon Road,** which is home to a lot of good galleries with objets d'art at all price ranges.

Buy jewelry directly from the Pueblo Indians along the portal of the **Palace of the Governors.**

Taos

A nice day trip from Santa Fe to Taos, take the back road through the small villages of **Truchas** (where *Milagro Beanfield War* was filmed) and **Las Trampas.** The scenery is spectacular with wonderful old churches.

Taos Pueblo just outside town is centuries old and a must-see.

Ledoux Street off of the **Plaza** is a pedestrian street of galleries and a lovely wander in the summer.

Navajo Gallery on Ledoux Street has the most comprehensive collection of Navajo artist R.C. Gorman's work.

Continue on the main road through Taos to the bridge that overlooks the **Rio Grande Gorge.** Park your car and walk onto the bridge and look down— breathtaking view.

Albuquerque

Old Town offers wonderful food and shopping and is a favorite among locals as well as tourists. The **Plaza,** bordered on the north by the historic **San Felipe de Neri Catholic Church,** is magical when lined with glowing *luminarias* during Christmas evenings.

The **University of New Mexico** campus must be viewed by a walk-through to fully appreciate its Southwestern flavor and beauty. The **Zimmerman Library** and the **Anthropology Building,** both built during the 1930s with WPA funds, are fine examples of classic Pueblo architecture.

The **Rio Grande Zoological Park** houses 235 species, including two extremely rare white Bengal tigers (with three offspring). A major aquarium and botanical gardens have opened there as well.

The **Indian Pueblo Cultural Center** is home to magnificent art, food, and dances, representing New Mexico's 19 Pueblos.

Few views are more spectacular than one atop the **Sandia Mountains** via the **Sandia Peak Aerial Tramway,** the world's longest of its kind. Travelers are lifted from 6,500 to over 10,300 feet, where skiing, dining, or just observing the wide expanse of Albuquerque and far beyond are experiences not soon forgotten.

Betty Hahn
Photographer/Mixed Media Artist

Just cruising along **Central Avenue** in Albuquerque (famous as **Route 66**) you can still get your kicks by:

Having lunch at **Duran Central Pharmacy.** They serve New Mexican food great with either the red or green chile (a little on the hot side for the very faint-hearted).

Attending almost anything at the **KiMo Theatre** or even just looking at the delightful Pueblo Deco architecture restored both inside and out. Fine, small dance companies appear here as well as other more eccentric productions.

Hanging out at the **Frontier.** Incredible fresh squeezed orange juice, sinful homemade cinnamon rolls, and good New Mexican favorites such as *huevos rancheros.*

Splurging (well, for Albuquerque) for dinner at **Scalo Northern Italian Grill.** Virtually the only Italian restaurant in town, its speciality is Northern Italian cooking, and, even though it's usually noisy and crowded, the food is always good. You do get what you pay for. Also deserving a try is their place across the street, **Il Vicino.** Good pizza and big salads.

Having any kind of coffee and pastry at the **Double Rainbow.** A popular hangout because you can sit around and read magazines off their racks and nobody runs you off for staying too long. Everything here always tastes good and fresh.

Pomona Hallenbeck
Artist, Sketchbox Studio, Santa Fe

Old Santa Fe Trail Books & Bistro features a plethora of book, magazine, cassette, and video options, as well as giant exotic muffins, a fine bar, and a splendid menu including my favorite, a huge portobello mushroom sandwich on sesame bun.

Madrid, an old mining town with great selection of shops/galleries, good foods, restored miners' dwellings.

El Rancho de las Golindrinas, a delightful slice of Indian/Spanish colonial history with defensive tower, molasses mill, blacksmith and wheelwright shops, winery, gift shop, picnic area.

Downtown

When the railroad whistled its way into New Mexico in 1880, Albuquerque was still a small adobe village huddled around a traditional Spanish plaza on the banks of the Rio Grande. But eager to cash in on the economic gains predicted by the dawn of modern transportation, merchants and residents packed up and moved closer to the tracks. The original settlement—the site of today's Old Town—was practically abandoned. And **New Town**, two miles east of the original town site, quickly took over.

As the population grew, New Town blossomed into Downtown, the city's central business, government, and social hub. By the turn of the century, as businesses bustled, saloons and gambling houses flourished, and tourists arrived in droves, Albuquerque began to lose its small-town feel. **Route 66** came to Albuquerque in 1926 and cut a swath through Downtown along **Central Avenue**. Dubbed by John Steinbeck as the "Mother Road," the highway linked Chicago with the West Coast and transformed Central Avenue into a neon haze of motels, truck stops, diners, and more.

During the next 20 years, Downtown thrived as restaurants, stores, and movie houses multiplied, and major companies moved in. But in the mid-1950s, appealing new residential and commercial developments in the northeast quadrant of town caused the city's business and population center to shift to the sprawling neighborhoods and shopping centers of Albuquerque's Northeast Heights—and they sent Downtown downhill.

Like many of America's once thriving downtown areas, Albuquerque's central business district became dormant for nearly 20 years, although it continued as the seat of city government. Then, in the late 1970s, residents longing for the nostalgia and charm of Downtown's golden age began to revitalize the area. Slowly, old buildings were restored, new businesses settled in, and shoppers appeared again on the sidewalks of Central Avenue.

Although a few cheap motels, greasy-spoon diners, and old-fashioned gas stations inspire sentimental thoughts of Route 66, Downtown today leans more toward the contemporary: 20-story buildings stretch skyward, first-rate restaurants feature innovative combinations of native and nouvelle cuisines, nightclubs pulse with new and alternative sounds, and galleries tout contemporary painting, sculpture, photography, and other fine art.

But Downtown hasn't snubbed all of its roots. A delightful mix of old adobe and Victorian-style neighborhoods still borders Downtown on all sides, and architectural wonders such as the Pueblo Deco–style **KiMo Theatre**, a one-of-a-kind 1927 picture palace, and **La Posada de Albuquerque**, Conrad Hilton's 1939 Spanish-style showpiece hotel, are well-preserved landmarks. Strolling through the "new" Downtown presents visitors with an interesting blend of sights and sounds that range from the upscale to the casual, the corporate to the funky, and the ultraconservative to the downright weird.

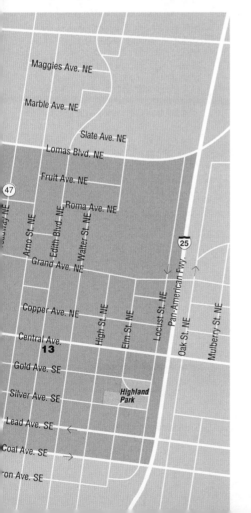

STEPHENS

1 Stephens ★★★$$$$ This Southwestern/American cafe packs in the let's-make-a-deal lunch crowd but also draws folks from throughout the city seeking a much less stressful dining experience. There are three elegant areas in which to eat: an enclosed patio, a large Santa Fe–style room with a view of the open kitchen, and a formal dining room with an exposed brick wall dating from the original 1915 building in which the restaurant stands. Chef Robert Boone is classically oriented but offers a little bit of everything. The menu ranges from a delectable rack of lamb and roasted duckling to excellent grilled fish, chicken, veal, seafood, and pasta. The special spa menu offers dishes low in cholesterol, sodium, and calories, including an incredible Wiener schnitzel. Baked brie or bread pudding should fit the bill for those wanting their calories in fat. The service is notable, as is Albuquerque's only award-winning list of more than 300 fine wines. ◆ Southwestern/American ◆ M-F lunch and dinner; Sa-Su dinner. Reservations recommended. 1311 Tijeras Ave NW (at Central Ave). 842.1773 ⅃

2 El Rey Theatre Once a popular movie house and long owned by a great-niece of famed opera composer Giacomo Puccini (Virginia Puccini Doyle), this renovated 1941 theater now bustles as a house of spirits with live music and dance. With its huge screen, red-velvet curtains, and classic 1940s decor, "The King" reigned as the monarch of

115

Downtown movie houses until the modern theaters of the 1960s moved into the city. After falling into disrepair, the **Puccini Building,** as it was known then, was renovated in the early 1970s, and 15 years ago reopened as a neighborhood nightclub and bar. Today, the stage spotlights live musicians at least three times weekly—with many of the biggest national and international acts to pass through the state—in performances that include blues, rock, alternative, jazz, metal, and country sounds. The high ceilings provide great acoustics, while dance floors are featured on both levels of the two-story space. Those not into dancing can head over to the **El Rey Liquor Establishment** (242.9300), the corner bar. Once one of the most popular soda fountains in the city, the tiny one-room tavern is now an equally famous watering hole. Free movies are shown in the theater on Sunday. ◆ Cover for shows. Shows: Call ahead for schedule. Bar: daily 10AM-2AM. 624 Central Ave (between Sixth and Seventh Sts NW). 243.7546, Ticketmaster 884.0999

2 Golden West Saloon Just like **El Rey Theater,** this swinging nightclub and bar is owned by Puccini's great-niece. It's named after one of the composer's famous operas, *Girl of the Golden West,* but it doesn't cater to opera fans (the walls, however, are plastered with original posters of famous Puccini opera pics). Featuring loud live music every night (with at least two national acts a week), club managers Charles and Sulie Connelly concentrate on making their casual nightspot a center for live music (in the 1950s, it was a lively saloon). A small indoor grill and ornate wooden bar offer affordable food and drink specials, including 19 beers on tap, while a huge hardwood dance floor provides plenty of room for moving to different musical styles every day. ◆ Cover for shows. Bar: daily 10AM-2AM. Shows: Call ahead for schedule. 620 Central Ave (between Sixth and Seventh Sts SW). 243.7546, Ticketmaster 884.0999

3 Lookie Loos Named after the slang term for book lovers who browsed—but never bought—in bookstores in the 1920s and 1930s, this hodgepodge of quality antiques and modern-day collectibles offers lots to look at and prices so affordable a "lookie loo" might actually be tempted to buy. John Gallegos's fascinating selection (it's the only antiques store in Downtown) includes furniture, glassware, jewelry, and art plus an impressive array of vintage hats, clothing, and accessories. He also offers local artists free exhibit space on store walls; if their work doesn't sell, they just come and take it down. ◆ M-Sa. 519 Central Ave (between Fifth and Sixth Sts NW). 242.4740

3 Rio Bravo ★★★★$$ With its black ceiling, white linen–covered tables, and stark contemporary art, this restaurant is more Manhattan cool than Albuquerque casual, but locals pack the place every night. Owners Dave and Lisa Smith have created an unusual menu of exquisite flavors, using New Mexican–grown fruits, vegetables, and spices. Everything has a new twist, like *chiles rellenos* stuffed with goat cheese or mesquite-grilled artichokes with smoked chile aioli. Don't miss the corn cakes filled with roasted corn, scallions, and roasted peppers, or the melt-in-your-mouth filet mignon stuffed with jalapeño chile. Master brewer Brad Kraus turns out four to five different delicious light and dark beers daily from his microbrewery in the bar, and the Andrew Paul Jazz Duo keeps things hot with live smokey jazz on Tuesday and Thursday evenings. The staff, mostly graduate students at the **University of New Mexico,** provide excellent service. ◆ New Mexican/American ◆ Daily. 515 Central Ave (between Fifth and Sixth Sts NW). 242.6800 &

4 University Art Museum This downtown branch of the **Albuquerque University Art Museum** features 19th- and 20th-century art, Spanish Colonial artworks, photography, and work from the *Tamarind Print Archives,* a collection of historic lithographs. Audio tours are available, and the gift shop has some nice art and jewelry items. ◆ Tu-Sa 11AM-4PM. 516 Central Ave (between Fifth and Sixth Sts SW). 242.8244

4 Richard Levy Gallery With one of the world's most diverse collections dedicated exclusively to modern and contemporary prints and works on paper, this large, well-lit gallery represents artists of regional, national, and international standing. Featured here are the works of Christopher Brown, Wes Mills, Lorna Simpson, James Casebere, David Levinthal, and Stewart Arends. A staunch supporter of new printmaking styles, owner Richard Levy's focus is on the unusual, and his displays of waterless lithographs are both new and unique. ◆ Tu-Sa 11AM-4PM. 514 Central Ave (between Fifth and Sixth Sts SW). 766.9888

5 Skip Maisel Wholesale Indian Jewelry & Crafts This large, warehouselike store may not be incredibly attractive, but it's packed with quality Indian arts and crafts at genuine wholesale prices. Gigantic **Cochiti Pueblo** drums, for instance, go for at least half the price of those found elsewhere. Other main attractions include authentic **Zuni, Navajo,** and **Santo Domingo** jewelry, some crafted in-shop; pottery from the pueblos of **Jemez, Acoma,** and **Santa Clara;** kachina dolls, rugs, painting, sculpture, and more. ◆ M-Sa. 510 Central Ave SW (between Fifth and Sixth Sts). 242.6526

6 KiMo Theatre Built by Italian immigrant Oreste Bachechi, this architectural masterpiece (illustrated below) fulfilled his dream of bringing a unique picture palace to his adopted city. The year was 1925: Art Deco was in, and picture palaces were all the rage. Bachechi, a film buff who had come to Albuquerque in 1885 and made his fortune as a grocer, wanted to repay the city with a premier theater. Native American themes had appeared in only a handful of theaters thus far, so Bachechi chose "Pueblo Deco," a flamboyant but short-lived style that fused the spirit of Southwest Indian culture with the exuberance of the Roaring '20s.

Bachechi hired Hollywood theater architect **Carl Boller** to design a building that would evoke the arts, culture, and traditions of New Mexico and the American Indian. **Boller** traveled extensively throughout the state, visiting the Indian pueblos of **Acoma** and **Isleta** as well as the Navajo reservation. Back in Albuquerque, he then created an outrageous rendering that combined traditional Indian motifs and Spanish Mission styles with such garish touches as garlanded longhorn steer skulls with eerie, glowing amber eyes. Bachechi loved it, and one year and $150,000 later, his peculiar picture palace opened. On 19 September 1927 the theater was christened the **KiMo,** a Pueblo Indian expression meaning "King of Its Kind."

As opening-night visitors poured into Bachechi's two-story dreamworld, they must have thought they were the ones who were dreaming. The outside facade was covered in terra-cotta Indian shields, and inside, door handles took on the shape of Indian kachina dolls, air vents were painted to look like Navajo rugs, and stylized wrought-iron waterfowl descended the stairs. Overhead, plaster ceiling beams were decorated with thunderbirds, rain clouds, and other geometric designs, all of which were illuminated by chandeliers in the shape of war drums and glowing steer skull sconce lights. All of the Native American symbols had precise historical significance, and even the color scheme was based on abstract Indian meanings: yellow stood for the setting sun, white the approaching morning, and black the darkening northern clouds. Crowning the lobby ceiling were seven murals by Carl von Hassler, dean of the Albuquerque art colony. In trompe l'oeil style, the murals represented a panoramic view of low mountains, cloud-filled skies, and peaceful Indian pueblos.

An elaborate $18,000 Wurlitzer organ was also purchased to accompany silent films. In addition to movies, the theater became home to weekly bingo games, vaudeville acts, and other live performances. Several up-and-coming talents got their start here, including Vivian Vance, who played Ethel Mertz in the "I Love Lucy" TV series. Other stars to grace the stage included Ginger Rogers, Tom Mix, Gloria Swanson, and Sally Rand.

Bachechi died just one year after the theater opened, but it remained a popular entertainment venue until the late 1960s. By that time, however, the original building had been altered several times to keep up with current architectural trends, and modern movie houses were in full swing. The **KiMo** was closed as a picture palace, and during the next 10 years was used for office space and occasional live performances. Then in 1977 the City of Albuquerque purchased the theater and restored it to its original flamboyant elegance. The theater is now a thriving performing-arts center for local and national acts and is listed on the National Register of Historic Places. ◆ Tours: M-F. 423 Central Ave (at Fifth St NW). 848.1370

KiMo Theater

M. BLUM

La Posada

7 La Posada de Albuquerque $$ Hotel mogul and New Mexico native Conrad Hilton chose this spot to become the highlight of his hotel chain and the hospitality hub of Downtown Albuquerque. The 10-story hostelry was built to ooze Southwestern architectural charm and featured a lavish two-story lobby with whitewashed arches, Mexican tile floors, ceiling vigas (exposed wooden beams), and hand-carved corbels. It was the first air-conditioned building in New Mexico as well as the 1949 honeymoon spot for Hilton and his famous bride-of-the-moment, Zsa Zsa Gabor.

Restored as **La Posada de Albuquerque** under new ownership in the 1980s, the 114-room hotel today is listed on the National Register of Historic Places and has retained its original charm. The lobby floor has an ornate brass-and-mosaic fountain, while ceilings are anchored by old-fashioned etched glass and tin chandeliers. A hand-carved wooden balcony circles overhead, and murals of Native American war dancers grace the downstairs halls. Southwest and Indian themes are carried over into the large earth-toned guest rooms, which feature hand-crafted furniture and Mexican tile, and wood-shuttered windows (some have fireplaces). Limited-edition prints by R.C. Gorman and Amado Peña hang on whitewashed walls, while Hopi pottery dots tables and shelves. Health club facilities are available adjacent to the hotel, and golf and tennis are 10 minutes away. ♦ 125 Second St NW (at Copper Ave NW). 242.9090, 800/777.5723; fax 242.8664 &

Within La Posada de Albuquerque:

Conrad's ★★★$$$ This restaurant feels like springtime, with its white walls and table linen, large windows, and bird of paradise plants. Specialties include *chuletas de cordero y camarones* (lamb chops and shrimp) and salmon *con salsa de mango* (salmon fillet with a sweet mango salsa). Three paellas are served, including a vegetable-only version. In the evenings, classical Spanish music is played by a different guitarist every month. ♦ New Southwestern ♦ Daily breakfast, lunch, and dinner. Reservations recommended for lunch and dinner. 242.9090 ext 25, 26 &

Lobby Bar A favorite local hangout for weekday Happy Hour, this is one of the only places in town to hear live jazz. ♦ Happy Hour: M-F; live music: F-Sa 9PM-midnight. 242.9090 &

8 Hyatt Regency $$$ Open since 1990, Albuquerque's newest major hotel towers 20 stories above Downtown in understated desert tones. Boasting Neo-Classical decor with a Southwestern flair, this modern and luxurious facility offers 395 spacious guest rooms and suites decorated in mixed shades of mauve, burgundy, and tan, with mahogany furnishings and all the standard Hyatt amenities. The lobby features a palm-shaded fountain bathed in natural light, while original Frederic Remington sculptures and other classic Southwestern art are spotlighted throughout the hotel. Also included are a full-service health club, spa, outdoor pool, two lounges, and a shopping promenade. ♦ 330 Tijeras Ave NW (at Third St NW). 842.1234, 800/233.1234; fax 766.6710 &

Within the Hyatt Regency:

McGrath's ★★★★$$$ This award-winning establishment—considered by many to be the best hotel restaurant in Albuquerque—was named after Lizzie McGrath, the madam of a "parlor house" on this site from 1880 to 1914 who became one of Albuquerque's most influential businesswomen of the era. The emphasis is on traditional dishes made with a Southwestern touch: filet mignon is brushed with red-chile butter; the rack of lamb is made with garlic and Mexican oregano; and the seared Norwegian salmon is served with an avocado-and-lime relish. Other wild and wonderful dishes include Texas blue crab cakes, roasted-duck quesadilla with sweet potato and black-bean puree, and a tangy Caesar salad that just may be the best in town. There's also a *cuisine naturelle* menu that offers great low-fat, low-calorie items including breast of chicken with mixed greens, followed by a fresh fruit basket served in a baked, crispy shell with a strawberry coulis for dessert; calories, carbohydrates, and percent of calories from fat are all given. Those who don't mind high-calorie splurges can choose crème brûlée. Kids get an activity book and crayons along with pizza, burgers, and fries. The restaurant's cherry wood appointments add to its intimate atmosphere. ♦ New Southwestern/Continental ♦ Daily breakfast, lunch, and dinner. Reservations recommended. 766.6700 &

9 Civic Plaza The "front yard" of Albuquerque City Hall, this wide-open landscaped space is the centrally located site of Downtown arts-and-crafts fairs, musical events, and other outdoor performances. The highlights of these events include the big annual Cinco de Mayo celebration and the annual Summerfest series—weekly Saturday night celebrations held from June through August that feature food, entertainment, and arts and crafts from one of Albuquerque's many ethnic communities. Greek Night, Italian Night, and of course, New Mexico Night are always hits. ♦ Bounded by Tijeras and Marquette Aves NW, and Third and Fourth Sts NW. Event information 768.3490

10 Albuquerque Convention Center In addition to nearly 168,000 square feet of exhibition space (106,000 square feet is column-free), a 2,500-seat auditorium, and 30 meeting rooms, this windowed complex has a two-story central atrium and a landscaped park area. ♦ 201 Second St NW (between Tijeras and Marquette Aves NW). 268.6060 ♿

DOUBLETREE

11 Doubletree Hotel of Albuquerque $$$ Located next to the **Albuquerque Convention Center,** this hotel boasts a convenient location and a friendly staff. The 15-story structure features 294 comfortable guest rooms in pastel hues with custom-made Southwestern furnishings and other regional touches. The pillared lobby is drenched in marble elegance and includes a two-story waterfall that cascades down a marble backdrop. Visitors can also take a dip in an outdoor swimming pool or forge their way through a fully equipped fitness room. Courtesy shuttle service is available to the airport and Old Town, and complimentary chocolate chip cookies await visitors in every room. ♦ 201 Marquette Ave NW (at Second St NW). 247.3344, 800/528.0444; fax 247.7025 ♿

Within the Doubletree Hotel of Albuquerque:

La Cascada Restaurant ★★$$ Sitting at the foot of a streaming waterfall, this restaurant is an airy, intimate dining space serving Southwestern specialties, fresh seafood, soups, and salads. The patio is ideal for casual dining while the adjacent **Bistro Bar** also offers light snacks. ♦ Southwestern ♦ Daily breakfast, lunch, and dinner. Reservations recommended. 247.3344 ext 1605 ♿

12 First Plaza Galeria Located in the heart of Albuquerque's business and government district, this seven-story retail mall covers an entire block and is conveniently located next to the **Albuquerque Convention Center** and two of Downtown's finest hotels. Courtyard fountains, native landscaping, and a two-story lobby and atrium greet visitors, while escalators and elevators provide easy access to shops and covered parking lots. The award-winning building, designed by **Harry Weese,** boasts contemporary geometric motifs and includes an exclusive athletic club, restaurants, galleries, gift shops, hair care and beauty services, and upscale clothing boutiques. Of particular note are **La Esquina Restaurant and Bar** (242.3432 ♿), which features good New Mexican food and great margaritas in a relaxed Southwestern ambience, and the eclectic collection of Southwest traditional and fine art at **Concetta D. Gallery** (243.5066). The **Albuquerque**

Convention and Visitors' Bureau (842.9918, 800/733.9918), open Monday through Friday, is in Suite 601. ♦ Most shops: M-Sa. At Second St NW and Tijeras Ave NW. 242.3446

Within First Plaza Galeria:

¡Explora! Much of **First Plaza Galeria**'s lower level is taken over by this colorful, kids-oriented 9,000-square-foot science museum that is full of such hands-on exhibits as a flight simulator, a Bernoulli ball (a big ball suspended by air currents that demonstrates a theorem by mathematician Daniel Bernoulli), and lots of computers. During the week it can be crowded (and noisy) with youngsters from rural schools throughout New Mexico, thanks to a state program that provides the transportation. At press time the museum was expected to relocate in 1998 to a $10-million facility near the **New Mexico Museum of Natural History & Science** in Old Town. ♦ Admission. W-Sa; Su noon-5PM. 842.6188 ♿

13 Artichoke Cafe ★★★★$$$ One of the best things about this upscale, intimate restaurant is that dining can be as fine or as casual as you like: Ordering a full meal or a mix of appetizers is equally acceptable to the friendly, unpretentious staff.

Given the marvelous modern American menu, however, sampling a little of everything is highly recommended. At both lunch and dinner, head chef Patty Keene (and co-owner, along with her husband Bob) alternates beautifully between the classic and the experimental with dishes that range from hearty and heavy to heart-healthy. Appetizers include roasted garlic with goat cheese and grilled red pepper; grilled rabbit, sausage, and pancetta in a red-wine, demi-glaze sauce; and steamed mussels and clams in a light broth of white wine, garlic, leeks, tomatoes, and herbs. A particularly good main course is the baked free-range chicken breast with wild mushrooms in a pesto of fresh basil, parsley, garlic, and olive oil served in a sea of fresh crushed tomato concassé sauce garnished with gorgonzola and walnuts. Also recommended is the egg fettuccine with a sauce of sautéed lobster, rock shrimp, shiitake mushrooms, shallots, brandy, cream, tarragon, and chives. The ingredients are organically grown, which explains why everything tastes so incredibly fresh. And while the wine list is not large, it's more than adequate. Specials are offered on weekends. The enclosed patio adds to the art-filled atmosphere. ♦ American ♦ M-F lunch and dinner; Sa dinner. Reservations recommended. 424 Central Ave (between Walter St NE and Edith Blvd NE). 243.0200 ♿

University of New Mexico/Nob Hill

In the 1880s a new generation of Albuquerque businesspeople shared a vision that would chart the economic future of the city and state. Looking to ensure Albuquerque's long-term growth and profits, they appealed to the territorial legislature to establish a university in their town. But New Mexico had yet to become a state, and public education was rare; thus, legislators nearly laughed the entrepreneurs out of the capital of Santa Fe. Still, money was on the minds of even the harshest critics in the poverty-stricken territory, and in the waning hours of the 1889 legislative session, the **University of New Mexico (UNM)** was born.

UNM took root two miles east of the Downtown railroad tracks on a sandy, yucca-studded tableland, where a three-story redbrick Romanesque building—today's **Hodgin Hall**—was erected as the school's first hall of academia. In 1901 university president William Tight initiated the transformation of the desert campus into "the pueblo on the mesa," a shady oasis of native plants and trees dotted with adobe buildings that reflected the architectural styles of surrounding Indian villages. But when he decided to integrate the original Romanesque structure into the distinctive campus design— ordering laborers to plaster over the redbrick with earth-colored stucco and replace gables and chimneys with vigas, corbels, and a flat roof—he was run out of office by those who considered his architectural vision too primitive for their up-and-coming town.

Almost a century later, it is **UNM's** unique architectural character, along with noted programs in anthropology, medicine, and Latin American and Southwest studies, that attract about 25,000 students from around the globe to make it the state's largest university. Ironically, the Pueblo Revival style that led to William Tight's professional demise was later adopted as the official campus design; the total transformation of the campus to the Pueblo Revival style began in the mid-1930s and was headed by famed Santa Fe architect **John Gaw Meem**, who served as the university's architect for 25 years. Today, the beautifully landscaped 700-acre campus is filled with some of the finest examples of Pueblo Revival architecture in the state, including the **Zimmerman Library, Scholes Hall, Alumni Memorial Chapel,**

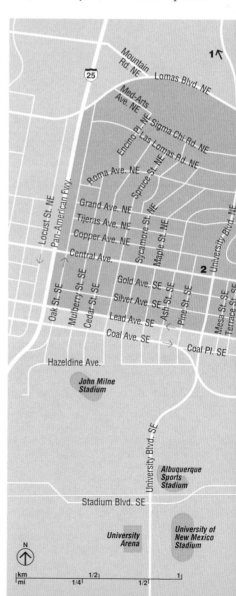

and the once-controversial **Hodgin Hall**. A series of plazas and pathways woven throughout the central campus makes these structures easily accessible by foot.

Beyond the university's borders is the usual college landscape of coffee shops, bookstores, pizzerias, and other cheap places to eat, drink, and study. While many of these spots are appealing to some visitors, others prefer to head farther east along Central Avenue to the trendy specialty shops, restaurants, and galleries of the historic Nob Hill district.

When it was built in 1947 at what was then the edge of town, the **Nob Hill Business Center** was the city's first car-oriented shopping center. The **Central Avenue** stretch of clothing and variety stores flourished until the early 1960s, when the arrival of the interstate drove shoppers to new outlying malls. Then in 1985, the district was one of eight commercial areas in the nation chosen for a government-funded redevelopment project. Galleries, restaurants, and boutiques sprang up along Central Avenue again, and those who once sought the enclosure of the glossy mall scene returned to a renewed Nob Hill.

Today's Nob Hill is a seven-block strip that stretches along Central Avenue from **Washington** to **Girard;** Art Deco–style arches straddle the strip to designate the district borders. Neon signs and eye-catching store facades encourage foot traffic, and the area's budding gallery and music scene brings Nob Hill hobnobbers out after dark. The district attracts trend-setters and trend-haters alike and is commonly referred to by Nob Hill residents as Albuquerque's Melrose Avenue. A stroll through Nob Hill is still the best way to witness the increasing urbanization and ever-changing character of Albuquerque.

1 Albuquerque Hilton $$ This 253-room chain hotel lies beyond the university's borders, but offers probably the best contemporary lodgings in the immediate area. The large rooms are pastel shaded and decorated with regional art and wooden appointments. Interiors throughout the rest of the hotel feature Native American and Western motifs—the white stuccoed corridors are hung with petroglyph-style paintings—while the high ceilings and arched doorways echo regional architectural styles. Indoor and outdoor swimming pools, a fitness center, and a sauna and whirlpool offer relaxing options. The hotel provides free transportation to and from the airport, bus, and train stations. ♦ 1901 University Blvd NE (at Menaul Blvd NE). 884.2500, 800/HILTONS; fax 889.9118 &

Within the Albuquerque Hilton:

Ranchers Club ★★★$$$$ Built in the style of a British hunting lodge, this cozy, elegant restaurant is the quintessential steak house: The fireplace is always blazing, and a buffalo head looms above the mantel. Lunch features excellent salads and such pastas as the spicy Southwest pasta with green-chile cream sauce. Dinner, however, is the restaurant's forte, with offerings of gigantic steaks, as well as other prime meats, poultry, and seafood, grilled over aromatic woods that customers select themselves. Exotic woods include piñon, hickory, apple, cherry, sassafras, and mesquite. These are complemented by grilled vegetables and one of more than 20 gourmet sauces. The wine list is extensive, and the bar features live entertainment. ♦ Steak/Southwestern ♦ M-F lunch and dinner; Sa dinner; Su brunch. Reservations recommended. 884.2500

Casa Chaco ★★$$$ At breakfast and lunch, this casual eatery serves standard coffee-shop fare. But at dinner, its original Southwestern cuisine served by tuxedoed waiters at candlelit tables draws raves. Try the grilled Rocky Mountain lamb with Dijon mustard and seasoned breadcrumbs served over green chile with a shallot beurre blanc sauce. ♦ Southwestern ♦ Daily breakfast, lunch, and dinner. 884.2500 &

2 66 Diner ★$ Take a nostalgic trip back to the days of soda jerks, hopscotch, and jukebox tunes in this 1950s diner. Once a transmission shop on the old Route 66, the fun Art Deco establishment now features such blue plate specials as liver and onions, meat loaf sandwiches, and chicken-fried steak. The old-fashioned burgers are great, and the milk shakes and sundaes are rich and gooey. ♦ American ♦ Daily breakfast, lunch, and dinner. 1405 Central Ave (between Pine St NE and University Blvd NE). 247.1421 &

3 University of New Mexico (UNM) The 700-acre campus of the state's largest university features some of the finest examples of Pueblo Revival architecture in New Mexico and is studded with native flora, grassy knolls, and large-scale sculptures by internationally renowned artists. The university is known for excellence in

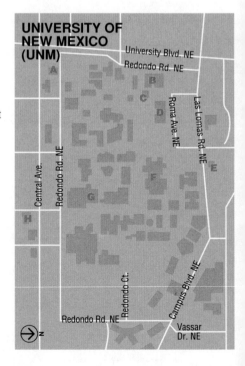

UNIVERSITY OF NEW MEXICO (UNM)

Hodgin Hall

anthropology, medicine, and Southwest and Latin American studies. Its outstanding museums and galleries—free to the public—shouldn't be missed. And its array of performing arts venues plays a major role in the city's thriving arts-and-culture scene.
♦ Bounded by Central Ave and Marble Ave NE, and Girard and University Blvds NE. 277.0111

Within the University of New Mexico (the green letters below correspond to the map on page 122):

A Hodgin Hall Erected in 1892 as the first building on the campus, **Hodgin Hall** (pictured above) was transformed from its original redbrick Romanesque design to the flat-roofed Pueblo Revival style in 1908. Named after former faculty member Charles Hodgin, the three-story structure underwent an extensive renovation in 1983. Its traditional architectural elements of ceiling vigas and hand-carved wooden corbels make it one of the jewels of the **UNM** campus. ♦ M-F. Redondo Rd (between Terrace St NE and University Blvd NE)

B Maxwell Museum Founded in 1932 as the first public museum in Albuquerque, this incredible museum of anthropology is a renowned repository for more than 2,500,000 artifacts from the United States, the Arctic, Mexico, Central and South America, Africa, India, Pakistan, Southeast Asia, New Guinea, Australia, and Oceania. Located in the **UNM Anthropology Building** on the campus's west side, the museum's two galleries give a special emphasis to the Native cultures of the Southwest. The *Ancestors* exhibit chronicles four million years of human emergence, while *People of the Southwest* documents 11,500 years of art, life, and culture in the American Southwest. The **Maxwell's Photographic Archive** houses more than 250,000 images, including many of the earliest photographs of Southwest Pueblo and Navajo Indian peoples. The museum shop features high-quality Native American art, publications, and folk art from other indigenous peoples worldwide.
♦ Free. Daily. UNM Anthropology Building, Redondo Rd NE (between Grand Ave NE and Las Lomas Rd NE). 277.4405

C Alumni Memorial Chapel Designed by renowned Santa Fe architect **John Gaw Meem** and completed in 1962, this small chapel (pictured below) sits in the shade of tall cottonwoods and is patterned after the pueblo

Alumni Memorial Chapel

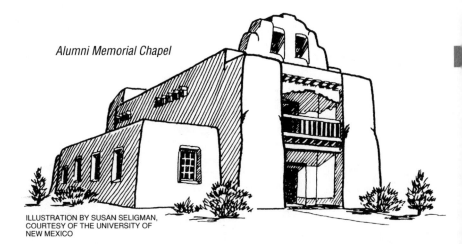

Images carved in Zimmerman Library ceiling Beams

ILLUSTRATION BY SUSAN SELIGMAN, COURTESY OF THE UNIVERSITY OF NEW MEXICO

mission churches erected by Franciscan friars throughout the state during the 17th and 18th centuries. The eastern tablet on the chapel's south wall is etched with the names of alumni killed in World Wars I and II and the wars in Korea and Vietnam. ♦ Behind the Maxwell Museum. 277.5808

D **Scholes Hall (UNM Administration Building)** Listed on the National Register of Historic Places, this 1936 building (pictured below) was **John Gaw Meem**'s first campus project. The Pueblo Revival structure is named for the late France Scholes, one of the Southwest's leading historians and **UNM**'s first academic vice president. The east wing

features a beautiful fresco, *Union of the Americas,* painted by Jesus Galvan in 1943. ♦ M-F. Roma Ave NE (between Yale Blvd NE and Redondo Rd NE)

E **Jonson Gallery** Located on the north side of campus in the former home and studio of the late modernist painter Raymond Jonson, this intimate space presents changing exhibits of more than 2,000 of his works, as well as those of the Transcendentalist painters and other contemporary artists. Retrospectives of Jonson's work are presented each summer, and gallery talks are held on the first Tuesday evening of the month. ♦ M-F. 1909 Las Lomas Rd NE (near Yale Blvd NE). 277.4967

F **Zimmerman Library** Another **John Gaw Meem** gem, this central campus facility was completed in 1938. **Meem**'s original core structure integrates murals and hand-carved wooden motifs into the Pueblo Revival design. Massive beams straddle library ceilings and feature abstract Native American images of birds and animals carved deeply into the surface. A four-panel mural in the lobby depicts the tricultural heritage of the region, while a stairwell mural runs up the library's four floors and charts the historical development of the alphabet. Named after former **UNM** president James Fulton Zimmerman, the original **Meem** library has undergone numerous additions through the years and today houses more than a million books. ♦ Daily during the school year; call for summer hours. Roma Ave NE (near Yale Blvd NE). 277.2003

G **University Art Museum** Since its establishment in 1963 as a department of the **UNM College of Fine Arts,** this attractive multilevel museum has amassed the largest fine arts collection in the state, with more than 23,000 paintings, drawings, prints, photographs, and sculptures. The permanent collection includes Spanish Colonial art, Old Master paintings and sculpture by such artists as Rembrandt, and works by 19th- and 20th-century American and European artists ranging from Picasso to O'Keeffe. The museum's collection of prints and photographs, including works by pioneers in the field, is one of the most extensive in the country. Gallery talks are held on Tuesday

Scholes Hall

ILLUSTRATION BY SUSAN SELIGMAN, COURTESY OF THE UNIVERSITY OF NEW MEXICO evenings. ◆ Free. Daily. UNM Fine Arts Center (off Cornell Dr NE, on southern edge of campus). 277.4001

H Tamarind Institute Artists from around the world who want to learn the complex process of lithography are lured to this esteemed workshop and gallery run by the university. The staff of certified Master Printers is on hand to assist in the printmaking process, and the in-house gallery displays contemporary lithographs created by professional and novice artists alike. Free guided tours are held on the first Friday of the month; reservations are required. ◆ M-F. 108 Cornell Dr SE (between Silver Ave SE and Central Ave). 277.3901

4 EJ's Coffee & Tea Co. ★★$ Coffee and customers are in constant flow at this popular coffeehouse. The high ceilings and hardwood decor create an inviting ambience for hard-working students as well as other confirmed coffee addicts. Besides more than 20 specialty coffees and teas, the establishment offers breakfast, lunch, and dinner, plus live poetry, music, and other esoteric entertainment. The menu leans toward healthy and vegetarian fare, with recommendations going to the scrambled tofu and enormous homemade bagels for breakfast, and the daily pasta or stir-fry specials at dinner. The eight different cheesecakes, in flavors like baklava and fuzzy navel, probably aren't so healthy, but they go great with a cup of fresh-roasted java. ◆ Health food/Cafe ◆ Daily breakfast, lunch, and dinner. 2201 Silver Ave SE (at Yale Blvd SE). 268.2233 &

5 The Quarters ★★$$ One of the most popular spots for barbecue in the city, this casual restaurant serves heaping helpings of spicy ribs and chicken, plus huge sandwiches and fabulous fries. Also try the tender catfish, plump knockwurst, or classic Reuben sandwiches. Top it all off with a brew from the largest selection of imported beer in town. ◆ Barbecue ◆ M-Sa lunch and dinner. 801 Yale Blvd SE (at Coal Ave SE). 843.7505 &

6 El Patio ★★$ University students craving a home-cooked New Mexican meal flock to this hot chile spot a half-block from campus. The New Mexican menu features plump *chiles rellenos* (whole green chiles stuffed with cheese and deep-fried), tender *carne adovada* (pork marinated in red chiles), and possibly the best green-chile chicken enchiladas in town. Vegetarians opt for the tasty avocado burrito, and the red and green chiles can also be ordered without meat. Other draws include nightly guitar music and a pleasant enclosed patio, which is open year-round. The creamy flan is incredible. ◆ New Mexican ◆ Daily lunch and dinner. 142 Harvard Dr SE (at Silver Ave SE). 268.4245

OLYMPIA CAFE

7 Olympia Cafe ★★$ This restaurant doesn't have much atmosphere, but it does boast a fabulous array of Greek specialties, including shish kebab, spanakopita (spinach and feta cheese in phyllo), moussaka (ground meat and eggplant), and hummus. The classic gyro, tangy Greek salad, and sweet-and-sticky baklava are established cafe favorites. And the large portions and low prices rank high with the college crowd. ◆ Greek ◆ M-Sa lunch and dinner. 2210 Central Ave (between Harvard Dr SE and Yale Blvd SE). 266.5222 &

FRONTIER

8 Frontier ★★$ Home of the famous Frontier sweet roll, a messy and moist mouthful of butter, cinnamon, and dough, this enormous barnlike building covers nearly an entire city block and has been a home-away-from-home to thousands of university denizens since 1971. Although it looks like a fast-food coffee shop, patrons here get real plates and utensils with their home-cooked meals and have their choice of seating for 325 amid a hodgepodge of Western art. Twenty-four hours a day, students spread their books out on tables and drink pots of coffee around meals of burgers, burritos, and old-fashioned bacon and eggs. Besides the sweet rolls, the *huevos rancheros* (fried eggs on corn tortillas smothered with chile salsa and topped with grated cheese), Western-style hash browns (topped with cheese and green chiles), and other New Mexican dishes are favorites here. Chiles and salsa are the most popular condiments here; the management roasts 2,200 sacks of chiles a year, and the salsa sits in a jug next to the sugar and cream. There's even an ATM if you're out of cash. ◆ New Mexican ◆ Daily 24 hours. 2400 Central Ave (at Cornell Dr SE). 266.0550 &

As the turn of the century approached, Albuquerque sought to enhance its image in order to gain statehood for the New Mexico territory. One improvement was the University of New Mexico, established in 1889. Today the university has a total enrollment of almost 25,000 students, and is known for its engineering and anthropology departments, as well as its extensive cancer research facility.

9 Dartmouth Street Gallery Works by New Mexican artists, including Frank McCulloch, Angus Macpherson, and Carol Hoy, are spotlighted in this established contemporary art gallery. ♦ M-Sa 1-5PM; or by appointment. 3011 Monte Vista Blvd NE (between Dartmouth Dr NE and Central Ave). 266.7751

10 Fred's Bread & Bagel ★★$ This has to be the only bagelry in the world where green-chile bagels are as popular as pumpernickel or cinnamon raisin. Always bustling, this place features more than a dozen bagel flavors, including oat bran, sourdough rye, and the popular green-chile cheese or green-chile blue corn. Bagel buyers also can choose from a host of "Fred's Spreads," creamy cream cheese spreads in flavors like garlic olive, honey nut, and, of course, green chile. But don't ask for Fred. Owner Aaron Hendron admits he just needed a name for his bakery that rhymes with bread. ♦ Bagels ♦ Daily breakfast, lunch, and dinner. 3009 Central Ave (between Richmond and Dartmouth Drs NE). 266.7323

11 Bow Wow Records Andy Horwitz's shop spins alternative sounds by independent labels only and features an impressive selection of used records, CDs, and cassettes. A host of music accessories including books, videos, T-shirts, and posters also leans toward the alternative, and the back of the shop serves as an art-space for local artists. Whether you're looking for a classic Miles Davis or the latest from Brian Eno, the shop's staff will be more than helpful. ♦ Daily. 3103 Central Ave (between Bryn Mawr and Richmond Drs NE). 256.0928

11 Martha's Body Bueno Forget the gym. Lotions, potions, and sensual notions is Martha Doster's good body motto, which she translates into an aromatic selection of body oils, bath gels, lotions, soaps, shampoos, and more. Silky-skin lovers choose from either the Body Bueno brand of natural skin-care products, which come in chamomile, coconut, and a host of other tantalizing smells, or the standard Crabtree & Evelyn selection. Or if none of those scents suit your senses, staffers are on hand to mix personalized body oils and other products. The shop also features shameless lingerie, unusual jewelry, and off-color, under-the-counter greeting cards. ♦ Daily. 3105 Central Ave (between Bryn Mawr and Richmond Drs NE). 255.1122

11 Peacecraft Handmade arts, crafts, and clothing from the Third World are on sale at this nonprofit gallery. The shop's emphasis is on traditional handicrafts of cultural significance, and the selection includes beautiful handwoven clothing, baskets, hats, and textiles from Mexico, Africa, and Guatemala; exquisite Peruvian pottery; and an unusual array of other ethnic, folk, and tribal arts. The shop is run by an all-volunteer staff, and all money goes back into purchasing more goods. ♦ M-Sa. 3107 Central Ave (between Bryn Mawr and Richmond Drs NE). 255.5229

12 Larry's Hats The old-time art of millinery lives on in Larry Koch's wonderful world of hats. An accomplished hat maker, Koch fashions old and new styles to fit the heads of teenagers and adults alike. His classic collection includes a number of antique hats, but mostly Koch custom-makes a fascinating range of shapes that tower overhead, sit low above the brow, or fall any-which-way the wearer wants. Just as fascinating is Koch's large selection of jewelry and accessories, which includes unusual costume jewelry, antique gloves, and old **Santo Domingo Pueblo** Indian pieces. The jewelry counter alone is worth a visit. ♦ M-Sa. 3102 Central Ave (at Richmond Dr SE). 266.2095

12 In Crowd One of Nob Hill's most outrageous outfitters features funky fashions in natural materials and wild prints and colors; the great 1960s go-go collection even makes polyester look good. They also carry a wide array of unusual accessories. And it's the only place in town selling sculptures, paintings, and pottery made by inmates of the Santa Fe Prison. ♦ M-Sa; Su noon-4PM. 3106 Central Ave (between Bryn Mawr and Richmond Drs SE). 268.3750

13 Off Broadway The best vintage clothing store in the state is big on Western and formal vintage wear dating from the turn of the century to the 1960s. Especially notable are the 1940s sequined sweater collection, the vintage hats, and the funky hand-painted Mexican skirts. The shop also does a brisk rental business, just in case you left your Roaring '20s flapper fashions at home. ♦ M-Sa; Su noon-4PM. 3110 Central Ave (between Bryn Mawr and Richmond Drs SE). 268.1489

Tinseltown Among the Tumbleweeds

The rolling, piñon-studded hills and sandy arroyos of Northern New Mexico have long attracted filmmakers in search of a place to shoot old- and new-fashioned Westerns. Among the films that brought actors and camera crews to the Santa Fe/Taos/Albuquerque area are the following:

Butch and Sundance: The Early Days (1979) This "prequel" to the 1969 blockbuster (see below) features Tom Berenger and William Katt.

Butch Cassidy and the Sundance Kid (1969) Paul Newman and Robert Redford dashingly rob their way through the Southwest and into Central and South America, until showdown time in Bolivia.

City Slickers (1991) Billy Crystal, among others, is an urbanite who signs on to a cattle drive for his vacation.

Easy Rider (1969) This tough and tender road movie about two lost souls on motorbikes stars Peter Fonda and Dennis Hopper.

Fool for Love (1985) Based on a Sam Shephard play and featuring him along with Kim Basinger, Randy Quaid, and Harry Dean Stanton, this heavy drama-in-a-hotel deals with incest between half-siblings.

The Fortune (1975) This thriller about a rich heiress, set in the 1920s, stars Jack Nicholson, Warren Beatty, and Stockard Channing.

The Last Outlaw (1993) Set in 1870, this Western is about an ex-Confederate soldier—now an outlaw—who is hunting his bank-robbing buddies who betrayed him. Shot in **Abiquiu** and **Nambe,** it stars Mickey Rourke and Keith David.

The Man Who Fell to Earth (1976) David Bowie is the tragic protagonist of this visitor-from-another-planet science fiction film.

The Milagro Beanfield War (1988) Robert Redford directed this tale of a battle over precious land in New Mexico starring Sonia Braga and John Heard.

The Muppet Movie (1979) Yes, even Kermit the Frog has visited New Mexico—on his way to Hollywood.

Outrageous Fortune (1987) Bette Midler competes with a female rival for a lover; the FBI and CIA want him, too.

Santa Fe (1996) An offbeat comedy about a man (Gary Cole) who survives a cult experience, falling in love along the way with a beautiful New Age philosopher (Lolita Davidovich) who lives in **Santa Fe**.

Silkwood (1983) Meryl Streep plays Karen Silkwood, a real-life victim of radiation and corporate conspiracy; Cher plays a morgue cosmetician.

Twins (1988) A perfect (genetically engineered) Arnold Schwarzenegger discovers he has an all-too-imperfect "twin" (Danny DeVito).

White Sands (1992) A small-town sheriff gets in over his head when he tries to solve a murder with links to the FBI and CIA. Starring Willem Dafoe, Mickey Rourke, Mimi Rogers, and Mary Elizabeth Mastrantonio, this adventure was filmed in Santa Fe, **Taos, Estancia,** and **White Sands National Monument.**

Wyatt Earp (1994) Directed by Lawrence Kasdan and starring Kevin Costner, Dennis Quaid, and Gene Hackman, this remake documents the life and times of the famous lawman.

---

13 Sachs Appeal Boutique What appeals to shopkeeper Renee Sachs is an assortment of new and used clothing and accessories that ranges from garish skull-and-crossbones T-shirts to funky Spandex shapes to conservative business suits. The small but high-quality selection of handmade silver belts, bracelets, button covers, and rings gives a nod to Southwest style. ♦ M-Sa; Su noon-5PM. 3112 Central Ave (between Bryn Mawr and Richmond Drs SE). 266.1661

14 Monte Vista Fire Station ★★★$$$ This fine restaurant served as local Fire Station No. 3 for 36 years before it started cooking some of the best contemporary American cuisine in town. Remodeled by owner Kerry Rayner to its original Pueblo Revival architectural style, the two-story restaurant today is also one of the city's outstanding examples of classic New Mexico adobe architecture—brass fire pole and all.

Chef Harry Cavanaugh explores an array of cuisines—from new Southwestern to traditional French and Italian to new American—making for an exotic, ever-changing menu in a casual Art Deco atmosphere. Usual lunch and dinner features include pasta, grilled meats, poultry, and seafood. The crab cakes with goat cheese make frequent appearances as appetizers, and the silky white-chocolate mousse in a fudge crust is a must-eat for chocolate lovers. Upstairs—what was once the fire station's sleeping quarters—is one of the city's most popular indoor/outdoor bars. ◆ International ◆ Restaurant: M-F lunch and dinner; Sa-Su dinner. Bar: daily 2PM-1:30AM. Reservations recommended. 3201 Central Ave (at Bryn Mawr Dr NE). 255.2424

15 Aja Eclectic natural-fiber clothing and one-of-a-kind handmade accessories give this affordable women's boutique an alternative appeal for women who like to create their own style. ◆ M-Sa. 3215 Central Ave (between Wellesley and Bryn Mawr Drs NE). 255.7804

16 Il Vicino ★★$ Owned by the same folks who run **Scalo Northern Italian Grill** (see below), this neighborhood pizzeria features fresh and fabulous European-style pizza baked in wood-fired ovens. Forget your run-of-the-mill pepperoni and try the pizza *rustica* (a buttery cornmeal crust topped with roasted garlic, artichoke hearts, calamata olives, capers, fresh tomato sauce, oregano, and mozzarella). The menu features 12 other house pizzas, and customers can create their own designer pies from a choice of 25 gourmet toppings. A few salads and pasta dishes are additional options, and wine comes by the bottle or glass. ◆ Pizza/Italian ◆ Daily lunch and dinner. 3403 Central Ave (at Tulane Dr NE). 266.7855

Albuquerque resident and best-selling mystery author Tony Hillerman started his writing career penning commercials for Purina Pig Chow. He then went on to a career in journalism, and in the late 1960s, while teaching journalism at the University of New Mexico, wrote his first novel, *The Blessing Way*. It was the first in what would be a long line of mysteries set in the Navajo Indian reservation for which Hillerman has won worldwide acclaim. When he sent the original manuscript to his New York agent, she had this advice, "Just get rid of all the Indian stuff."

Restaurants/Clubs: Red   **Hotels:** Blue

Shops/ ♥ Outdoors: Green   **Sights/Culture:** Black

16 Guild Cinema Albuquerque's only art cinema screens art, independent, and foreign flicks and serves popcorn drenched in real butter. ◆ 3405 Central Ave NE (between Amherst and Tulane Drs NE). 255.1848

17 Double Rainbow ★★$ The famous San Francisco-based Double Rainbow ice cream is sold in this brightly lighted place, which also offers great salads, sandwiches (try the grilled gouda and artichoke), and pastries. The chocolate-mousse cake is renowned as one of the most decadent desserts in town, while the huge selection of magazines includes New Age and Italian fashion rags that outsell *People* and *Time*. The place is always packed. ◆ Ice cream/Cafe ◆ Daily breakfast, lunch, and dinner. 3416 Central Ave SE (between Amherst and Tulane Drs SE). 255.6633

17 Wargames West Adventure is the name of the game(s) in Wayne R. Godfrey's incredible specialty store. Brimming with an inventory of more than 6,000 different "games that make you think" and the accessories that go with them, Godfrey's collection is considered by his international clientele of avid adventure gamers to be one of the largest of its kind in the world. But Godfrey's games are not the typical department store kind; these brainy board puzzlers—no electronic gadgets on sale here—are created to challenge the minds and imaginations of fantasy gamers. The selection ranges from the best-selling "Dungeons and Dragons" to science fiction to mystery and traditional war games. ◆ M-Sa. 3422 Central Ave (between Amherst and Tulane Drs SE). 265.6100, 800/SAY.GAME

18 Wear It! The style in Janet Moses's popular women's clothing store is contemporary and comfortable, and the service is as impeccable as the fine linens and silks found here. She also carries a great selection of denim, cotton, and rayon, plus fun accessories and designer names. ◆ M-Sa; Su noon-5PM. 107 Amherst Dr SE (at Central Ave). 266.7764

19 P.T. Crow Trading Co. Walk into this custom cowboy boot shop, and chances are when you walk outside again, you'll be wearing a pair of shoes that are at least 20 years older than the ones you wore in. Specializing in vintage cowboy boots, shop owners Ron and Linda Linton have rummaged through flea markets, garage sales, and the closets of cowboy boot collectors to put you into a pair of Old West footwear—their extensive classic collection of vintage boots is well worn but well preserved. If you prefer a new pair, boots can be custom-made to look like vintage. Most popular are colorful reproductions of the flamboyant designs of the 1930s and 1940s worn by the likes of Tom Mix and Roy Rogers, but customers are free to conceive of creative designs to suit their own Wild West style. ◆ M-Sa. 114 Amherst Dr SE (at Silver Ave SE). 247.2693, 800/657.0944

20 Nob Hill Business Center Built in 1947 as the city's first auto-oriented shopping center, this building is a streamlined architectural display of contemporary and regional design styles of the era. It is also the hub of the resurrected Nob Hill district and is listed on the National Register of Historic Places. ♦ 3500 Central Ave (between Carlisle Blvd SE and Amherst Dr SE)

Within the Nob Hill Business Center:

Scalo Northern Italian Grill ★★★$$ The trendy Nob Hill set congregates at this informal but elegant Italian restaurant. The food is straightforward but solid, with good fresh pasta specials and meat, chicken, and fish entrées. Notable eatables include the *ravioli di magro al basilico* (filled with spinach and ricotta cheese in a basil cream sauce), *agnello alla griglia splendido* (grilled lamb with red onions and garlic), and *salmone al forno* (roasted salmon fillet with savoy spinach and toasted squash polenta). The carpaccio appetizer, homemade desserts, and Italian wines are good anytime. ♦ Italian ♦ M-Sa lunch and dinner; Su dinner. 255.8782 ♿

Geckos Gallery and Grill ★$ Excellent sandwiches, burgers, pizza, and pasta are on order in this upbeat neighborhood bar with a casual bistro atmosphere. Sit outdoors on the patio for the pulse of the Nob Hill scene. ♦ Cafe ♦ Daily lunch and dinner. 262.1848 ♿

Beeps With its huge selection of gifts for all personalities and occasions, this fun card and novelty store is the ultimate gift shop. Gifts here range from genuine to gag and include everything from silk ties to satin boxers to rubber cockroaches. The best-selling T-shirt selection is one of the largest in Albuquerque, and the one-of-a-kind greeting card line runs the gamut from very tasteful to completely tasteless. ♦ M-Sa; Su noon-6PM. 262.1900

21 Cafe Zurich ★★$ Local European wannabes fill this dainty Deco corner cafe. Covered in checkerboard black and white, this small European-style establishment is best known for its wide selection of hot espresso drinks, cool Italian sodas, and wickedly luscious desserts.

Chocoholics swear by the *caffè mocha* paired with a piece of the chocolate torte. Soups, salads, sandwiches, and great gourmet pizzas are also featured, with kudos going to the French onion soup and the pesto pizza. Regular art exhibits, specialty magazines, and hip hairdos round out the eclectic feel, but sidewalk seating on congested Central Avenue doesn't even come close to Paris. ♦ Cafe/Pizza ♦ Daily lunch and dinner. 3513 Central Ave (between Carlisle Blvd NE and Amherst Dr NE). 265.2556 ♿

21 Nirvana ★★$$ This Nob Hill eatery specializes in the vegetarian cuisine of southern India, a cooking style that is miles away from the tangy curries and grilled meats of the northern part of that country. Ravi Goradi's cooking distinguishes itself by the absence of animal meats and animal by-products. Try the huge *masala dosai* (a graham flour crepe filled with onions, potatoes, nuts, and tomatoes) or the *oothapam* (cashews, onions, green chile, bell peppers, and raisins on a lentil sourdough pancake). Dishes come with wheat flatbreads plus coconut-ginger chutney or a yogurt-based soup. The service is gracious but unhurried, which gives you time to relax amidst a tasteful decor of gray relief wall sculptures. ♦ Southern Indian ♦ Tu-Sa lunch and dinner. Reservations recommended for dinner. 3523 Central Ave (between Carlisle Blvd NE and Amherst Dr NE). 265.2172 ♿

22 University Lodge $ Situated eight blocks east of **UNM** in the middle of Nob Hill, this 53-room hotel is clean and comfortable but average. The pastel rooms are adequately sized with standard motel furnishings, and rooms for people with disabilities are also available. The food in the hotel's small restaurant is decent, and an outdoor swimming pool is open during the warmer months. ♦ 3711 Central Ave (between Solano and Hermosa Drs NE). 266.7663 ♿

23 Outpost Performance Space This funky storefront performance space is a popular venue for some of the best music, dance, readings, and other live performances in Albuquerque. Hosting roughly 80 events annually, the intimate space seats up to a hundred people—on folding chairs in an alcohol- and smoke-free environment—and is best known for its eclectic blend of musical events, including folk, jazz, and world beat by local, national, and international acts. ♦ Hours vary. 112 Morningside Dr SE (between Silver Ave SE and Central Ave). 268.0044

24 Classic Century Square Three floors of antiques, arts and crafts, and collectibles by some 70 independent dealers are featured in this antiques extravaganza—a great spot to find old Indian collectibles and Western memorabilia. ♦ M-Sa; Su noon-5PM. 4616 Central Ave (at Jefferson St SE). 265.3161

Additional Highlights of Albuquerque

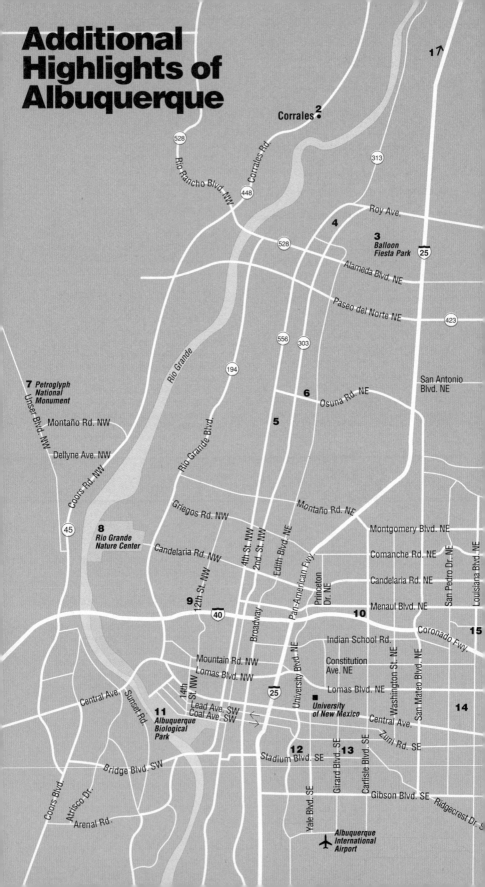

17 ↗

Corrales 2

528
Rio Rancho Blvd. NW
Corrales Rd.
448
313
Roy Ave.
4
3 Balloon Fiesta Park
528
Alameda Blvd. NE
25
Paseo del Norte NE
423
556
303
194
San Antonio Blvd. NE
7 Petroglyph National Monument
Unser Blvd. NW
6
Osuna Rd. NE
Montaño Rd. NW
5
Rio Grande
Dellyne Ave. NW
Rio Grande Blvd.
Coors Rd. NW
Griegos Rd. NW
Montaño Rd. NE
45
8 Rio Grande Nature Center
Montgomery Blvd. NE
Candelaria Rd. NW
Comanche Rd. NE
4th St. NW
2nd. St. NW
Edith Blvd. NE
Candelaria Rd. NE
San Pedro Dr. NE
Louisiana Blvd. NE
9
12th St. NW
40
Broadway
Pan-American Fwy
Princeton Dr. NE
Menaul Blvd. NE
10
15
Coronado Fwy
Indian School Rd.
Mountain Rd. NW
University Blvd. NE
Constitution Ave. NE
Washington St. NE
San Mateo Blvd. NE
Central Ave.
Lomas Blvd. NW
Lomas Blvd. NE
14
Sunset Rd.
14th St. NW
Lead Ave. SW
University of New Mexico
11 Albuquerque Biological Park
Coal Ave. SW
Central Ave.
Zuni Rd. SE
12
13
Stadium Blvd. SE
Girard Blvd. SE
Carlisle Blvd. SE
Gibson Blvd. SE
Ridgecrest Dr. S
Bridge Blvd. SW
Coors Blvd.
Atrisco Dr.
Yale Blvd. SE
Arenal Rd.
Albuquerque International Airport

A variety of interesting things to do and see awaits those who venture beyond the borders of the three walking areas in Albuquerque highlighted in the earlier chapters. For glimpses into the city's fascinating history, the village of **Corrales** provides a feel for the region's pre-urban past, and the **Petroglyph National Monument** transports people back to prehistoric times. Nature lovers won't want to miss the lush **Rio Grande Nature Center**, nostalgia buffs will get a kick out of the memorabilia-filled **Ernie Pyle Memorial Library,** and those who are fascinated by Native American culture will want

La Luz Trail

21
Sandia Crest
10,678 ft.

Tramway – **20** Sandia Peak ■
Ski Area

556
Tramway Rd.

Paseo del Norte Dr.   423

16
San Antonio Dr. NE

Ventura St. NE

Pino Trail

536

Crest Hwy.

19

Academy Rd. NE

Cibola
National
Forest

Osuna Rd. NE

SANDIA MOUNTAINS

Montgomery Blvd. NE   **17**

Comanche Rd. NE

Candelaria Rd. NE   556

Menaul Blvd. NE

Wyoming Blvd. NE

Indian School Rd. NE

Eubank Blvd. NE

Juan Tabo Blvd. NE

Chelwood Park Blvd. NE

Tramway Blvd. NE

14

Los Altos
Park   Lomas Blvd. NE

Turquoise Trail

Central Ave.

40

F St.
18 H St.
↓

N
↑

km   2
mi   1   2   4

to visit the extraordinary **Indian Pueblo Cultural Center.** The **Albuquerque Biological Park** includes the **Rio Grande Zoo,** the new **Rio Grande Botanic Garden** and **Albuquerque Aquarium,** and the **Tingley Aquatic Park.** To sample the best New Mexican food in town, visit **El Pinto** and **Rio Bravo.** And for the ultimate view of Albuquerque, take the thrilling 2.7-milelong **Sandia Peak Aerial Tramway** to the city's highest point.

PRAIRIE STAR

1 **Prairie Star** ★★★$$$ Sunset is prime time to take in the incredible view of Albuquerque's Sandia Mountains from the patio of this rambling 1940s adobe hacienda. Located approximately 15 minutes north of Albuquerque in the town of Bernalillo, the 6,000-square-foot Mission-style home sits on a rural site leased from the **Santa Ana Pueblo.** Outside, the Rio Grande meanders nearby as high plains stretch into the distance, while inside, diners are surrounded by regional art and traditional New Mexican architectural motifs: vigas with smaller *latillas* (peeled wooden poles) wedged in between, blazing kiva fireplaces, and *bancos* (small benches that gracefully emerge from thick adobe walls). The menu offers an exquisite range of New American, Southwestern, and classical cuisine, including stuffed poblano chiles, a tender lamb loin, and a hearty trout. Homemade bread and desserts are featured daily. The wine list is extensive, but the tangy margaritas are still the favorite for sipping as the sun slips behind the Sandias. ♦ American/Southwestern ♦ M-Sa dinner; Su brunch and dinner. Reservations recommended. 255 Prairie Star Rd, Bernalillo. Take I-25 north to Bernalillo exit 242, turn left on NM 44, cross the Rio Grande, turn right a half-mile past the river onto Jemez Dam Rd, and drive a half-mile north. 867.3327 ♿

2 **Corrales** A drive through this tiny village gives visitors a taste of what Santa Fe, Taos, and yes, even Albuquerque, were once like. A largely agricultural hamlet filled with farm fields, horse corrals, and ancient adobe homes, the area today is also an artists' haven and home to wonderful farmers' markets, specialty shops, restaurants, and other attractions sprinkled alongside Corrales Road, the village's main thoroughfare. ♦ Take I-40 west to Coors Rd and continue north to Corrales

Within Corrales:

Desert Rose ★★$ This small cafe is a popular breakfast spot for bicyclists, balloonists, and other locals in the know. Try the Desert Rose steak (12 ounces of rib eye with lots of red or green chile, topped with melted cheddar cheese) or the *paparito* (potatoes, eggs, and chorizo in a flour tortilla smothered in red or green chile), another favorite. ♦ American/New Mexican ♦ Tu-Sa breakfast, lunch, and dinner; Su breakfast and lunch. 4515 Corrales Rd. 898.2269

Casa Vieja ★★★$$$ Classic French and Northern Italian cuisine is offered in the warm adobe setting of the oldest house in Corrales, built circa 1706. Daily specials feature poultry, beef, and seafood plus a selection of several wonderful pasta dishes; interesting seasonal entrées include sautéed soft-shell crab in the summer and wild boar in the fall. The back of the restaurant doubles as a gourmet pizzeria, where the unusual red-chile cheese pizza gets rave reviews. There's also an extensive selection of French and California wines, with a reserve wine list that predates World War II. ♦ Continental ♦ M lunch; Tu-Su dinner. Reservations recommended. 4541 Corrales Rd. 898.7489

Las Nutrias Vineyard and Winery The grapes grown here have won numerous awards for this winery's distinctly New Mexican wines. Complimentary tastings let your own palate decide the quality of the vintage. The enchanting scenic rural setting surely deserves some awards, too. ♦ W-Su noon-6PM; or by appointment. 4627 Corrales Rd. 897.7863

Old San Ysidro Church Once the center of Corrales, the original **San Ysidro Church,** named after the patron saint of agriculture, was washed away during the Rio Grande flood of 1868. Some of the original church timbers, however, were recovered and used in the beautiful adobe Mission-style structure seen today. ♦ Old Church Rd. Turn east off of northbound Corrales Rd and continue about three minutes east. No phone

3 **Balloon Fiesta Park** Every October the largest gathering of balloonists in the world convenes in this 200-acre park, the new venue for the Albuquerque International Balloon Fiesta. (For more information on this event, see "Fiesta in the Sky" on page 134.) It is also used year-round by local balloonists to launch flights. On sunny weekends, you can hear the dragonlike roar of hot-air balloons as they skim just above the rooftops of surrounding suburbs. ♦ 9450 Jefferson St NE (north of Alameda Blvd NE) ♿

4 **El Pinto** ★★★★$ One of the city's most beautiful—and affordable—restaurants, dining here is like being entertained in a grand Spanish hacienda: cascading waterfalls, lush

greenery, hand-carved chairs, and roaring fireplaces all create a sensational ambience. Enjoy a meal alfresco overlooking the abundant Southwestern gardens or inside in the lovely dining room. Owners Jim and John Thomas credit the success of their ever-popular and always-crowded-on-weekends restaurant to their Grandma Griggs for her ancestral New Mexican recipes, and to Chef Mary Martinez, who has been cooking chiles here for over 25 years. Everything is made from scratch, from the roasted chiles to the *calabacitas* (squash casserole). Notable dishes include chile con carne enchiladas, chicken *adovada* (chicken breast marinated in red-chile sauce), and a new low-fat enchilada with steamed corn tortillas (instead of fried) and low-fat cheese. Live music nightly varies from Flamenco jazz to traditional mariachi. Classical guitarist Antonio Mendoza plays on Wednesday, in between his concerts in Europe, and his rendition of "Dios Nunca Muere" is so mesmerizing you might forget to eat (don't!). ◆ New Mexican ◆ Daily lunch and dinner. 10500 Fourth St NW, Alameda (between Alameda Blvd and Roy Ave). 898.1771 ⓓ

5 **Sadie's** ★★★★$$ This favorite North Valley restaurant serves some of the best New Mexican food in town—the servings are massive, and the chile is authentic and hot. Try the red-chile cheese enchiladas, the *guaco* chicken (guacamole and chicken) tacos, or green-chile stew. Everything comes with chips and scorching salsa, crispy *papitas* (fried potatoes), and fresh fluffy sopaipillas made to drench in honey. There's usually a line, but it's worth the wait. ◆ New Mexican ◆ Daily lunch and dinner. 6230 Fourth St NW (at Solar Rd NW, 6 blocks north of Montaño Rd). 345.5339 ⓓ

hacienda antigua

6 **Hacienda Antigua** $$ Innkeepers Melinda Moffitt and Ann Dunlap have turned a 200-year-old hacienda into an oasis of beauty and comfort. The five guest rooms, each with a fireplace and private entrance, are decorated with sumptuous Persian rugs, antique furniture, and Melinda's collection of dolls made by her grandmother. Lace curtains and clawfoot tubs add to the romantic ambience. The walled courtyard blooms with iris, roses, and lamb's ears throughout spring and summer, and guests can enjoy the outdoor pool, hot tub, and a very inviting hammock. Hearty breakfasts feature whole-wheat pancakes and spicy chile dishes. Enjoy the photos of Mabel Dodge Luhan and Georgia O'Keeffe on the living room walls, or curl up with one of their many travel books, such as "Indiscreet Journeys—Stories of Women on the Road" from the library. ◆ 6708

Tierra Drive (off Osuna Rd, between I-25 and Second St) 345.5399

7 **Petroglyph National Monument** A glimpse into the fascinating world of some of the area's earliest Indian inhabitants can be found along this ancient 17-mile stretch of volcanic rock on Albuquerque's West Mesa. Here on the site of five extinct volcanoes, more than 17,000 petroglyphs (prehistoric rock drawings) dating back as early as AD 1300 provide a record of Native American hunters who camped along the lava flows and etched their heritage into the dark basalt. For years, the area stood as a state park, but in 1990 Congress designated it the country's first site for the preservation of prehistoric rock art. Four hiking trails take visitors along the escarpment through miles of symbolic images of birds, horned serpents, shield bearers (see illustration above), flute players, and more, while plaques tell observers whether they represent human, animal, or ceremonial forms. Though somewhat strenuous, the **Mesa Point Trail** provides some of the best viewing. ◆ Fee per vehicle. Daily. 6900 Unser Blvd NW. Take I-40 west to Coors Rd and follow the signs. 897.8814

8 **Rio Grande Nature Center** All manner of fauna and flora can be viewed year-round in this stunning sanctuary for birds and migratory fowl in western Albuquerque. Located in a cottonwood forest on the east bank of the Rio Grande, the beautiful space features two miles of riverside trails where roadrunners (New Mexico's state bird), pheasant, skunks, beavers, and other wildlife frolic in their natural habitats. Free guided trail walks are held every weekend. The unique **Antoine Predock**–designed visitors' center is built half-above and half-below ground, providing fascinating over-and-under-the-surface views of the frogs, ducks, birds, and turtles that live in the center's three-acre pond. During migration months, the center is also a popular resting spot for fowl such as snow geese and sandhill cranes. ◆ Nominal admission; children under age 6 free. Daily. 2901 Candelaria Rd NW (at the Rio Grande; Candelaria dead ends in the park). 344.7240 ⓓ

The Pueblo Indians of the Rio Grande Valley call the Sandia Mountains *Oku Pin* (Turtle Mountain). Such deities as Wind Woman and the Twin War gods are thought to live here, and sacred shrines still exist high among the crags.

Fiesta in the Sky

Since 1972, when 13 balloons ascended from the parking lot of a local mall, the city has been home to the Kodak Albuquerque International Balloon Fiesta, today's largest gathering of balloonists in the world. Every year during the first and second weekend in October, the city's azure skies and wide-open spaces are the backdrop for a nine-day aerial extravaganza featuring some 850 of the world's most talented balloonists who fly their hot-air and gas balloons through eye-dazzling events.

Pilots from around the planet flock to the fiesta to enjoy some of the best flying conditions in the world. Flanked by mountains on all sides, the city's unique wind and weather patterns create what is known as the "Albuquerque Box Effect," a phenomenon that allows balloonists to traverse the city in different directions and at varying altitudes. With an estimated 1.4 million spectators—plus pilots representing numerous countries including the United States, Switzerland, England, Germany, Canada, Russia, Australia, France, and Japan—the event ranks as New Mexico's biggest, and Albuquerque proudly wears the title "Balloon Capital of the World."

R. CORUJO

Held on the city's northeast side at the new 200-acre **Balloon Fiesta Park,** the event features amazing mass ascensions on both weekends. Balloonists gather at dawn and take to the skies in droves just as the sun rises. After the sun sets on the first Sunday of the fiesta, the breathtaking "Balloon Glow" takes place; on the second Saturday is the "Night Magic Glow." Remaining tethered to the ground, the balloons are illuminated, lighting up the night like giant light bulbs.

Throughout the week, pilots compete in a number of events, including the difficult "Key Grab," in which they attempt to steer their balloons from more than a mile away toward a 30-foot-high pole, where a set of shiny new car keys waits to be snatched from the top. On two weekday afternoons, the "Special Shapes Rodeo" takes place, and pilots parade their balloons in such outrageous forms as Santa Claus, the Cow Jumping Over the Moon, Broom Hilda, and a very large tennis shoe. Meanwhile, some of the city's commercial balloon pilots are on hand during the week to take visitors up, up, and away.

The **Balloon Fiesta Park** is located on Jefferson Street NE between Alameda Boulevard NE and Roy Ave. For more information on the Albuquerque International Balloon Fiesta, call 821.1000.

9 Indian Pueblo Cultural Center The life and culture of the Native American peoples of New Mexico's 19 Indian pueblos are highlighted in this spectacular, two-story, open horseshoe structure. (It is said to be a contemporary interpretation of the design of **Pueblo Bonito,** the prehistoric ruin that is considered the high point of Chaco Canyon Indian architecture.) Jointly owned and operated by the pueblos as a nonprofit organization, the center is a short drive north of Old Town, but the mood is miles away from Albuquerque's bustling city life. Murals depicting traditional Indian life line the walls while drumbeats drone from a central courtyard where ceremonial dances are performed for visitors most weekends and holidays. (Unlike dances held at the pueblos, picture-taking is allowed here—and at no charge.) Downstairs, a permanent exhibit charts the evolution of the pueblos from prehistoric times to the present, while the center's upper level showcases the distinctive arts and crafts of the individual pueblos. Visitors can see videos of the late **San Ildefonso** potter Maria Martinez demonstrating her renowned black pottery technique or read instructions on how to bake bread in a traditional Indian *horno* (mud oven). The gift shop features the largest collection of Indian arts and crafts in the Southwest and some of the best buys found anywhere on authentic Indian jewelry, textiles, painting, sculpture, baskets, leather works, and pottery. The center's small restaurant is also the best place to sample authentic Native American and Mexican cuisine, including *posole* (corn-based stew), tamales, and fluffy Indian fry bread. ◆ Admission for museum. Daily. 2401 12th St NW (between Indian School Rd NW and Menaul Blvd NW, just north of I-40). 843.7270

10 Rudy's Country Story and Bar-B-Q ★★★$ The indoor restaurant sign proclaims "Real people eat meat," and that's what everyone is here for: pit-smoked barbecued brisket, pork, prime rib, and sausage (although turkey and rainbow trout are also offered). Nothing fancy, just long tables swathed in red-and-white plastic, where meat lovers dip smoked meat into pools of Rudy's spicy sauce. Owner Blake Brown, a tall, blue-eyed Texan, greets many customers by first name in his smooth southern drawl. The walls are fire-engine red, which is how your taste buds feel after a mouthwatering meal at this family fun spot. Try some ice cream for dessert to quench the flames. ◆ Barbecue ◆ Daily breakfast, lunch, and dinner. 2321 Carlisle Blvd NE (between I-40 and Menaul Blvd NE). 884.4000 ⑤

**Albuquerque
Biological
Park**

11 Albuquerque Biological Park Set along
three miles of the Rio Grande *bosque*
(wooded area) a short distance from
Downtown, this park offers a variety of
attractions, including the existing zoo and
three newly created sister facilities.

Within the Albuquerque Biological Park:

Rio Grande Zoological Park Home to
more than 1,100 animals from around the
world, this 60-acre zoo (see map below) sits
amid ancient cottonwoods on a stretch of
bosque. Known for its lush native landscaping
and naturalistic spacious design, the zoo's
newest exhibits include the **Elephant
Watering Hole** and **Australia—the Island
Continent,** featuring koalas. It is also
internationally recognized for focusing on the
psychological and physical needs of animals
native to New Mexico—bison, mountain lions,
and grizzly bears—as well as endangered

species worldwide. Stop for a bite at the
Southwestern **Cottonwood Cafe** and browse
at the **Conservation Gift Shop.** ♦ Admission.
Daily. 903 10th St SW (at Atlantic Ave SW).
764.6200 &

Rio Grande Botanic Garden Scheduled
to open at press time, this lovely garden
showcases formal walled areas that illustrate
traditional Spanish-Moorish and English
landscape design. A 10,000-square-foot
glass conservatory features plants from the
Sonoran and Chihuahuan Deserts in one
wing and flora from the Mediterranean in
another. A **Demonstration Garden** boasts a
red flat-bed Chevy that shows New Mexico
truck farming at harvest time. The gift shop
stocks botanical gifts. ♦ Admission. Daily.
2601 Central Ave (at New York Ave NW).
764.6200 &

Albuquerque Aquarium Scheduled to
open at press time, this state-of-the-art
aquarium features a walk-through moray-eel
tunnel, a combined stingray and shore bird
exhibit, a coral reef habitat, and a 285,000-
gallon shark tank with a floor-to-ceiling
window view. Another exhibit traces a drop
of water in its journey from the headwaters
of the Rio Grande in southern Colorado to
the Gulf of Mexico 1,185 miles away.
♦ Admission. Daily. 2601 Central Ave (at
New York Ave). 764.6200 &

Tingley Aquatic Park Walkways and piers
provide easy fishing access over a lake at this
water park. There's also a model boat lake.
♦ Daily dawn to dusk. Tingley Dr SW and
Central Ave. 764.6200 &

12 Albuquerque Sports Stadium The only
known sports stadium with a drive-in
spectator area is home to the **Albuquerque**

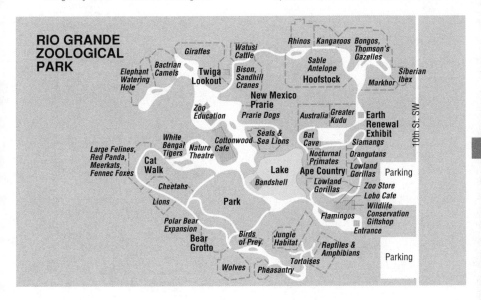

RIO GRANDE ZOOLOGICAL PARK

Dukes, the top Triple-A farm team of the **Los Angeles Dodgers.** Every April through September **Dodger** hopefuls take on their **Pacific Coast League** rivals in the 30,000-seat, city-owned stadium. ◆ 1601 Stadium Blvd SE (between Buena Vista Dr SE and University Blvd SE). 243.1791

13 Ernie Pyle Memorial Library A bust of beloved World War II correspondent Ernie Pyle greets visitors to the memorabilia-filled home of the Pulitzer Prize–winning writer who won the loyalty of readers worldwide with his "Worm's Eye View" of the war overseas. Pyle moved with his wife, Jerry, to the little white clapboard house in 1940 and returned there between assignments until his death at the hands of a sniper on the Pacific island of Ie Shima on 18 April 1945. Today, the house is home to the smallest branch of the **Albuquerque Public Library** and is a tribute to his illustrious writing career. On display are Pyle's Stetson, his pewter mug, and his favorite chair, plus photos, Pyle's hand-written articles, and news clippings of his career and his untimely death. ◆ Free. Tu-Sa. 900 Girard Blvd SE (between Santa Clara Ave SE and Coal Ave SE). 256.2065

14 New Mexico State Fairgrounds/The Downs at Albuquerque This spot doubles as the site of the annual New Mexico State Fair, one of the state's largest events, and as home to horse racing at the **Downs at Albuquerque.** Every September the fair features two weeks of down-home entertainment and cuisine, including one of the top professional rodeos in the country, a carnival, cooking contests, and animal exhibits, plus displays of the arts and culture of the state's Native American and Hispanic populations. Be sure to sample the native foods in the fair's Spanish and Indian villages.

The fair also kicks off a "mini" horse-racing season at the **Downs at Albuquerque,** where a substantial purse attracts the best thoroughbred and quarter horse talent in the Southwest. Races are simulcast daily year-round from tracks around the country. Live races are run in the spring and fall; call ahead for schedules. The glass-enclosed, climate-controlled grandstand is ideal for watching the jockeys chase some of the world's fastest equine athletes. ◆ Bounded by Louisiana Blvd NE and San Pedro Dr NE, and Central Ave and Lomas Blvd NE. New Mexico State Fairgrounds 265.1791. Race track 266.5555

15 Uptown Shopping If you absolutely *must* go to a mall, Albuquerque's two major shopping centers are located in the fast-paced Uptown business district on Louisiana Boulevard between I-40 and Menaul Boulevard. **Coronado Center,** the state's largest mall, houses more than 160 stores, including **The Gap, Foley's,** and **Victoria's**

Secret. Down the road at **Winrock Center, Dillard's** and **Montgomery Ward** mix with fast food, books, and sporting goods. ◆ Daily. Coronado Center: 6600 Menaul Blvd NE (at Louisiana Blvd NE). 881.2700; Winrock Center: Louisiana Blvd NE (just north of I-40). 883.6132

Enchanted Vista

16 Enchanted Vista $ Panoramic views of the Sandia Mountains and Albuquerque's city lights make this a delightfully located bed-and-breakfast, especially for skiing in winter or enjoying mountain gardens in summer. This is the private home of Tillie and Albert Gonzales, master gardeners who've lovingly landscaped their property with flowers, outdoor decks, bunny trails, and comfortable chairs underneath fruit trees. The two suites are large enough for a long stay, and many European guests do linger for several weeks. Each boasts a modern decor and features a refrigerator and eating area. ◆ 10700 Del Rey Ave (2 blocks north of San Antonio Dr NE, between Browning St and Eubank Blvd). 823.1301

17 Page One Billed as New Mexico's largest locally owned bookstore, this place offers 5,000 international and domestic magazines, 125 newspapers from around the world, and books in every category from biography to travel. There is also an extensive computer game department and a wide variety of CDs and audio cassettes featuring jazz, rock 'n' roll, country western, hip hop, and R&B music. Owners Yvette and Steve Stout encourage patrons to stay a while—a cafe with a drop-dead view of the Sandia Mountains serves sandwiches, soups, desserts, wine, and beer. ◆ Daily 7AM-midnight. 11018 Montgomery Blvd NE (at Juan Tabo Blvd NE). 294.2026; 800/521.4122 &

18 National Atomic Museum This Kirtland Air Force Base museum traces the history of the nuclear age and New Mexico's role in it, beginning with the top-secret Los Alamos–based Manhattan Project of the 1940s through today's development of nuclear technology and the problems of nuclear waste. Exhibits include replicas of the "Fat Man" and "Little Boy" bombs, full-scale models of the B-52 and F105D bombers, and historic flying machines. The classic documentary *Ten Seconds that Shook the World* (on the World War II atomic bomb story) is shown daily, while other displays and films deal with fusion, alternative energy, and peaceful applications of nuclear technology. ♦ Free. Daily. Wyoming Blvd and L St, Kirtland Air Force Base. 284.3243 ♿

19 Tinkertown Museum Bob and Carla Ward own this marvelous miniature world of animated hand-carved figurines. Located 20 minutes east of Albuquerque on the winding road to Sandia Crest, the museum is the result of more than 30 years of collecting and carving by Bob, a fan of the traveling miniature circus shows of the 1950s, and Carla, who has been crafting her own functional pottery since 1975. Together, the two have amassed a delightful collection of more than 900 carved wooden characters, complete with a tiny Western town and a circus with trapeze artists, dancing bears, fire-eaters, and a merry-go-round. Other museum highlights include wedding cake couples; an eerie mechanical Boot Hill Cemetery, where lightning crackles as an angel and devil battle over poor lost souls; and the gift shop's selection of Carla Ward's hand-thrown stoneware. All is enclosed between walls constructed of more than 40,000 glass bottles, another Ward hobby honed long before recycling became fashionable. ♦ Daily Apr-Oct. Sandia Park, NM 536. Take exit 175 north from I-40. 281.5233 ♿

20 Sandia Peak Aerial Tramway The best view of Albuquerque is from atop the world's longest aerial tramway ride. The spectacular 2.7-mile trip to the top of 10,400-foot-high Sandia Peak climbs 4,000 feet from the northern outskirts of the city through four of the Earth's seven life zones, the equivalent of traveling from Mexico to Alaska in biological terms. The 20-minute ride features dramatic vistas of high desert flora, jagged granite outcroppings, and pine-covered peaks, where elk, bear, bighorn sheep, and golden eagles roam. The observation deck at the summit provides an 11,000-square-mile panoramic view of Santa Fe, Los Alamos, and other distant sites. In winter, the tram whisks skiers to the Sandia Peak ski area, which features six lifts and 25 miles of beginner and intermediate slopes. The Sandias are also popular for cross-country skiing, hiking, and mountain biking, with various trails accessible by tram or by car. ♦ Fee. Daily. 10 Tramway Loop. From I-40, take Tramway Rd exit 167 and head north approximately 9 miles; from I-25, take Tramway Rd exit 234 and head approximately 5 miles east. 298.8518, 296.9585 ♿

At Sandia Peak Aerial Tramway:

Pier 66 ★★$$$$ Located at the base of the **Sandia Peak Tramway,** this casual restaurant also provides good city views from its outdoor deck, plus steak and seafood cooked over a mesquite grill. An old steam-powered fire engine doubles as a bar. ♦ Steak/Seafood ♦ Daily lunch and dinner; deck and bar: noon-11PM. Reservations recommended. Next to the base of the tramway. 856.3473 ♿

High Finance ★★$$$$ Perched two miles above Albuquerque atop Sandia Peak, this restaurant offers a breathtaking view plus a good selection of beef, seafood, and pasta in an elegant but casual setting. The fettuccine alfredo, Santa Fe chicken (with green chile, tomatoes, onions, and melted cheese), and prime rib are sure to satisfy. Dinner reservations include a discount tramway ticket to the top. ♦ Continental ♦ Daily lunch and dinner. Reservations recommended. 243.9742

21 Sandia Crest House Gift Shop ★$ Yet more wonderful views are offered at this place at the top of Sandia Crest. Have a snack—nachos, hot dogs, hamburgers—outdoors or inside, and peruse the gift shop. This spot provides good access to hiking trails, too. ♦ Snacks ♦ Daily. Sandia Crest. From I-40, take exit 175 north, follow NM 14 north, and head west on NM 536 to the summit. 243.0605

Sandia means "watermelon" in Spanish. Formed between 5 and 25 million years ago, layers of limestone cap the tops of the Sandia Mountains like a banded rind, contrasting with the rugged granite below that glows watermelon pink at sunset.

New Mexico, famous for its high altitudes and dry climate, was covered by shallow inland seas teeming with marine life 75 million years ago. At that time, Albuquerque's Sandia Crest, now towering above the city at an elevation of 10,678 feet, was hundreds of feet *below* sea level.

Restaurants/Clubs: Red | **Hotels:** Blue
Shops/ Outdoors: Green | **Sights/Culture:** Black

Albuquerque Day Trips

Escape from urban Albuquerque to a meandering mountain road or a historic Indian pueblo is possible in anywhere from three minutes to three hours. Those who really want to get out of town quickly should hit the beautiful **Turquoise Trail**, which winds through some of the most scenic and eclectic towns in the state and eventually leads to Santa Fe. And don't miss some of the area's other natural and historic wonders that are farther afield.

Some of the most notable getaways include the ruins of the capital of the Anasazi people at **Chaco Culture National Historic Park**, the spectacular bird sanctuary at the **Bosque del Apache Wildlife Refuge**, the ancient lava-crusted landscapes of **El Malpais National Monument and Conservation Area**, the massive sandstone mesa at **El Morro National Monument**, and the **Fort Sumner State Monument**, where the infamous Billy the Kid was gunned down and buried. Finally, both ancient Indian ruins and the modern-day homes of 11 of the state's Pueblo Indian tribes are situated throughout the area. The stunning **Acoma Pueblo** and the 17th-century **Salinas National Monument** are prime recommendations, although a day trip to any of the surrounding Indian sites will undoubtedly be insightful and memorable.

1 Turquoise Trail If you prefer backroad scenery over freeway frenzy, this historic trail should be your route of choice to Santa Fe. Beginning at I-40's Cedar Crest exit on Albuquerque's east side, NM 14 meanders north some 46 miles to Santa Fe, snaking through the old mining towns of Golden, Madrid, and Cerrillos, where miners once coaxed mass quantities of gold, coal, silver, lead, zinc, and turquoise from nearby hills. When World War II sent these men to war, the mines went bust, and the towns went to the ghosts. Then during the 1960s, the sleepy villages reawakened to a new generation of residents—hippies, artists, writers, and the like—whose own frontier spirit has

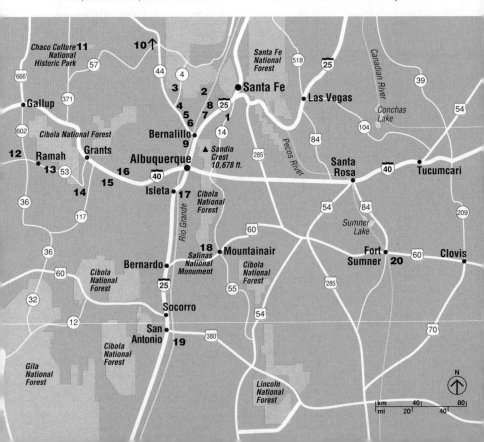

transformed the towns into historic centers steeped in a relaxed old-time atmosphere of art, music, theater, and more.

Winding through the shadows of Albuquerque's majestic Sandia Mountains, the trail makes its way past Cedar Crest and **Sandia Park** until the tiny village of Golden comes into view about 10 miles north. Once a bustling gold-mining town—and the site of the first gold rush west of the Mississippi in 1825—Golden sits on the northern edge of the San Pedro Mountains. Today a general store and a rock shop sit by the highway along with a smattering of restored houses; most of the old homes, however, remain dilapidated and abandoned. Golden's architectural gem is the **St. Francis Church,** which rests on a hill at the edge of town. Built in the 1830s in honor of St. Francis of Assisi, the simple adobe mission contains beautiful hand-carved statues and holds services twice yearly—the Feast of St. Peter on 29 June and the Feast of St. Francis on 4 October.

About 12 miles north of Golden, in the mineral-rich Ortiz Mountains, is the renowned little coal town of Madrid, the only place in the country where hard (anthracite) and soft (bituminous) coal exist side by side. Once boasting a production of 500 tons of coal a day, Madrid was a thriving company town of about 2,500 people from 1893 to 1954. In the 1930s it was known worldwide as the City of Lights for its extraordinary annual Christmas display of more than 150,000 lights (the town owned the power company). Hillsides and streets were transformed into a giant toyland, a miniature Bethlehem, and other spectacular settings filled with Santa and scores of animated characters. So incredible was the spectacle that commercial airline pilots detoured through the area so their passengers could view it from above. In recent years, Madrid residents have begun lighting up the town again at Christmas, though on a much smaller scale than before.

Today Madrid is home to some 300 people who have converted old company stores and wooden houses into intriguing galleries, restaurants, and shops featuring works by local artisans, native foods, custom clothing, and imported goods. Recommended are the **Tapestry Gallery** (471.0194) for handwoven rugs and clothing; **Maya Jones** (473.3641) for Guatemalan imports; **Primitiva** (no phone) for local pottery, rugs, baskets, and folk art. Plan to stop for lunch at the **Mineshaft Tavern and Giftshop** (473.0743 &), where the live entertainment and blue-cheese burger can't be beat. The **Old Coal Mine**

Museum (473.0743) features artifacts and memorabilia of Madrid's mining heyday. It's open daily (tours are given), and there's an admission charge. The **Engine House Theater** (473.0743) stages hilarious melodramas before the backdrop of an old steam locomotive. And in the summer, a superb series of outdoor concerts is held at Madrid's old ballpark.

A few more miles north is the still-sleepy village of Cerrillos, whose hills once bore some of the finest turquoise in the world and whose boomtown-era residents once supported 21 saloons. The town retains an Old West ambience and has provided the setting for a number of Westerns, including the "Young Guns" and "Lonesome Dove" TV series. Highlights include the **Turquoise Trail Trading Post** (471.0629), where you can purchase miniature adobe bricks and tie-dyed T-shirts; and **Casa Grande** (471.2744), a rambling 21-room adobe that features a petting zoo, turquoise-mining museum, and the **What Not Shop,** which carries antiques, old rocks, and Indian jewelry. From Cerrillos the trail continues another 15 miles to Santa Fe and I-25. ♦ NM 14, from I-40 at Tijeras Ave to I-25 in Santa Fe

2 Cochiti Pueblo The famous pottery *Storyteller* figurine originated here in the 1960s when pueblo potter Helen Cordero was inspired by memories of her grandfather spinning the ancient tales of the Cochiti tribe. Soon, other pueblo artists were creating their own versions of the openmouthed narrator whose lap is piled with listening youngsters, and the Storyteller became the distinctive symbol of the villagers' fine pottery skills. Craftspeople at this Keresan Indian pueblo are also praised for their traditional drums, which beat hypnotically each 14 July, when the tribe gathers for its annual feast day to perform the ceremonial Corn Dance in honor of their patron saint, San Buenaventura. The church erected in 1628 in his honor still stands regally here amid squat modern pueblo homes.

Cochiti also is known for its prime recreational facilities, including Cochiti Dam, one of the largest earth-and-concrete dams in

San Buenaventura, Cochiti Pueblo

JOHN DEL GAIZO

the country. The dam created Cochiti Lake, a beautiful seven-milelong warm-water lake that is a windsurfer's wonderland and an angler's paradise, stocked with rainbow trout, bass, crappie, and pike. But don't bring a motor boat, as this is a no-wake lake. The pueblo's commercial center, tennis courts, and 18-hole championship golf course offer other alternatives. ♦ Free. Daily. Cameras, recorders, and sketchbooks prohibited. Take I-25 north 45 miles to the Cochiti exit, then follow the signs west. 465.2244

3 Jemez Pueblo This picturesque pueblo, located northwest of Albuquerque in the foothills of the Jemez Mountains, became the state's sole Towa-speaking pueblo after **Pecos Pueblo** was abandoned in the 1830s. Today the ceremonials of both pueblos are observed here; the Feast of Our Lady of the Angels, highlighted by the Old Pecos Bull Dance, is held on 2 August, while on 12 November the pueblo honors its patron saint, San Diego. Three miles north is the **Red Rock Scenic Area** (NM 4, no phone), where the pueblo's noted crafts—sculpture, pottery, jewelry, moccasins, drums, and baskets made from

yucca fronds—are sold. The 88,000-acre reservation also includes fishing and hunting sites, permits for which must be purchased from the **Jemez Pueblo** game warden. ♦ Free. Daily. Photographs and sketches prohibited. Follow I-25 north 20 miles to Bernalillo, then go northwest about 20 miles along NM 44 and follow the signs to Jemez Pueblo. 834.7359

3 Jemez Springs/Jemez State Monument
Twenty miles north of the pueblo, in the spectacular red sandstone Jemez Canyon, is Jemez Springs, an old resort town filled with bubbling hot mineral springs that attracts health-seekers from miles around. On NM 4 is **Jemez Springs Bath House** (829.3303). Built in 1870, today it is a modern health spa with hot mineral baths and massage. On the northern edge of the springs is **Jemez State Monument,** the site of the spectacular ruins of the prehistoric Jemez Indian pueblo of **Giusewa** (Place of the Boiling Waters). Also preserved here is the **San Jose de los Jemez Church** (no phone), a great stone structure built in 1622 as a place of worship and a fortress with eight-foot-thick rock walls and an octagonal bell tower. The **Laughing Lizard Cafe** (829.3108), open Tuesday through Sunday for lunch and dinner, serves homemade pizza, chicken tacos, and spinach-and-black-bean burritos.

For those wanting to spend a day or two, spend the night at **Jemez River B&B Inn** (16445 NM 4, 829.3262) or **Dancing Bear** (NM 4, 829.3336).3108). ♦ Jemez State Monument: admission; free for those under age 15. Daily. 20 miles north of Jemez Pueblo along NM 44. 829.3530

Jemez Springs/Jemez State Monument

JOHN DEL GAIZO

4 Zia Pueblo The ancient Zia sun sign (pictured above) that is the symbol of this small Keresan village is also the official emblem that appears on the New Mexico state flag and license plates. Likewise, the Zia bird and the double rainbow design both are distinctive **Zia Pueblo** symbols and figure prominently in the exquisite polychrome pottery created here. The pueblo is also known for its outstanding painters, some of whom are internationally recognized for their watercolors and oils. Located at its present site since the early 1300s, the pueblo honors its patron saint, Our Lady of the Assumption, every 15 August with an all-day Corn Dance. Zia arts and crafts are sold at the tribe's **Cultural Center.** And two miles west of the village, Zia Lake offers fishing, with permits available at the site. ◆ Free. Daily. Photos, recorders, and sketchbooks prohibited. Take I-25 north 20 miles to Bernalillo, then go 17 miles northwest on NM 44. 867.3304

5 Santa Ana Pueblo The old village of this Keresan Indian pueblo houses few of its current tribal members; most of them live in modern stuccoed homes in nearby Bernalillo or surrounding farmlands. Nonetheless, the village comes alive each year when residents return for their annual 26 July feast day and pay homage to their patron saint, Santa Ana, with the daylong Corn Dance. Other ceremonial dances are held here on 1 and 6 January, Easter Sunday, 24 and 29 June, and 25-28 December. Visitors are encouraged to attend the ceremonials because that's the only time the ancient community opens to the public. Nearby, however, the new village of Santa Ana bustles with activity year-round. At the **Ta Ma Myia Cooperative Association** (no phone), native craftspeople sell their fine woven belts and bold polychrome pottery, along with other arts and crafts. And the tribe's 27-hole **Valle Grande Golf Course** (Bernalillo, 867.9464) draws golfers from around the state. ◆ Free. The old pueblo is open during annual ceremonials only; contact the tribal governor's office for the best times to visit the new village. No photographs, recordings, or sketching permitted. Take I-25 north 20 miles to Bernalillo, then head northwest 8 miles on NM 44. 867.3301

6 Coronado State Monument and Park
Explorer Francisco Vásquez de Coronado wintered here in 1540 during the first exploration of the area by the Spanish as they searched for the elusive Seven Cities of Cibola, rumored to be made of gold. What they found instead was the ancient Tiwa-speaking people of Kuaua, whose awesome 1,200-room pueblo on the west banks of the Rio Grande represented the tribe's architectural sophistication. More than a thousand people once lived amid this maze of rooms and sacred underground kivas, which were painted with elaborate murals of ancient Indian symbols and plant and animal life. The pueblo was abandoned near the end of the 17th century, and its mud walls remained buried for 250 years until its excavation in 1935. The monument was created in 1940 to preserve the ruins, and today visitors can walk among the pueblo's crumbling rock walls and descend into an ancient kiva. A small archaeological museum displays ancient Kuaua murals and artifacts. Adjacent to the monument is the **Coronado State Park,** which features picnic shelters, campsites, and more Indian ruins. A good time to visit is during the fall; when the trees change to their glistening autumn hue, you might indeed think you've discovered cities of gold. ◆ Admission; children under age 6 free. Daily. Take I-25 north 20 miles to Bernalillo, then head northwest a few miles on NM 44. 867.5351

7 San Felipe Pueblo One of the most traditional of the Rio Grande pueblos, this Keresan Indian community is renowned for its beautiful ceremonials. Most notable is the Green Corn Dance held on 1 May, when hundreds of men, women, and children honor their patron saint, San Felipe, singing ancient chants and dancing about in brilliant costumes on a central plaza that has been well-worn by generations of dancing feet. The craftspeople here are known for their exquisite beadwork and pottery; permission to walk around the village to talk to native artisans or other pueblo residents must be granted from the tribal office. ◆ Free. Call the tribal office for the best times to visit. No cameras, sketching, or recording permitted. Take I-25 north 20 miles to Bernalillo and follow the signs another 10 miles north. 867.3381

Partly because of their stable, agrarian lifestyle, the Pueblo people were able to attain a sophisticated culture characterized by superb skill at stone masonry, breathtaking arts and crafts, and extensive knowledge of solar and lunar astronomy. Pueblo culture reached its zenith in the Chaco Canyon area of Northwestern New Mexico.

Restaurants/Clubs: Red   **Hotels:** Blue
Shops/ Outdoors: Green   **Sights/Culture:** Black

8 Santo Domingo Pueblo The largest of the eastern Keresan Indian pueblos is famous for its fine *heishi* (intricately ground shell, pronounced *he*-she), turquoise, and silver jewelry. Once a thriving farming community, it is now known for its marketing skills; more than 350 pueblo artisans sell their arts and crafts at roadside stands, on the **Palace of the Governor**'s portal in Santa Fe, and during the pueblo's annual Labor Day weekend arts-and-crafts fair. The community also performs one of the most dramatic Indian ceremonials in the area— more than 500 pueblo singers, dancers, and drummers participate in a colorful all-day Corn Dance on 4 August. The elaborate dance features "Koshare" clowns—nearly naked men who paint their bodies in black-and-white stripes and pester spectators—as well as men, women, and children tinged in orange and turquoise paint and clad in traditional ceremonial belts, animal skins, and headdresses. A small museum and **Tribal Cultural Center** are also located at the pueblo. ◆ Free; donations accepted. Daily. No photographs, sketching, or tape recording permitted. Take I-25 north 31 miles to Santo Domingo exit 259 and follow the signs. 465.2214

9 Sandia Pueblo Perhaps the most striking feature of this tiny Tiwa-speaking community is its huge Las Vegas–style bingo hall that's open round the clock. The pueblo's long history, however, is much more traditional: originally called **Nafiat**, the village was founded circa 1300. In 1540, after a visit by Spanish explorer Francisco Vásquez de Coronado, it was dubbed Sandia, which is Spanish for watermelon, the color of the surrounding mountains at sunset. The pueblo was abandoned after the 1680 Pueblo Revolt, but tribal members returned to the village in later years—the ruins of the old pueblo are still visible near the present-day church.

The pueblo maintains a reputation as one of the most industrious in the state, with its bingo, horseback-riding stables, and the **Bien Mur Indian Market Center,** which includes arts and crafts from all of the New Mexican pueblos. The 40-acre **Sandia Lakes Recreation Area** also features fishing for bass, trout, and catfish; permits are available at the site. The pueblo's St. Anthony feast day is 13 June. Among other things, St. Anthony is the patron saint of good husbands, and on the annual feast day, pueblo mothers bring their single daughters in hopes the saint will find them a good match. ◆ Free. Daily. No photographs, sketching, or recording permitted. Follow I-25 north toward Bernalillo to tramway exit, then head north on NM 313 for a few miles. 867.3317

The Zia believe a man has four sacred obligations: he must develop a strong body, clear mind, pure spirit, and devotion to the welfare of his people.

10 Aztec Ruins National Monument The spectacular maze of rooms comprising these prehistoric communal dwellings were named incorrectly by 19th-century settlers who mistakenly believed they had been built by the Aztec Indians of Mexico. The ruins are actually the remnants of an ancient Anasazi pueblo that once bustled with activity. Built on a rise overlooking the turquoise waters of the Animas River, the ruins are highlighted by a two-acre U-shaped village, where visitors follow a self-guided trail to peer through decaying walls into underground kivas and crawl through tiny doorways. The 12th-century **Great Kiva,** which was restored to its original condition in 1934, features a timbered roof packed with mud and offers modern-day visitors a place to rest, listen to Navajo chants, and contemplate the lives of the ancient ones. ◆ Admission. Daily. Follow I-25 north 20 miles to Bernalillo, then head north 160 miles on NM 44 to Aztec. 334.6174

11 Chaco Culture National Historic Park Set in the heart of the flat San Juan Basin, Chaco Canyon was the site of the largest city (more than 5,000 people) in the Southwest during the Classic Anasazi period (about AD 1000-1200). The Chaco people also established "outlier" colonies across an area of more than 10,000 square miles of New Mexico and southern Colorado. These outposts were necessary because timber and food had to be brought into the arid San Juan Basin to support the city. Archaeologists debate endlessly about why the Anasazi chose to locate their capital in this place. One likely theory is that smoke from the city's signal fires, announcing the arrival of trade caravans from Mexico or heralding religious ceremonies, could be seen by lookouts for great distances across the San Juan Basin, as no mountains obstructed the view. The extraordinary number and size of ceremonial kivas suggest Chaco Canyon was a spiritual center for the region. **Pueblo Bonito,** the largest of the several pueblo ruins within walking distance of one another in the canyon, contained more than 800 rooms at its heyday and is said to have been the largest residential building in the world in the 12th century. ◆ Admission. Daily. Fill the gas tank in Cuba; there is no gas, food service, or lodging in the park. Follow I-25 north to Bernalillo, then take NM 44 north 115 miles to Nageezi Trading Post and follow the unpaved park road west for about 29 miles. 786.7014, 988.6716

12 Zuni Pueblo Legends of the brilliant sunlit walls of the pueblo dwellings of Hawikuh, the ancient village of the Zuni Indians, are what prompted Francisco Vásquez de Coronado to begin exploring New Mexico in 1540 in search of the fabled Seven Cities of Cibola. When he arrived, however, he found no cities of gold, just the sophisticated Zuni Indian tribe. For more than a century, the Zunis grudgingly accepted the Spanish presence and the Christianity forced upon them, but after the 1680 Pueblo Revolt, Hawikuh was abandoned. In 1692 the Zuni resettled 12 miles north of Hawikuh.

With more than 8,000 members, this is the largest of the state's 19 pueblos and is renowned worldwide for its fine jewelers. Their unique inlay, overlay, and minute "needlepoint" styles combine silver with such rich stones as turquoise, black jet, coral, opal, lapis, and sugalite. Jewelry is for sale, at very expensive prices, in pueblo shops and at the tribe's **Zuni Arts and Crafts Market.**

At the **Old Zuni Mission Church** (Sandy Hill Rd and Plaza Cir), artists Alex and Ken Seowtewa have spent 25 years creating stunning murals of lifesized kachinas. Brilliantly colored costumes, exotic face masks, and bowls of feathered prayer sticks depict important Zuni religious rites amidst mesas and desert landscapes. The church is usually locked, but a polite telephone call to **St. Anthony's Mission** (782.2888) usually results in someone meeting you there with the key during the week. A donation is appreciated. The pueblo is also well known for its annual all-night Shalako Ceremony, during which dancers wear larger-than-life masks that evoke the pantheon of Zuni gods. The ceremony takes place in late November or early December. ◆ Free. Daily. Photos, sketches, and recordings prohibited on feast days; cameras are allowed on other days for a fee. Take I-40 west about 120 miles to Gallup, then head 34 miles south on NM 602 to NM 53. Zuni Pueblo is several miles west on NM 53. 782.4481

13 El Morro National Monument For nearly a thousand years, New Mexico explorers, traders, soldiers, and settlers traveling an ancient Indian trade route couldn't resist taking a break in the shadow of a 200-foot-high sandstone mesa and etching their marks into its smooth surface. A portion of the pale cliff, known as **Inscription Rock,** is a virtual guest register of Southwestern history with its prehistoric Indian petroglyphs and signatures

of prominent passersby. When Juan de Oñate went through in 1605, he wrote: "Passed by here the Governor Don Juan de Oñate, from the discovery of the Sea of the South (the Gulf of California) on the 16th of April 1605." And Diego de Vargas, on his journey to reclaim the area after the 1680 Pueblo Revolt, noted: "Here was the General Don Diego de Vargas who conquered for our Holy Faith, and for the Royal Crown, all of New Mexico at his own expense, year of 1692." A natural water basin sits at the base of the towering mesa, while unexcavated Anasazi ruins, dating from the late 1300s, rest up top. The site also features a visitors' center, from which guided tours depart regularly, and a picnic area. ◆ Admission; children under 17 free. Daily. Follow I-40 west about 68 miles to Grants, then exit on NM 53 and continue about 40 miles west toward the village of Ramah. 783.4226

14 El Malpais National Monument and Conservation Area One of the most recent lava flows in North America—the remnants of five now-dormant volcanoes—is preserved at El Malpais, a 114,000-acre lava rock valley known as the **Land of Fire and Ice.** A succession of trails through the rugged lava beds leads to a number of volcanic wonders ranging in age from 700 to 50,000 years old, including volcanoes, ice caves, and the longest lava tube system in the world. The 7.5-mile **Zuni-Acoma Trail,** an ancient Indian trade route, crosses all five of the major lava flows, allowing visitors to walk on a chunky lava called *aa* and a ropelike lava known as *pahoehoe.* The lava is so hard that even though the trail has been in use for more than 800 years, there is little sign of wear (unlike the soles of your shoes when you're done with this walk). The five extinct volcanoes still loom overhead; visitors can peer down into the 800-foot-deep **Bandera Crater,** which last erupted one million years ago, or journey 75 feet below its jagged edge to a 31-degree ice cave, a freak of nature that early settlers used to store perishable foods. A must on any jaunt is **La Ventana Natural Arch,** located at the eastern end of the lava flow. The massive sandstone arch was formed after years of wind and water permeated the soft stone surface, creating a 125-foot-high by 165-foot-wide opening in the rock—a spectacular natural window to the world. Backcountry camping in the area is permitted, and a visitors' center is located 10 miles to the north in Grants at 620 East Santa Fe Avenue (285.4506). ◆ Free. Daily. Take I-40 about 58 miles west and exit south onto NM 117 at the Quemado exit. The lava flow area lines the west side of NM 117. Monument headquarters 285.4641

Nuestra Señora de Guadalupe, Zuni Pueblo

JOHN DEL GAIZO

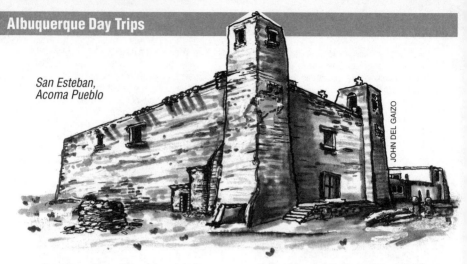

San Esteban,
Acoma Pueblo

JOHN DEL GAIZO

15 Acoma Pueblo Considered by many to be the most incredible of the state's 19 pueblos, **Acoma** sits 7,000 feet above sea level atop a 367-foot mesa—the **Rock of Acuco**—and provides a dreamy panoramic view of chamisa, juniper, red sandstone cliffs, and an endless azure sky. Appropriately called the "Sky City," the pueblo's Keresan residents are estimated to have lived here since AD 1075, making it the oldest continually inhabited city in the country. The village's multistory rock-walled dwellings occupy 70 acres of the mesa top, along with a magnificent mission church. Villagers once scaled the mesa by an ancient rock stairway and a system of handholds and toeholds chipped into the cliff. Both the pueblo and its mission are listed as National Historic Landmarks on the National Register of Historic Places.

While several thousand Indians once lived here, today the pueblo is home to about 50 residents who continue to live without water or electricity, hauling their daily necessities—even dirt for their cemetery—along a narrow road that leads from below. The other 4,000 pueblo members now live in the surrounding villages of Acomita, Anzac, and McCarty's. They return to the mesa for annual ceremonials, especially the elaborate San Esteban Feast Day held on 2 September, when residents of all ages don traditional garb and perform the Harvest Dance throughout the day. The jewel of the pueblo is the massive church, the **Mission of San Esteban del Rey,** erected in honor of the pueblo's patron saint. The church's whitewashed walls and dirt floor contrast beautifully with its 17th-century altar paintings and hand-carved wooden saints. The giant 40-footlong ceiling beams that cross overhead were cut in the mountains 30 miles away and hauled back to the mesa on the backs of the village men.

The only way to see the pueblo is by guided tours, which depart regularly from the visitors' center at the mesa's base. The center also includes a snack bar and a small museum, which gives the history of the pueblo and its prized thin-shelled pottery. Made from white clay, the pots are embellished with orange and black optical art line patterns and Mimbres (an ancient tribe that was a forerunner of the Pueblo people) designs and are valued by collectors worldwide. Pots are for sale in the visitors' center's crafts shop, at outdoor booths, and at the ancient pueblo.♦ Admission. Daily. Cameras are permitted only on non-feast days; there's a fee. Take I-40 about 52 miles west to the Acoma exit, then head another 11 miles southwest on Indian Rd 23. 552.6604

16 Laguna Pueblo The largest of the Keresan Indian pueblos, it includes six villages scattered over thousands of acres: Old Laguna, Paguate, Mesita, Paraje, Encinal, and Seama. The pueblo is also one of the state's most enterprising, bringing income to its residents through such innovative economic development projects on the reservation as the prosperous Laguna Industries, which manufactures communications shelters for the US Army. The pueblo was also once the site of one of the world's richest uranium mines, and the ongoing Laguna Reclamation Project is dedicated to restoring the mine lands to again provide mining jobs for pueblo residents. Clay is also excavated on pueblo land, and the production of the pueblo's traditional polychrome pottery—which incorporates distinctive geometric and plant and animal designs—also provides income for pueblo artists. While each of the Laguna villages celebrates its own feast day, the entire pueblo turns out at Old Laguna on 19 September to celebrate St. Joseph's Day with Corn, Buffalo, and Eagle dances and an arts-and-crafts fair. During fishing season, permits for the Paguate Reservoir can be purchased in that village. ♦ Free. Daily. Photography regulations vary in each community. Take I-40 west 46 miles, and follow the signs to the individual villages. 552.6654, 243.7616

17 Isleta Pueblo This 16th-century pueblo is the largest of the Tiwa-speaking pueblos and home to the **San Augustín Church,** one of the oldest missions in the US. Erected about 1613, the massive adobe facade boasts two towers, a small belfry in the center, and a smaller bell hanging just above the entrance. Tribal legend has it that Fray Juan Padilla, a Spanish priest who was buried in the sanctuary of the church, periodically leaves his cottonwood coffin and comes to the surface of the sanctuary to reveal his remains to the pueblo people, many of whom regard him as a saint. The tribe also holds two annual feast days in honor of its patron saint, San Augustin, on 28 August and 4 September.

Located on the west banks of the Rio Grande just south of Albuquerque, the original pueblo was abandoned during the 1680 Pueblo Revolt. Villagers returned later and built a new **Isleta** (little island), which today has grown to over 4,000 residents scattered among several settlements. Pueblo artisans are known for their polychrome pottery—red and black on a white background—while the pueblo's large bingo hall and camping and fishing areas lure many visitors to the reservation. One of the largest of the state's pueblos, in 1986 **Isleta** became the first to elect a woman as tribal governor, although not without creating considerable controversy. Camping, fishing, and picnicking permits must be purchased on site. ♦ Free. Daily. Photographs are allowed (for free) except on feast days. Follow I-25 south 13 miles, then follow the signs east to Isleta. 869.3111

18 Salinas National Monument The ruins of three abandoned 17th-century Indian villages represent the classic encounter between European civilization and prehistoric Indian tribes. This 645-acre monument is the site of three magnificent villages—**Quarai, Abo,** and **Gran Quivira**—that were abandoned in the 1670s after the arrival of the Spanish. Each of the villages features the

remains of spectacular earthen Spanish-style missions erected before their inhabitants left. The area was situated near a salt lake, which was an important source of salt for early residents and traders, and the pueblos in its vicinity became known as the Salinas (Spanish for saline) tribes. Today, the villages are located within a 25-mile radius of Mountainair.

The **Quarai** ruins, with red sandstone walls five feet thick and forty feet high, are some of the most beautiful in the monument. There, the well-preserved 1630 church of **La Purisima Concepción de Cuarac** continues to tower 100 feet across and 40 feet above a grassy plain. Seventeen miles to the southwest at **Abo**, the 30-foot-high bright red sandstone mission of **San Gregorio** boasts stone buttresses that represent the tribe's sophisticated building techniques. Nearby, the Abo River flows past the ancient Indians' three-story rock-walled homes. Still farther south is the awesome village of **Gran Quivira**, once home to a thriving community of 1,500. Here, Indians farmed beans and squash, hunted bison, and fashioned pottery. In 1659 they built the massive mission of **San Buenaventura** atop a windswept mesa with 30-foot-high limestone walls standing six feet thick. The multilevel ruins also are scattered with underground kivas, where villagers worshiped their traditional gods. Self-guided tour pamphlets are available at the monument's visitors' center (847.2585) in the **Shaffer Hotel** (Hwy 60, 847.2888) in Mountainair or at the individual sites. ♦ Free. Daily. Take I-25 south 50 miles to Bernardo, then take Hwy 60 about 35 miles to Mountainair, at the junction of Hwy 60 and NM 55. Quarai is 10 miles north of Mountainair off NM 55. Abo is 7 miles west of Mountainair on Hwy 60. Gran Quivira is 25 miles south of Mountainair on NM 55

San Agustín, Isleta Pueblo

JOHN DEL GAIZO

Salinas National Monument

JOHN DEL GAIZO

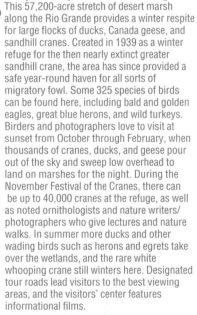

19 Bosque del Apache Wildlife Refuge

This 57,200-acre stretch of desert marsh along the Rio Grande provides a winter respite for large flocks of ducks, Canada geese, and sandhill cranes. Created in 1939 as a winter refuge for the then nearly extinct greater sandhill crane, the area has since provided a safe year-round haven for all sorts of migratory fowl. Some 325 species of birds can be found here, including bald and golden eagles, great blue herons, and wild turkeys. Birders and photographers love to visit at sunset from October through February, when thousands of cranes, ducks, and geese pour out of the sky and sweep low overhead to land on marshes for the night. During the November Festival of the Cranes, there can be up to 40,000 cranes at the refuge, as well as noted ornithologists and nature writers/ photographers who give lectures and nature walks. In summer more ducks and other wading birds such as herons and egrets take over the wetlands, and the rare white whooping crane still winters here. Designated tour roads lead visitors to the best viewing areas, and the visitors' center features informational films.

Bring your camera; you'll be sorry if you don't. ♦ Admission. Visitors' center: daily; tour loop: daily one hour before sunrise to one hour after sunset. Take I-25 south 103 miles to the San Antonio exit. In the town of San Antonio, you'll come to a yellow blinking light; turn south (right) onto NM 1 and follow it 8 miles to the refuge. 835.1828

20 Fort Sumner State Monument

The crumbling ruins of **Fort Sumner**'s **Bosque Redondo Reservation** are a harsh reminder of the incarceration of more than 9,000 Mescalero Apache and Navajo from 1863 to 1868 by the US Army. Moved from their homes in Canyon de Chelly, the Indians were forced to endure the infamous "Long Walk" to the site, as well as the wretched living conditions at the fort on the state's rugged eastern plains. When a treaty was signed five years later, those who had survived were allowed to return to Arizona. The fort was later sold and converted into a large ranch—the same ranch where Pat Garrett gunned down Billy the Kid after the infamous outlaw's escape from the Lincoln County Jail in 1881. The Kid was buried in the military cemetery nearby, but because the fugitive's fans keep trying to steal his tombstone, a chain link fence now surrounds the marker. Adjacent to the cemetery is the **Billy the Kid Museum** (355.2380), housing a collection of photographs and memorabilia of the state's most notorious outlaw. ♦ Admission. M, Th-Su. Follow I-40 east about 113 miles to Santa Rosa, then take Hwy 84 south for 45 miles and follow the signs. 355.2573

Santo Domingo Pueblo, 25 miles south of Santa Fe, is considered the least altered of any Indian village in America. Ladders are still used to reach many of the second-story homes.

Although mistakenly referred to as Mexican food or Tex-Mex, the dishes commonly identified with New Mexico reflect a blend of Hispanic and Indian cultures. Virtually all Southwestern dishes make use of the tortilla, pinto beans, cheese, and chiles.

Restaurants/Clubs: Red   **Hotels:** Blue
Shops/ ♥ Outdoors: Green   **Sights/Culture:** Black

History

2,000 years ago The Anasazi, ancestors of today's Pueblo Indians, come to live in Northern New Mexico, building villages and farming.

1100-1550 The Anasazi erect stone houses in mountain cliffs for protection. Most homes were a few stories high.

1536 During an expedition to colonize Florida, the Spaniard Cabeza de Vaca is shipwrecked off the coast of Texas. After six years as a slave of Indians in the area that is now Galveston, he and Esteban the Moor—a Moorish slave—escape and perhaps wander through Southeastern New Mexico.

1539 The Franciscan friar Marcos de Niza and Esteban the Moor explore the area near today's Gallup. Fray de Niza tries to claim the **Zuni Pueblo** for Spain, thinking that the adobe buildings are gold. Esteban is killed during this unsuccessful attempt.

1540 Setting out 150 miles south of Mazatlán, Mexico, looking for the fabled Seven Cities of Cibola, Francisco Vásquez de Coronado begins exploration and conquest of New Mexico in his quest for gold.

1590 Spaniard Gaspar de Sosa makes the first attempt to colonize New Mexico (all others before him were only looking for gold) in the **Pecos Valley.**

1598 Juan de Oñate claims "all of the kingdom and the province of New Mexico on the Rio del Norte" for Spain and founds **San Juan de Los Caballeros** near the **Chama River,** the first Spanish settlement in the state.

1610 Pedro de Peralta, governor of New Mexico, founds the city of **Santa Fe,** making it the capital of the Spanish province of New Mexico. The **Palace of the Governors** is built.

1617 After being kicked out of the **Taos Pueblo** after their unsuccessful attempt to convert the Indians, Fray Pedro de Miranda and other Spanish settlers move to what is today **Taos.**

1680 Led by Popé, a Tewa medicine man from the **San Juan Pueblo** in exile in Taos, Pueblo Indians revolt against the Spanish. Almost 500 are killed, and the settlers flee Santa Fe to El Paso del Norte, in what is now Texas. In this, the only successful major Native American rebellion in North American history, the Indians eradicate Spanish-Christian influences in New Mexico and bring back native traditions and religion.

1680-92 Indians rule Santa Fe from the **Palace of the Governors.**

1692-96 Governor Diego de Vargas reconquers New Mexico, killing many Indians in the process.

1706 Francisco Cuervo y Valdes founds the city of **Albuquerque.**

1710 Santa Fe's **San Miguel Mission** is rebuilt after being destroyed during the 1680 Pueblo Revolt.

1776 Franciscan friars Francisco Silvestre Vélez de Escalante and Francisco Dominguez open the first section of the **Old Spanish Trail.** It runs from Santa Fe to Los Angeles.

1793 The first school text in New Mexico is printed by Antonio Jose Martinez, a priest and schoolteacher from Taos.

1821 Mexico wins its independence from Spain; New Mexico becomes a Mexican province.

1822 The **Santa Fe Trail** opens when a trader, William Becknell, brings the first shipment of goods from Independence, Missouri to Santa Fe.

1833 The first gold mine west of the Mississippi River is discovered at **Sierra del Oro,** in the **Ortiz Mountains** between Santa Fe and Albuquerque.

1837 After Governor Albino Perez, a Mexican officer left in charge of New Mexico, imposes new taxes and takes away self-government, New Mexican farmers and Indians band together and revolt against the governor and the Mexican Army. Perez is killed during this incursion, known as the Chimayó Rebellion.

1846 The United States declares war on Mexico, winning a battle at Brazito. US General Stephen W. Kearny occupies Santa Fe and builds **Fort Marcy.** Charles Bent is appointed governor; Colonel Alexander Doniphan defeats Mexican forces at the Battle of El Brazito, south of Las Cruces.

1847 Fearful of losing their land, angry Hispanics and Indians kill Governor Bent, starting the Taos rebellion.

1848 With the signing of the Treaty of Guadalupe-Hidalgo, Mexico cedes New Mexico and California to the US.

1849 The **Stage Line** between Santa Fe and Independence, Missouri begins.

1850 New Mexico is designated a territory after being denied statehood. James C. Calhoun is named governor in 1851.

1851 The first English-language school is founded in Santa Fe.

1853 The Gadsden Purchase adds the Gila River area in the southern part of today's state to New Mexico.

1861-62 Confederate soldiers from Texas invade and occupy Santa Fe. The Battle of Glorieta near Santa Fe ends Confederate control in New Mexico.

1862-67 Some Navajo and Apache are relocated to **Bosque Redondo** near Fort Sumner, 160 miles southeast of Albuquerque. Colonel Kit Carson defeats the Navajo in 1864 northeast of Fort Defiance.

1870 New Mexico's population exceeds 90,000.

1878 The railroad comes to New Mexico, bringing farmers and miners. Cattle is shipped to eastern markets by train.

1881 Billy the Kid is killed by Sheriff Pat Garrett at Fort Sumner.

1886 Indian chief Geronimo is captured and surrenders to the US Army in Arizona, ending Apache raids.

1892 The **University of New Mexico** opens in Albuquerque. The **Territorial Capitol Building** in Santa Fe burns down and is rebuilt eight years later.

1900 The state population is over 195,000.

1912 On 6 January, New Mexico becomes the 47th state of the US. Santa Fe is designated the official capital.

1922 Large oil fields are discovered in San Juan County in Northwestern New Mexico. Black gold becomes New Mexico's main mining product.

1945 The world's first atomic bomb is produced at **Los Alamos National Laboratory.**

1950 Uranium is discovered near **Grants** by Navajo Paddy Martinez.

1962 The **Navajo Dam** on the **San Juan River** is completed, enabling Indians to farm the surrounding area.

1967 Spanish-Americans revive a 120-year-old land grant feud to reclaim acreage in what is today the **Carson National Forest.**

1969 *House Made of Dawn,* a novel by Native American N. Scott Momaday, wins the Pulitzer Prize for Literature.

1975 Jerry Apodaca becomes the first Spanish-American elected governor since 1918.

1977 Using electron beams, the first fusion reaction in the US is conducted in Albuquerque.

1978 The *Double Eagle II* balloon leaves Albuquerque and is the first to successfully cross the Atlantic Ocean.

1985 The Great Plains is plagued by record-breaking infestations of grasshoppers.

1988 Severe drought and wind erosion damage more than 1.4 million acres in New Mexico.

1994 New Mexican voters say yes to video gambling and a state lottery. Monies from the gambling and lottery are earmarked for education and other state projects.

1995 Despite budget constraints, President Clinton orders the US Department of Energy to keep **Los Alamos National Laboratory** open. The lab lays off 1,500 workers to consolidate the work done here and at two other major labs in the country.

Gary Johnson, a novice politician, becomes governor and signs casino gaming contracts with 14 Indian tribes. Disputes arise over the legality, and US Attorney John Kelly orders casinos shut down. At press time, the controversy was in the courts, but the casinos run by the Indian tribes were allowed to continue operating.

A federal judge halts 15 logging operations in New Mexico after environmentalists sue to protect the Mexican spotted owl.

1996 After a campfire is not properly put out, a fire rages for 10 days throughout Northern New Mexico, destroying 17,000 acres of forest in and around **Bandelier National Monument.**

The Spanish expedition of 1540 into what is now New Mexico was undertaken in search of gold, but it found little more than salt and some turquoise. Later forays went through the Rio Grande and Pecos Valleys passing ore deposits that would have made the Spanish rich beyond their fondest dreams. The Spanish, however, followed their Indian guides along the streams to avoid what they saw as hostile heights.

While the country waited in suspense, Billy the Kid hid with friendly Hispanic sheepmen on the range around Fort Sumner. Sheriff Pat Garrett and two deputies stole into the fort on the night of 14 July 1881 looking for him. At midnight Garrett slipped into the bedroom of Pete Maxwell, a New Mexico rancher living at the fort, to question him about Billy's whereabouts. Entirely by coincidence, Billy also entered the room. "Who is it? Who is it?" were Billy's last words as Garrett fired twice.

Index

Index

Restaurants

Only restaurants with star ratings are listed below. All restaurants are listed alphabetically in the main (preceding) index. Always call in advance to ensure a restaurant has not closed, changed its hours, or booked its tables for a private party. The restaurant price ratings are based on the average cost of an entrée for one person, excluding tax and tip.

★★★★ An Extraordinary Experience
★★★ Excellent
★★ Very Good
★ Good

$$$$ Big Bucks ($20 and up)
$$$ Expensive ($15-$20)
$$ Reasonable ($10-$15)
$ The Price Is Right (less than $10)

Index

Hotels

The hotels listed below are grouped according to their price ratings; they are also listed in the main index. The hotel price ratings reflect the base price of a standard room for two people for one night during the peak season.

$$$$ Big Bucks ($250 and up)

$$$ Expensive ($175–$250)

$$ Reasonable ($100–$175)

$ The Price Is Right (less than $100)

Features

Bests

Maps

Page	Entry #	Notes